REV.
ST.
274
CORNING

*His*
*Word*
*Resounds*

# His Word Resounds

Reflections on the Sunday Gospels —Cycles A-B-C

*Albert Cylwicki, CSB*

ALBA · HOUSE    NEW · YORK

SOCIETY OF ST. PAUL, 2187 VICTORY BLVD., STATEN ISLAND, NEW YORK 10314

*Library of Congress Cataloging-in-Publication Data*

Cylwicki, Albert.
  His Word Resounds.

  1. Church year meditations.   I. Title.
  BX2170.C55C92      1988        242'.3      87-33468
  ISBN 0-8189-0528-X

Nihil Obstat:
Rev. Harry S. Benjamin, S.T.L., S.S.L.
Censor Librorum

Imprimatur:
† Most Rev. Matthew H. Clark, D.D.
Bishop of Rochester
January 11, 1988

---

Designed, printed and bound in the United States of
America by the Fathers and Brothers of the
Society of St. Paul, 2187 Victory Boulevard,
Staten Island, New York 10314, as part of their
communications apostolate.

---

© *Copyright 1988 by the Society of St. Paul*

---

**Printing Information:**

Current Printing - first digit   1   2   3   4   5   6   7   8   9   10   11   12   13   14   15   16   17   18   19   20

Year of Current Printing - first year shown
           1988   1989   1990   1991   1992   1993   1994   1995   1996   1997   1998   1999   2000   2001   2002

# FOREWORD

The gospels and the documents of Vatican II encourage us to "read the signs of the times." This collection of reflections offers some examples of discerning how God's word resounds in films, plays, television programs, books and newspapers.

Some examples used to introduce these reflections on God's word are of enduring value—great historical figures, classic literature, landmark films, etc. Other examples are of necessity quickly outdated—election results, current awards, recent disasters, etc.

The latter are offered to suggest to the reader areas where more contemporary examples can be found by keeping abreast of current events.

To show the connections between Scripture and contemporary life, I've tried, on the one hand, to avoid getting too technical or theoretical, and, on the other hand, to focus on practical applications.

Without the constant encouragement of two Sisters this math teacher would never have tried his hand at writing a book. My deepest appreciation to Sr. Nolantia Zola, SSJ-TOSF, my eighth-grade teacher in literature, and the late Sr. Emma Hvozdovic, SSCM, my teaching colleague for many years.

Also, I thank Dorothy Kubik and Anita Tortorella who with their criticisms and corrections, helped prepare the manuscript, and the following pastors who welcomed me into their rectories during my sabbatical so I could complete this work: Msgr. Edward Creighton of San Diego, Fr. Frank J. McNulty of Roseland, N.J., Msgr. Anthony Jaworowski of Philadelphia, and Fr. Casimir Szatkowski of Chicago.

Finally, I am grateful to my own Basilian teachers and confreres who have inspired me over the years, and to Bishop Ricardo Ramirez for writing the introduction.

This book is dedicated to my parents, Vincent and Victoria, in whom God's word resounded so strongly that the echoes are still heard in my life.

*Albert Cylwicki, CSB*

# INTRODUCTION

It is a pleasure to introduce this valuable volume of homilies based on the Gospel readings. Not only will this collection provide good resource material for homilies, but it will also serve as a meditation guide for those who will not be preaching God's word. This book is an excellent means for growth in spirituality and an opportunity to follow God's word throughout the liturgical year.

These short meditations are successful in bringing the light of God's word to real life situations, and making the word of God alive. As a matter of fact, this is what good homilies are supposed to do.

Fr. Cylwicki's background as a high school teacher, university instructor and preacher is obvious in the way these homilies have been written. He has provided his readers with great clarity and order in these meditations and has done it interestingly. One cannot teach without keeping one's hearers interested.

Fr. Cylwicki concentrates his thoughts remarkably well in a few words. At the same time, he remains faithful in directing his readers to the challenges of the Gospel. The Gospel does not simply console or pacify, it basically challenges and points out directions for personal and communal growth. Fr. Cylwicki is faithful to this principle.

Pope Paul VI in his apostolic exhortation, *Evangelii Nuntiandi*, raised these difficult questions:

> What is the effectiveness today of the innate force of the Gospel message which can penetrate to the depth of man's conscience?
> To what extent and in what manner is the power of the Gospel able to transform the minds of the men of this century?
> What methods and approaches should we employ in preaching the Gospel to insure that it will achieve its full effect? (no. 4)

Pope Paul VI answers his own questions beautifully. Part of the answer is in these words:

It is necessary to keep before our minds the heritage of the faith which the Church must translate whole and entire and at the same time seek to present this heritage to the men of our time in the form which is at once clear and convincing. (no. 3)

Homilists of these post-Vatican II times are more and more responding to challenges such as those made by our recent popes when they exhort us to zealous preaching of the Gospel. Our parishioners themselves are demanding good homilies more and more. The current emphasis on good preaching is why books such as those by Fr. Cylwicki are so important. They assist us in bringing together the word of God and the life of people. In this way, the preaching of God's word remains vitalizing in our times.

I read once that a homilist has to have the intuition and the skill of a poet. With the intuition of the poet goes the ability to see every bush as a burning bush and hear God's voice everywhere. Poets can see in every bush the burning presence of God and in every happening his protective hand.

Fr. Cylwicki has certain poetic qualities. His examples are, as we mentioned above, crystal clear and fit beautifully in the totality of the message which he wants to convey. Like a poet, a good homilist has to be clever with words, not in order to be popular or to capture the attention of hearers, but to bring freshness and timeliness to God's word in our day. Fr. Cylwicki provides us with good models for doing this.

May the words of these pages serve as an inspiration, especially to the bearers of God's word.

*Bishop Ricardo Ramirez*
*Diocese of Las Cruces, New Mexico*
*April, 1987*

# ACKNOWLEDGMENTS

Quotations from the following works were used by permission.

Barclay, William. *The Daily Study Bible Series*. Philadelphia: Westminster, 1958.
   *The Gospel of John*.
   *The Gospel of Luke*.
   *The Gospel of Mark*.
   *The Gospel of Matthew*.
Brett, Laurence. *Share the Word*. Washington: The Paulist Fathers.
Cylwicki, Albert W. "Homilies on the Liturgy of the Sundays and Feasts." *Homiletic and Pastoral Review* Nov. 1972; April 1983; Nov. 1984; Oct. 1985.
*The Doubleday New Testament Commentary Series*. Garden City: Image Books, 1978.
   Achtemeier, Paul. *Invitation to Mark*.
   Karris, Robert. *Invitation to Acts*.
   Karris, Robert. *Invitation to Luke*.
   MacRae, George. *Invitation to John*.
   Senior, Donald. *Invitation to Matthew*.
*The Interpreter's Bible*. 12 volumes, Nashville: Abingdon Press, 1954.
*The Jerome Biblical Commentary*. Englewood Cliffs: Prentice-Hall, 1968.
*The Jerusalem Bible*. New York: Doubleday and Company, 1966.
*The New American Bible*. Washington: The Catholic Book Publishing Company, 1971.
*The Pelican New Testament Commentaries*. Baltimore: Penguin Books, 1968.
   Caird, J.B. *The Gospel of Luke*.
   Fenton, J.C. *The Gospel of Matthew*.
   Marsh, John. *The Gospel of John*.
   Nineham, Dennis. *The Gospel of Mark*.
Taylor, Michael. *John: The Different Gospel*. Staten Island: Alba House, 1983.

# TABLE OF CONTENTS

## CYCLE A

1st Sunday of Advent - *Waiting* ............3
2nd Sunday of Advent - *Do It Now* ...........4
3rd Sunday of Advent - *Key Questions* .......6
4th Sunday of Advent - *God Is With Us* ......7
Christmas Midnight Mass - *Be Not Afraid* ....9
Holy Family - *Shane* .......................11
January 1 - *Woman of the Year* .............12
2nd Sunday after Christmas - *Light In Darkness* ....................14
Epiphany - *Gifts* ..........................15
Baptism of the Lord - *Press Conferences* ...17
1st Sunday of Lent - *Winds of War* .........18
2nd Sunday of Lent - *Peak Experience* ......20
3rd Sunday of Lent - *Living Water* .........22
4th Sunday of Lent - *Spiritual Blindness* ..23
5th Sunday of Lent - *Death Be Not Proud* ...25
Palm Sunday - *Oberammergau* ................26
Easter - *Hold My Body Down* ................28
2nd Sunday of Easter - *Take Your Hands* ....29
3rd Sunday of Easter - *The Grass Is Greener* ..31
4th Sunday of Easter - *Gateways* ...........33
5th Sunday of Easter - *Do Not Be Troubled* ...34
6th Sunday of Easter - *Triple Crown Winners* ..36
Ascension - *Still With Us* .................37
7th Sunday of Easter - *Alfie* ..............39
Pentecost - *Fire* ..........................40
Holy Trinity - *Three, Yet One* .............42
Corpus Christi - *Food For The World* .......44
2nd Sunday of the Year - *Nicknames* ........45
3rd Sunday of the Year - *Fishermen* ........47
4th Sunday of the Year - *Be Happy* .........48
5th Sunday of the Year - *Salt and Light* ...50
6th Sunday of the Year - *Embody the Law* ...52
7th Sunday of the Year - *Love Your Enemy* ..53
8th Sunday of the Year - *Lilies of the Field* ..55
9th Sunday of the Year - *London Bridge* ....56
10th Sunday of the Year - *Second Chance* ...58

11th Sunday of the Year - *Give Your Gift* .....59
12th Sunday of the Year - *Do Not Be Afraid* ...61
13th Sunday of the Year - *Hospitality* ........63
14th Sunday of the Year - *Come To Me* .........64
15th Sunday of the Year - *Multiplying Good* ...66
16th Sunday of the Year - *Mustard Seeds* .....68
17th Sunday of the Year - *Treasure Hunts* ....69
18th Sunday of the Year - *Human Hungers* .....71
19th Sunday of the Year - *Walking on Water* ..72
20th Sunday of the Year - *Persistence* .......74
21st Sunday of the Year - *Public Images* .....76
22nd Sunday of the Year - *Losing* ............77
23rd Sunday of the Year - *Praying Together* ..79
24th Sunday of the Year - *Forgiveness* .......80
25th Sunday of the Year - *Word Parable* ......81
26th Sunday of the Year - *Brothers* ..........84
27th Sunday of the Year - *Unconditional Love* .85
28th Sunday of the Year - *Priorities* ........87
29th Sunday of the Year - *Trivial Pursuit* ...88
30th Sunday of the Year - *Leper Priest* ......90
31st Sunday of the Year - *Service* ...........92
32nd Sunday of the Year - *Timing* ............93
33rd Sunday of the Year - *Talents* ...........95
Christ the King - *Hale and Mills* ............97

## CYCLE B

1st Sunday of Advent - *Creative Waiting* ....101
2nd Sunday of Advent - *The Desert* .........102
3rd Sunday of Advent - *You Do Not Recognize* ....................104
4th Sunday of Advent - *Messiah* ............106
Christmas Mass at Dawn - *Come To The Stable* .......................108
Holy Family - *Star Trek* ...................109
January 1 - *Names* .........................111
2nd Sunday after Christmas - *Word Power* ...113
Epiphany - *Adventurers* ....................114

Baptism of the Lord - *Power Source* . . . . . . . 116
1st Sunday of Lent - *Training Periods* . . . . . 118
2nd Sunday of Lent - *Charles Rayburn* . . . . . 119
3rd Sunday of Lent - *Yamasaki* . . . . . . . . . . 121
4th Sunday of Lent - *Going On* . . . . . . . . . . . 123
5th Sunday of Lent - *The Grain of Wheat* . . . . 124
Palm Sunday - *Triumph and Tragedy* . . . . . . 125
Easter - *Do Not Be Amazed* . . . . . . . . . . . . . . 127
2nd Sunday of Easter - *Be An Inviter* . . . . . . 129
3rd Sunday of Easter - *Afterlife* . . . . . . . . . . 130
4th Sunday of Easter - *Laying Down One's Life* . . . . . . . . . . . . . . . . . . . . . . . . . 132
5th Sunday of Easter - *La Dolce Vita* . . . . . . 134
6th Sunday of Easter - *No Greater Love* . . . . 135
Ascension - *Solar Power* . . . . . . . . . . . . . . . 137
7th Sunday of Easter - *Sent In His Name* . . . . 139
Pentecost - *The Breath of God* . . . . . . . . . . . 140
Holy Trinity - *Faces of God* . . . . . . . . . . . . . 142
Corpus Christi - *Eucharistic Faith* . . . . . . . . 144
2nd Sunday of the Year - *Name Changes* . . . . 145
3rd Sunday of the Year-*Courage To Change* . . 147
4th Sunday of the Year - *Teaching With Authority* . . . . . . . . . . . . . . . . . . . . . . 148
5th Sunday of the Year-*Do What Jesus Did* . . . . 150
6th Sunday of the Year - *Faith and Healing* . . 151
7th Sunday of the Year - *Fellowship and Forgiveness* . . . . . . . . . . . . . . . . . . . . 153
8th Sunday of the Year - *Love Is Forever* . . . . 155
9th Sunday of the Year - *Law* . . . . . . . . . . . . 156
10th Sunday of the Year - *The Karate Kid* . . . 158
11th Sunday of the Year - *Seeds* . . . . . . . . . . 160
12th Sunday of the Year - *Storms* . . . . . . . . . 161
13th Sunday of the Year - *Death* . . . . . . . . . . 163
14th Sunday of the Year - *Prophets* . . . . . . . 165
15th Sunday of the Year - *Traveling Lightly* . . 166
16th Sunday of the Year - *Take Time To Rest* . . 168
17th Sunday of the Year - *Five Loaves and Two Fish* . . . . . . . . . . . . . . . . . . . . . . 169
18th Sunday of the Year - *Bread* . . . . . . . . . . 171
19th Sunday of the Year - *Living Bread* . . . . . 173
20th Sunday of the Year - *The Good Life* . . . . 174
21st Sunday of the Year - *Commitments* . . . . . 176
22nd Sunday of the Year - *Love in Action* . . . 178
23rd Sunday of the Year - *The Touch of His Hand* . . . . . . . . . . . . . . . . . . . . . . . . 179
24th Sunday of the Year - *Running Brave* . . . . 181
25th Sunday of the Year - *Mortality* . . . . . . . 182
26th Sunday of the Year - *Name Power* . . . . . 184
27th Sunday of the Year - *Marriage Model* . . 186
28th Sunday of the Year-*Sell What You Have* . . 187

29th Sunday of the Year - *True Greatness* . . . 189
30th Sunday of the Year - *Transformations* . . 190
31st Sunday of the Year - *Whole Being* . . . . . . 192
32nd Sunday of the Year - *Widows* . . . . . . . . . 194
33rd Sunday of the Year - *Tough Times* . . . . . 195
Christ the King - *Kingship Drama* . . . . . . . . . 197

CYCLE C

1st Sunday of Advent - *On Guard* . . . . . . . . . 201
2nd Sunday of Advent - *Rock Stars* . . . . . . . . 202
3rd Sunday of Advent - *Anticipation* . . . . . . . 204
4th Sunday of Advent - *Joy* . . . . . . . . . . . . . 205
Christmas Mass During the Day - *He Dwelt Among Us* . . . . . . . . . . . . . . . . . . . . . . 207
Holy Family - *The Cosby Show* . . . . . . . . . . . 209
January 1 - *Memories* . . . . . . . . . . . . . . . . . 210
2nd Sunday after Christmas-*Fullness of Life* . . 212
Epiphany - *The Star* . . . . . . . . . . . . . . . . . . 213
Baptism of the Lord - *Solidarity* . . . . . . . . . . 215
1st Sunday of Lent - *Wrong Reasons* . . . . . . 217
2nd Sunday of Lent - *Topaz* . . . . . . . . . . . . . 218
3rd Sunday of Lent - *One More Chance* . . . . . 220
4th Sunday of Lent - *Prodigal Son* . . . . . . . . . 222
5th Sunday of Lent - *The Scarlet Letter* . . . . . 223
Palm Sunday - *Fearless Resolve* . . . . . . . . . . 225
Easter - *A New Creation* . . . . . . . . . . . . . . . 226
2nd Sunday of Easter - *Breakthrough* . . . . . . 228
3rd Sunday of Easter - *Welcome Table* . . . . . 230
4th Sunday of Easter - *Abandoned? Never!* . . 231
5th Sunday of Easter - *Greatness* . . . . . . . . . 233
6th Sunday of Easter - *Pathfinders* . . . . . . . . 235
Ascension - *Soaring Higher* . . . . . . . . . . . . . 236
7th Sunday of Easter - *Stream of Consciousness* . . . . . . . . . . . . . . . . . . 238
Pentecost - *Language* . . . . . . . . . . . . . . . . . 240
Holy Trinity - *Trinitarian Comparisons* . . . . . 241
Corpus Christi - *Sharing* . . . . . . . . . . . . . . . 243
2nd Sunday of the Year-*The Best Is Yet To Be* . . 245
3rd Sunday of the Year - *Inaugural Address* . . 247
4th Sunday of the Year - *Unpopular Prophets* . 248
5th Sunday of the Year - *Launch Out* . . . . . . 250
6th Sunday of the Year - *Happiness Myth* . . . . 251
7th Sunday of the Year - *Forgiveness and Feelings* . . . . . . . . . . . . . . . . . . . . . . 253
8th Sunday of the Year - *True Excellence* . . . . 255
9th Sunday of the Year - *Chariots of Fire* . . . . 256
10th Sunday of the Year - *Widows and Only Sons* . . . . . . . . . . . . . . . . . . . . . . . . 258
11th Sunday of the Year - *Forgiveness Stories* 259

## Table of Contents

12th Sunday of the Year - *Suffering and
  Success* .........................261
13th Sunday of the Year - *World Class* ......263
14th Sunday of the Year - *Superstars* .......264
15th Sunday of the Year - *The Good
  Samaritan* .....................266
16th Sunday of the Year - *Tender Mercies* ...267
17th Sunday of the Year - *Ask, Seek and
  Knock* .........................269
18th Sunday of the Year - *Stockpiling* .......271
19th Sunday of the Year - *Sudden Death* ....272
20th Sunday of the Year - *A Fire To Kindle* ..274
21st Sunday of the Year - *The Last Will Be
  First* ..........................276
22nd Sunday of the Year - *Humility* ........277
23rd Sunday of the Year - *Bridge Building* ...279
24th Sunday of the Year - *Lost Sheep and
  Coins* .........................281
25th Sunday of the Year - *Money-Makers* ....282
26th Sunday of the Year - *Dear Abby* .......284
27th Sunday of the Year - *Faith* ...........286
28th Sunday of the Year - *Gratitude* ........287
29th Sunday of the Year - *Persistence in
  Prayer* .......................289
30th Sunday of the Year - *I'm OK, You're OK* ..291
31st Sunday of the Year - *Short and Tall* ....292
32nd Sunday of the Year - *The Day After* ....294
33rd Sunday of the Year - *Do Not Worry* ....295
Christ the King - *Charisma* ...............297

### SUPPLEMENT

Christmas Midnight Mass - *Tidings of Joy* ...303
Christmas Midnight Mass - *Giving* ........304
Easter - *He Is Alive* .....................305
Easter - *Death Leading To Life* ............307
Vigil of Pentecost - *Thirst* ................309
Pentecost - *Johnny Lingo* ................310
Vigil of the Assumption - *My Fair Lady* .....312
The Assumption of Mary - *Taj Mahal* ......314
All Saints - *Ordinary People* .............316
All Saints - *Dreamers and Doers* ..........317
Immaculate Conception - *Favored One* .....319
Immaculate Conception - *Misery and Glory* ..320

# A Cycle

1st Sunday of Advent                                    Is 2:1-5   Mt 24:37-44

# WAITING

Samuel Beckett's play *Waiting for Godot* focuses on two main characters, Vladimir and Estragon. They sit around waiting for the coming of a mysterious person known only as Godot. As they wait for him they try to recall exactly what their meeting is all about. They know that it is important and that their future depends on Godot's arrival, but that is all they can remember.

Then two other characters appear on the stage. Vladimir and Estragon are not sure if either one is Godot since they do not know how to recognize him. As the play ends, Vladimir and Estragon are left alone on a dark and empty stage, still waiting for Godot to come.

Today's liturgy ushers in the season of *Advent*, a word meaning, according to its roots, *coming*. Advent celebrates our Lord's coming in three ways: first, in past history, when he was born a man; second, in the present time, when he comes at Christmas; third, in the future, when he will return at the end of time.

The first reading from Isaiah speaks of the Old Testament waiting for the "days to come" when the Messiah would bring wisdom, light and peace. Jesus fulfilled this expectation when he came as man, an event which is now past tense for us.

The gospel makes a quantum leap into the future as Jesus speaks of his coming at the end of time. As we wait for this coming, Jesus urges us to be vigilant and ready, for his coming will occur when we least expect it.

In a sense, this final and future coming of Christ is a process, one that will begin for us personally when we die and time will end for us. For the moment, we are still living in a "mean-time," that is, the time between Christ's coming in past history to share our humanity and his coming in the future to lead us into glory.

Lest our waiting in this "mean-time" be empty and meaningless, as it seemed to be for Vladimir and Estragon in Beckett's play, we celebrate an Advent culminating in a Christmas each year to recall why we are waiting and whom we are awaiting.

Waiting plays a big part in our lives, and so it is important to learn how to wait. Children can't wait to grow up to stay out late; teenagers can't wait to drive a car; engaged couples can't wait to get married. All of us have something to wait for: a workday to end or a weekend to start; a sickness to pass or fun-time to commence; Christmas shopping to be finished or tree decorating to begin.

As human beings we always wait because our lives are never complete in themselves. There is always more to come. One of the purposes of Advent is to teach us how to wait—with patience, expectation and optimism. And while we wait we don't have to waste time. We can pray or make plans, or just simply relax and reflect.

Another purpose of Advent is to instruct us how to recognize our Lord's coming—in the duties we carry out, or in the things that happen to us, or in the people we meet.

It isn't only at the time of death or at the end of the world that our Lord's coming will happen when we least expect it. Our Lord comes in surprising ways even while we're waiting in a doctor's office for an appointment, or in a cashier's line at the supermarket, or in a bus station or airline terminal.

During Advent we have to discipline ourselves to see Christ in everyone and in every situation. Our waiting then will not be one of frustration, but rather one of readiness and anticipation.


2nd Sunday of Advent                                              Is 11:1-10   Mt 3:1-12

## DO IT NOW

According to its label, Drambuie was the liqueur of Prince Charles Edward, the famous "Bonnie Prince Charlie." In a recent magazine, Drambuie was advertised as: Why wait for your promotion or next raise? Why wait for the holidays? Why wait for tomorrow?

In other words, *now* is the time to enjoy Drambuie. *Now* is the time to sip this smooth liqueur. *Now* is the time to savor its distinctive taste. Typical of many ads, there is a note of urgency in the Drambuie commercial. Tomorrow may be too late. Act *now*!

Today's Scripture too has a note of urgency in it, not for the purpose of selling a liqueur, but for the purpose of arousing us to reform our lives. In the gospel John the Baptist appears with his spiritual commercial pitch: "Reform your lives. The reign of God is at hand . . . Prepare the way of the

Lord . . . Even now the ax is laid to the root of the tree."

In other words, John the Baptist is saying: "Why wait for the prophet Elijah to return? Why wait for the promised Messiah to come? Why wait for the Kingdom of God to be established? All these things are already happening. *Now* is the time to experience these events by reforming your lives. *Now* is the time to change your attitude and conduct. Tomorrow may be too late. Act *now*!"

More specifically, John the Baptist might be saying to us: "If you're planning on making a Christmas confession, do it soon and don't delay. If you're thinking about getting reconciled with someone, do it now and don't put it off. If you're wondering about doing something nice for someone, do it now and don't wait for tomorrow. If you're considering fasting a little and praying more, do it now and don't dilly-dally."

There is a verse written by Omar Ibn Al Halif which says: "Four things come not back—the spoken word, the sped arrow, time past, the neglected opportunity."

That's the same message as the Drambuie ad: Why wait for some important occasion to enjoy this liqueur? Do it now before the opportunity passes and may not come back. That's the theme of John the Baptist's message today: Why wait to reform your lives? The kingdom of God is at hand—right here, right now. Seize it before the opportunity disappears, never to return.

So why should we wait until we feel like it before we call, write, or invite a friend or relative we haven't seen or talked to in a long time? If we wait until we feel like it, one of us may die before it ever happens.

Why wait until the New Year before we start getting rid of some bad habits like excessive smoking or drinking, cursing or gossiping, or watching television too much? If we wait that long, even the desire to change will have disappeared by then.

NOW is the time—not tomorrow—to welcome Christ into our lives by doing good to other people. NOW is the time—not tomorrow—to become more Christ-like by making ourselves more loving and caring persons.

3rd Sunday of Advent                                          Is 35:1-6, 10    Mt 11:2-11

# KEY QUESTIONS

Some critics acclaim Shakespeare's *Hamlet* as the greatest play of the modern world. In this tragedy Hamlet is the prince of Denmark who learns from his father's ghost that he was murdered by his own brother Claudius, so that Claudius could take his place as king and marry Hamlet's mother.

Intent on avenging his father's assassination, Hamlet ponders what he should do in a soliloquy:

> To be, or not to be: that is the question. Whether 'tis nobler in the mind to suffer the slings and arrows of outrageous fortune, or to take arms against a sea of troubles, and by opposing end them? (Act 3, Sc. 1, l. 56)

Hamlet's perplexing question has become a Shakespearean classic. Scripture too poses some *key questions* about the mysteries of life, and today's gospel gives us a good example. John the Baptist sends his disciples to Jesus to ask the question: "Are you he who is to come, or do we look for another?"

This is by no means a casual question of identity, but a critical question whose answer affects our entire destiny. As such, it is a timeless question, a contemporary question, an ultimate question.

Today we are the ones who are asking: "Are you the expected one, Lord, who gives meaning to our life, brings us fulfillment, and completes our incompleteness? Or are we to look for another? Are we to look for meaning in materialism? Are we to find fulfillment in self-indulgence? Are we to seek our completeness in drug addiction? Are you he who is to come, or are we to look for another?"

During Advent we wait expectantly for the coming of Christ at Christmas. We wait expectantly because we are aware of our poverty and emptiness, conditions described in the first reading from the prophet Isaiah. In a sense, the landscape of our life is sometimes like a desert when we feel terribly lonely, or like parched land when our activity is barren of the fruit of good works.

At times our eyes are blind when we fail to see the opportunities we have in our present situation. Our ears are deaf when we do not listen to God's word or to the cry of the poor. Our hands are feeble and our knees weak when we lack courage to meet our commitments. Sometimes we become lame and a burden on society when we can carry our own load and don't. We become dumb when we can protest against injustice and don't.

But we must not allow our weaknesses and failures to discourage us. Rather, they should make us desire Christ's coming all the more. At least this is the attitude of the liturgy, and it should be ours too.

In the first reading we are told by Isaiah: "Things are going bad, but you will see the glory of the Lord. So be strong and fear not." In the gospel Jesus says: "Go back and report what you hear and see. The blind recover their sight and the deaf hear. Cripples walk and dead men rise to life."

In other words, we don't have to stay the way we are—weak, blind or crippled. Our Savior is coming at Christmas to bring us strength, light and healing. We don't have to look for another. Jesus is the one who is to come. We need no other. He is our way, our truth, and our life.

Moreover, our question becomes a mission. Once we've experienced his presence and power in our lives, we are sent to share these with others. "Go back to your homes and neighborhoods and places of work," our Lord says, "and report what you have seen and heard. Tell them too that I am indeed the one who was to come, and that they need look for no other."

4th Sunday of Advent                                      Is 7:10-14   Mt 1:18-24

## GOD IS WITH US

According to Russian author Aleksandr Solzhenitsyn, militant atheism is central to Communist policy. He says:

> To achieve its diabolical ends, Communism needs to control a population devoid of religious and national feeling, and this entails the destruction of faith and nationhood.

Nowhere is this more true than in Lithuania where there has been an ongoing 40 year persecution of the Catholic faith and an unrelenting effort to wipe out the ethnic heritage. For example, among Lithuania's growing list of persecuted priests is Fr. Alfonsas Svarinskas, who has been an outspoken agitator for religious freedom.

Fr. Svarinskas' prison record for defending Church and country against Communism is summarized on a clandestine Lithuanian holy card:

First term — 1946-1956.
Ordained in Abez special regime camp on Oct. 3, 1954.
Second term — 1958-1964.
Third arrest — Jan. 26, 1983.

Fr. Svarinskas' present sentence is for seven years of imprisonment to be followed by three years of exile in Siberia. In a letter smuggled out from prison he wrote:

> These ten years of want and suffering will be the crown of my priesthood. Let us pray for one another, so that we do not crumble under the cross of the Lord.

This Lithuanian priest's faith is similar to the prophet Isaiah's in today's first reading. The historical setting is the troubled reign of King Ahaz of Judah, the Southern Kingdom. On the one hand, Judah is threatened by a coalition between Israel, the Northern Kingdom, and Syria. On the other hand, the Assyrians were on the march threatening all three.

The prophet Isaiah is urging King Ahaz not to put his faith in foreign alliances, but in God. To persuade the king to have firm faith in God, Isaiah gives him a sign—a young woman will bear a son who will be named *Emmanuel*, a name which means "God is with us."

In other words, despite the impending foreign invasions, the child will be a sign that God would ultimately intervene to save his people. God would be *with them* and the nation would survive.

In the gospel, Matthew sees Isaiah's prophecy fulfilled in the birth of Mary's son Jesus. Jesus is truly *Emmanuel—God with us*—entering human history in human form.

This fact is so fundamental to Matthew's faith that the *Emmanuel* theme marks not only the beginning of his gospel with the birth of Jesus, but also its end with the ascension of Jesus: "Know that I am with you always to the end of time" (Mt 28:20).

It is faith in *Emmanuel* that enables Fr. Svarinskas and his Lithuanian people to survive in spite of apparent suppression. It is their belief that *God is with them* that enables people like the Lithuanians and Poles and Czechs to endure in spite of Communist oppression. How else can we explain their deep Christian devotion and fierce national pride after being plundered, persecuted and partitioned for so many centuries?

And what of us? Do we have faith in this central message of Christmas? Do we really believe that *God is with us*? As he was with the people of Judah at the time of Isaiah? As he was with the apostles at the time of Matthew? As he is with Fr. Svarinskas in his quest for justice and freedom?

The promise and fulfillment of *Emmanuel* is for us too. *God is with us* in moments of sorrow as well as joy; in situations of poverty as well as plenty; in times of worry as well as peace.

*God is with us* to see us through any struggle, to help us survive any setback, to strengthen us to endure any disappointment. Christmas is a yearly sign to reaffirm our faith that *God is still with us* and *will be with us* to the end of time.

Christmas — Midnight Mass (A, B, C)          Is 9:1-6    Lk 2:1-14

# BE NOT AFRAID

*One Magic Christmas* is a Walt Disney movie which tells the story of a Christmas skeptic, a young wife and mother named Ginnie Grainger. Hard times have come upon Ginnie: her husband Jack has been laid off; she is on the verge of losing her own job as a supermarket checker; they and their two children must move out of their company-owned house by New Year's Day.

It's easy to see why Ginnie has lost the Christmas spirit. But a Christmas angel named Gideon intervenes. In a dream or vision, Gideon takes Ginnie through some frightening experiences, including the apparent death of her husband.

With Gideon's help her little girl Abbie brings back a letter from the North Pole. When Ginnie reads the letter she realizes that it is the very letter she herself had sent to Santa Claus as a little girl 26 years ago. Ginnie then remembers and recovers the Christmas spirit.

As she awakens from her dream or vision she meets her husband, who, as it turns out, had really only gone for a long walk around the block. The miracle is completed when Ginnie can once again say and mean, "Merry Christmas."

One of the key lines in *One Magic Christmas* is the Christmas angel's words, "Don't be afraid," which he says to the little girl Abbie. These words were also spoken by the angel to the shepherds in the Christmas gospel: "Do not be afraid. Listen, I bring you news of great joy . . . Today in the town of David a savior has been born to you."

"Don't be afraid" was also the message of the Lord's angel when he spoke to Mary telling her that she would be the mother of Jesus, and again when he spoke to Joseph in a dream telling him to take Mary as his wife even though she was with child.

"Don't be afraid" is God's message to us this Christmas too. Times might be tough for us as they were for Ginnie in the movie. But whatever problems we have, whether in health, finances, work or relationships, the Lord's message is: "Don't be afraid. I bring you tidings of great joy. A savior is born for you."

In other words, we must never lose the Christmas spirit, for it is our faith in a savior that enables us to cope with any difficulty. Jesus may not save us from our problems in the sense of undoing a death, restoring some loss, or mending a broken marriage, but he will inspire us to discover fresh life, find other opportunities, and enter new relationships.

There is another way in which "Don't be afraid" could be God's Christmas message for us. Perhaps there is some decision we have to make about our home or education, or some challenge we're facing at work or on a parish committee, or some adventure we're hesitating to undertake.

Like Ginnie in the movie or the shepherds in the gospel, we may have to leave *fear* behind and step out in *faith* to make that decision, face that challenge, or begin that adventure.

There is nothing then that we need to be afraid of. We can always say and mean, "Merry Christmas"—not by magic—but by the mystery of God's grace. Christmas is the promise that God will be with us in our struggle—not with the make-believe problems and challenges of the movies—but with the real problems and challenges of our everyday lives.

Holy Family (A, B, C)   Si 3:2-6, 12-14   Mt 2:13-15, 19-23

# SHANE

The movie *Shane* starring Alan Ladd has become a frontier classic. Shane is a mythical American hero who fights for the rights of defenseless homesteaders being terrorized by a lawless cattleman and his hired gunmen. Shane himself is an ex-gunslinger who is searching for something to give meaning to his life.

At first he merely befriends the Start family, who take him in as a hired hand for their farm. But when trouble begins, Shane becomes their defender and savior. He risks his life for Joe and Marion Start and their son Li'l Joe in order to save their pride and property from the ruthless cattleman.

The movie *Shane* is more than a cowboy legend. It is also a modern parable about a Christ-figure and about family life. Shane is a Christ-figure in the story, not in the sense of his use of guns and fist fights, but in the sense of a celibate man who defends the powerless, risks his life for them, and then rides off alone to help someone else.

The film *Shane* also has much to say about family life, and even suggests some similarities between the Start family and the Holy Family. For example, the first names of the husband and wife—Joe and Marion—correspond to the names of Joseph and Mary in Matthew's gospel. Also, the violent threats to the Start family and their homestead are not unlike the dangers the Holy Family ran into with King Herod.

We may not be able to imitate the Starts in these respects, but there are other aspects of their family life in the movie *Shane* that we can emulate.

First, the Start's lifestyle was marked by *simplicity*. As frontier people they didn't have the luxuries that we enjoy. Yet, because they had to work hard for their basic necessities, they seemed to appreciate them more than we do. With few material comforts to distract them, they seemed to be more in touch with spiritual values.

Second, there was *solidarity* in the Start family. They tenaciously stuck together when the times got tough, and they supported their neighbors through adversity and death.

Third, the Starts enjoyed *intimacy*. There were a lot of deep feelings and signs of affection shared by the family members. They feared for and worried about one another's welfare and let this be known.

Fourth, a profound *loyalty* characterized their relationships. Joe and

Marion were so devoted to each other as husband and wife that Shane never appears as a rival but only as a genuine friend of the family. Their loyalty and purity have a healing effect on Shane. In spite of his shady past as a gunfighter, Shane is moved by his experiences with the Start family to do something noble and generous—not for himself this time, as he had always done in the past, but simply and purely for Marion, Joe and Li'l Joe.

Perhaps this sums it up. A good family life will be marked by *simplicity, solidarity, intimacy* and *loyalty*. But most of all it will bring out the best in us; it will reveal to us our hidden beauty and grandeur, our untapped powers and capacities. When we are loved by our family, we discover resources and strengths we never dreamed of, much as Joseph did in the gospel when his wife Mary and his child Jesus were threatened.

Moreover, when we have a sense of belonging to a family, we know that we have something to live for and that we will be mourned when we die. It was this that Shane searched for, and he found it in the Start family.

As a Christ-figure, the hero Shane became an integral part of the Start family and its protector and savior. May we never forget that Jesus plays this role for every family. But before he can be our family's protector and savior, we have to invite him in and allow him to become an integral part of our family life.

January 1 — Mary, Mother of God (A, B, C)     Nb 6:22-27   Lk 2:16-21

## WOMAN OF THE YEAR

Lauren Bacall once starred in a long-playing musical comedy entitled *Woman of the Year*. She played the role of a celebrated television talk show hostess, Tess Harding, who knows and interviews all the in-people like the president, the pope, Fidel Castro, Jean-Paul Sartre, and others. When Tess is selected by NOW, the National Organization for Women, for their *Woman of the Year* award, she sings a song by the same title.

Today we honor another woman as we begin a New Year. Her record is unbroken and unparalleled. For almost two thousand times in a row she has been singled out as the Church's *Woman of the Year*. She is Mary, the Mother of God.

Mary is not a celebrity like the fictional Tess Harding played by Lauren Bacall on Broadway, or like the real Barbara Walters who commands her own salary on television. But Mary is a saint, she was selected by God himself, and her son is Jesus, the Incarnate Word of God.

As St. Paul says in the second reading: "When the designated time had come, God sent forth his Son born of a woman" (Gal 4:4). Or, as the angels announced to the shepherds in Luke's Gospel, a Savior is born to them, the Messiah and Lord, and he is none other than Mary's infant lying in the manger in Bethlehem.

In one of his New Year's Day addresses, the late Pope Paul VI considered today's feast as a conclusion, a crowning of the Christmas mystery. In remembering the Nativity of Jesus, we can't help recalling the mother who gave birth to him. Moreover, Mary is given to us as our mother, too, so that she might teach and support us, especially as we start a new year.

We don't know how many more years we have left. After all, our present life is but a prelude to eternity. For some of our friends or relatives who died last year, there will never again be a new year, but only eternity.

So Mary is given to us as a mother to teach us how to use our remaining time wisely, not waste it; to spend it sensibly, not squander it; to employ it carefully, not recklessly.

We need Mary as mother to support us on our journey through the new year. We need her faith when we don't see a way; her hope when we run into a dead end; her love when others leave us. Pope Paul VI summed it up when he said that Mary is given to us as a mother "to accompany us on our tiring pilgrimage through life."

Mary won't win any awards this year like Lauren Bacall did, but can she at least win the affections of our hearts? Mary won't be seen on television this year like Barbara Walters will, but can she at least be seen in our lives by the way we practice her virtues? Mary won't ever be voted by NOW, the National Organization for Women, as their *Woman of the Year*, but can she at least have a vital part in our devotion?

May Mary's memory never leave us; may her image inspire us; and may her prayers bring us peace.

2nd Sunday After Christmas (A, B, C)                    Si 24:1-4, 8-12   Jn 1:1-18

# LIGHT IN DARKNESS

*The Lady of the Lamp* is a television movie in which Jaclyn Smith plays the role of Florence Nightingale. Although she was brought up in the elegant surroundings of high society in England, Florence Nightingale was obsessed with a desire to devote her life to humanitarian causes. She surrendered her social status to study nursing, and then began initiating reforms in health care throughout England.

When the Crimean War broke out in 1854, Florence was invited to go to the battlefields to organize nursing care for the wounded. It was her custom late at night to tour the wards with a lamp in her hand and offer comfort. Thus she became known as *The Lady of the Lamp*.

The way Florence Nightingale brought light into the darkness of hospital wards gives us some insight into the way Jesus brought light into the darkness of the world. Today's gospel says: "The real light which gives light to every man was coming into the world. The light shines on in the darkness, and the darkness did not overcome it."

Since these verses are part of the Prologue to John's gospel, they describe poetically the new creation taking place through Jesus. In the first creation story in Genesis, God made light when there was nothing but darkness. Now Jesus comes to re-create the world and dispel the darkness that still exists with the brightness of his light.

There are different kinds of darkness: the darkness of *deeds*—doing something evil or hateful, and then trying to hide it; the darkness of *ignorance*—not knowing what to do or say or where to go; the darkness of a *meaningless life*—not having any goal or sense of direction; the darkness of *disbelief*—not accepting Jesus into our lives as Savior; the darkness of *death*—dreading the event because we don't see any hope beyond the grave.

Jesus came as the light of the world to dissipate all these forms of darkness, and to give his light to every one of us so that we, too, can overcome them in our lives. With his revealing light we can see our *deeds* as they really are, acknowledge the wrongs we have done, and repair some of the damage or hurt we've caused.

The light of his truth and teachings removes *ignorance* as an excuse for not knowing who is the neighbor we should help, or for not speaking up in defense of human rights. The light of Jesus illumines the way we should walk to find *meaning* and *purpose* in life. He shows us how to lose our life in order to find it.

Jesus has the power to destroy the darkness of our *unbelief*, if only we open our hearts to receive the light of his gift of faith. The glory Jesus will manifest at his resurrection will drive out the darkness of *death*; this light too he will share with us so that we can overcome the darkness of the grave.

Like John the Baptist and Florence Nightingale, we are called to be witnesses of this light, and it doesn't mean just decorating our homes and trees with Christmas lights. It means carrying the light of Christ we bear in our minds and hearts into the world—the worlds of government and entertainment; the worlds of industry and the military; the worlds of finance and business. It means making the Christopher motto our own: "It is better to light one candle than to curse the darkness."


Epiphany (A, B, C)  Is 60:1-6  Mt 2:1-12

## GIFTS

In O. Henry's classic story "The Gift of the Magi," a wife sells her beautiful hair at Christmas time in order to buy a watch chain for her husband. He in turn sells his watch in order to buy a pair of combs for her hair.

Times have changed since O. Henry wrote that story. In recent years popular Christmas gifts for children have included Cabbage Patch dolls and Gentle Giant Mr. T kits, while for adults they've included home computers and videocassette recorders.

Christmas gift-giving began with the story in today's gospel. Astrologers from the east followed a star in search of a newborn king of the Jews. When they found the Christ-child they opened their coffers and presented him with gifts of gold, frankincense and myrrh.

In his commentary on this gospel, Fr. Laurence Brett points out that Matthew never tells us how many Magi there were, but the three gifts he mentions led to the conclusion that the Magi were three in number also.

Nor does Matthew make any mention of camels in connection with the

Magi. But since the first reading from Isaiah describes caravans of camels coming from Midian and Ephah, eventually the three Wise Men were pictured as riding on camels to make their journey.

Another author, Abbot Marmion, interprets the symbolism of the three gifts for us. First, gold is the most precious of metals, a symbol of *royalty*. The Magi acknowledged the newborn Christ as king, a title that would later appear above Christ's head on the cross. Second, incense is associated with prayer and divine worship. The Magi professed their faith in Christ's *divinity* as Son of God, the Word made flesh. Third, myrrh was used to dress wounds and embalm the dead. It symbolized the *humanity* of Jesus, his capacity to suffer and die for us.

But Abbot Marmion goes further. He says that the three gifts also symbolize what we should present to Christ. First, the gold signifies the loyalty and fidelity we owe to our Prince of Peace. Second, the frankincense symbolizes our prayers to the Lord and our worship of him in the liturgy. Third, the myrrh represents the gift of our suffering and sorrow whereby we share in his passion.

But what if our coffers are empty because we haven't been very faithful, or prayerful, or patient in suffering? Then we still have Jesus Christ to offer as our gift to the Father. In the Prayer over the Gifts we ask the Father: "Accept the offerings of your Church, not gold, frankincense and myrrh, but the sacrifice and food they symbolize: Jesus Christ, who is Lord forever."

In other words, though we might be poor in good works, Christ will enrich us with himself in the Eucharist. Though we may be destitute as far as devotion is concerned, Christ will supply what we lack.

We need never be discouraged, then, to approach the Father. He doesn't expect us to bring computers and video recorders as gifts. He wants our hearts to love him and our neighbor. He isn't interested in whether or not we have a Cabbage Patch doll to give him. He's interested in our prayers and in our problems.

The Father doesn't care where or how far we've come from. He wants to send us on our way like the Magi—overjoyed at having found his Son Jesus and strengthened for the rest of our journey through life.

Baptism of the Lord   Is 42:1-4, 6-7   Mt 3:13-17

# PRESS CONFERENCES

When likable Lou Holtz was announced as the new head football coach at the University of Notre Dame, he was touted as one who would restore the school's football program to its tradition of excellence.

Whenever a new leader appears on the scene, whether it is a new coach of a team or a new president of a corporation, a press conference is usually held to proclaim that leader's qualifications and potential. Such press conferences usually create some excitement about the leader's identity, and arouse our expectations with glowing promises about what this leader will accomplish.

Today's event of our Lord's baptism is something like this. It's as if God himself called a press conference to reveal his Son Jesus as the long-awaited Messiah and to give us a preview of what his mission will accomplish.

In the gospel, after Jesus is baptized, the Spirit descends like a dove upon him and a voice from heaven announces who he is: "This is my beloved Son. My favor rests on him."

In the first reading from Isaiah we hear the glowing promises of what Jesus will do: he will establish justice, open the eyes of the blind, bring out prisoners from confinement, and protect those who have been bruised.

Our Lord's baptism is part of the Epiphany cycle because it is a significant manifestation of his person. Jesus *appears* before John at the Jordan to be baptized, thus connecting the event to the star's *appearance* in last week's story of the Magi.

As already pointed out, there is a twofold dimension to our Lord's baptism. First, it declares *who* he is—God's own Son. Second, it declares what he will *do*—God's own works. Similarly our own baptism is also twofold. It not only proclaims publicly our new *identity* as members of the Church, but also empowers us to *do* good works as Jesus did.

In his book *Christian Sacraments and Christian Personality*, theologian Bernard Cooke comments on the anointing with chrism that takes place immediately after we are baptized with water.

> This anointing, this conferring of the Holy Spirit, this *Christ-ing* constitutes our appointment to the Christian vocation. Henceforth,

the baptized is irrevocably set aside for that apostolic life which Christ as Messiah initiated, and to which he admits us in order to complete his messianic work.

Cooke goes on to say that our baptism is not an action which happens once and has no further significance for our life. Rather, all the significance of this sacrament passes dynamically into the daily living of the Christian.

In other words, it is not enough for us just to accept baptism passively as something done to us. We must also allow it to become an operative power within us impelling us to act as Christ did: by bringing relief to people whose lives are like bruised reeds; by opening the eyes of people blinded by false promises; by freeing people imprisoned by social injustice.

It is not enough for us simply to be members in good standing by paying our parish dues. We must also put ourselves at the service of the parish: by showing sympathy to those who have lost a loved one; by assisting the sick and shut-ins; by volunteering our help in parish projects.

We may never become celebrities who can call press conferences to extol our successes. But we can become saints by living out our baptismal promises. We may never see any doves or hear any voices approving our good works. But that doesn't matter, because in faith we know that if we follow Jesus now in his ministry, later we also will share in his glory.

1st Sunday of Lent                    Gn 2:7-9, 3:1-7   Mt 4:1-11

## WINDS OF WAR

In the novel *Winds of War* the leading character, Capt. Victor (Pug) Henry, is tempted to commit adultery. It's war time, he's separated from his wife and family, and he has a military female companion named Pam. As his war time friendship with Pam becomes a threat to Pug's fidelity to his wife back home, Pug has to make a decision. He says,

> I know this kind of chance won't roll around again in my life. If I love you enough to have an affair with you behind my wife's back, then I love you enough to ask her for a divorce. To me the *injury* is the same.

Pug decides against adultery, and so he and Pam go their separate ways.

In today's readings we have two other temptation stories. In the first reading from Genesis, Adam and Eve are tempted by the serpent and fall. In the gospel, Jesus is tempted three times by Satan, but triumphs.

Commentators parallel the three temptations of Jesus with the desert experiences of Israel during the Exodus. Where the Israelites failed, Jesus—the new Israel—triumphs.

Our Lord's three temptations can be summarized under the heading of *substituting the lesser for the greater*. In fact, it seems that all temptations entice us to prefer a lesser good over a greater good, the superficial over the real, and the trivial over the tremendous.

For example, the first temptation to turn stones into bread is not so much a temptation to indulge one's appetite—whether a real appetite for food, for Jesus was hungry; or a symbolic appetite for sex, for Jesus was a man—but rather a temptation to substitute the lesser for the greater, namely, bread for the word of God.

When God provided manna in the desert for the hungry Israelites, he was teaching them that life—real life, the fullness of life—was not dependent on bread alone, but rather on his all-powerful word and promise. Jesus, too, proclaims this principle when he quotes the book of Deuteronomy: "Man does not live on bread alone, but on every word that comes from the mouth of God" (Dt 8:3).

In the second temptation Satan tries to lure Jesus into substituting his ways for God's ways, and his views for God's views. The Father wanted a Messiah who would be humble and minister to his people. Satan suggests being a Messiah who would be spectacular and do tricky things, like throwing himself off temple peaks to be caught by angels.

In the third temptation Satan tries to seduce Jesus into substituting worldly power and glory for God's power and glory. The Father wants Jesus to achieve power and glory through his suffering and death on the cross. Satan insinuates that Jesus can have instant success by simply worshiping him.

All three temptations are different attempts to *substitute some lesser good for a greater*. Where the Israelites failed in their tests in the desert, Jesus now triumphs. He is the new Israel forming a new people of God.

Today it is we who are the pilgrim people of God making our exodus from Lent to Easter in the narrow sense, and from time to eternity in the wider sense. We, too, experience the same temptations along the way. Sometimes we are attracted to infidelity like Pug in *Winds of War*, to excessive drinking, or to cheating in financial matters. At other times we are deluded into selfishly getting our own way, taking unfair advantage of others, or pretending people don't have real needs.

In all cases we are tempted to *substitute the lesser for the greater*, the superficial for the real, and the trivial for the tremendous. That's why we need *fasting* to focus on what is the greater, *prayer* to see what is really real, and *service* to others to experience the tremendous.


2nd Sunday of Lent                                    Gn 12:1-4   Mt 17:1-9

# PEAK EXPERIENCE

George Bernard Shaw once attended a concert given by the violinist Jascha Heifetz. Shaw wrote the following letter when he got home:

> Dear Mr. Heifetz, my wife and I were overwhelmed by your concert. If you continue to play with such beauty, you will certainly die young. No one can play with such perfection without provoking the jealousy of the gods. I earnestly implore you to play something badly every night before going to bed.

Beneath George Bernard Shaw's humor is a description of what psychologists term a *peak experience*. The violinist Heifetz had played with such beauty that his music moved Shaw and his wife to emotional depths they never knew existed. It was an evening of ecstasy for them, a peak experience they would never forget.

Today's gospel tells the story of another peak experience, namely, our Lord's transfiguration in the presence of his three disciples. The transfiguration story abounds with symbols which indicate that it was a peak experience for them.

The high mountain recalls the Mount Sinai revelations of the Old Testament. The dazzling face of Jesus suggests the face of Moses during the Exodus and the angels at the empty tomb of Easter. The cameo appearances of Moses and Elijah symbolize that the law and the prophets are now fulfilled in Christ. The falling down to the ground by the disciples anticipates their homage when they will behold the risen Lord later. Finally, only Matthew calls the whole experience a vision, reminiscent of the visions of the book of Daniel.

What was the purpose of this peak experience for the disciples? Why would Jesus give them a preview of his glory? To answer these questions we have to look at the context of the transfiguration story. It follows immediately upon our Lord's prediction of his own passion and death, and his declaration that his disciples must deny themselves and take up their cross.

Our Lord's transfiguration seems intended to strengthen the disciples' faith so that when Christ dies on the cross, they will be able to look beyond his death to his resurrection. Moreover, when they have to endure their own hardships for him, they will be able to see beyond their sufferings to the glory that awaits them.

When we have to experience hurt or pain, failure or brokenness, loss or death, we can survive because of our faith that all these things will ultimately be transformed. Our vision of the glory that awaits us will not remove our troubles and difficulties, but it will keep us believing and trying in spite of them.

When marathon runners "hit the wall" around the 20-mile mark, they feel like giving up. But if they can somehow envision the finish line and the cheering crowd awaiting them, then they can find deep down inside themselves the necessary strength to continue running to the end.

That's something like what the transfiguration does for us. It gives us a glimpse of the glory that lies ahead of us, a glimpse so powerful that it can keep us going when we want to quit, call up extra strength when we think that we have none left, and renew our hopes when everything seems hopeless.

Our memory of the transfiguration will not always be a peak experience, like listening to Heifetz play the violin, but it will empower us to carry our cross and follow the Lord. Regardless of the tasks or challenges that lie ahead of us, we can take them on with confidence because our Lord says to us as he said to his disciples: "Get up. Do not be afraid. Let us go to Jerusalem together."

3rd Sunday of Lent                                    Ex 17:3-7    Jn 4:5-42

# LIVING WATER

Hermann Hesse's book *Siddhartha* narrates the wanderings of a man in search of inner peace and self-realization. As a Brahman boy Siddhartha had everything—intelligence, handsome features, wealth—but he was restless. So he renounced his wealthy family and set off to seek happiness.

In succession he tried the asceticism of the Eastern monks, the way of enlightenment under the Buddha, the pleasures of sensual indulgence, and the luxuries of wealth, but all of these only left him disappointed and disillusioned.

Disgusted to the point of despair, Siddhartha considered committing suicide in a river, when he suddenly heard from the depths of his subconscious a Brahman word (Om) that begins and ends all prayers.

The remembrance of that word awakened Siddhartha's slumbering spirit to realize anew that all is divine and that loving devotion to the universe is the key to happiness. The water of the river helped him die a symbolic death to his old life of futility and emptiness and be born again to a new life of fulfillment and happiness.

In today's gospel, water is one of the main themes. Tired and thirsty from his journey, Jesus asks a Samaritan woman for a drink of water. This simple request for ordinary water becomes an occasion for Jesus to talk about another kind of water, namely, living water that becomes a fountain within us, springing up to provide eternal life.

In a booklet on the gospel of John, Fr. Raymond Brown writes:

> Living or running water, spring water, is greatly prized in Palestine, where, otherwise, during the long rainless months one must depend on cisterns which have stored up the previous winter's rains. In literature this precious living water became a symbol of divine wisdom and teaching. The Samaritan woman understands only natural water, but Jesus is referring to his divine revelation and to the Holy Spirit who will be given to those who accept that.

Like the Samaritan woman and Siddhartha, we thirst for meaning in life. Too often, though, we try to quench our thirst with stagnant water. We go to the cisterns of excess in drink, drugs, sex, work or material possessions. We think that five husbands, or five cars, or five stereos or five of whatever will satisfy our thirst for human fulfillment.

But none of these things satisfy us completely. They always leave us thirsting for better things—like the *peace* that comes from experiencing Jesus personally; or the *freedom* that comes from following him; or the *joy* that comes from serving his people.

When we drink of the water that Jesus gives—the water of his *word* in the Scriptures; the water of his *Spirit* in the sacraments; the water of his *presence* in prayer; the water of his *grace* in ministry—we will never be thirsty.

Instead, his life-giving waters will become a fountain within us, springing up to refresh people around us, to relieve the arid lives of the poor, and to nourish the hearts of the lonely.

Like a river, these life-giving waters will flow out from us to supply the needs of others and make them bloom. Following the lead of the Samaritan woman, we will go out and bring others to Jesus: "Come, see the Messiah, drink his water, and never be thirsty again."



4th Sunday of Lent                                    1 S 16:1, 6-7, 10-13   Jn 9:1-41

## SPIRITUAL BLINDNESS

Leonard Gershe's play *Butterflies Are Free* is about a young man who is blind from birth and about a lovely young lady who is a divorcee. To tear himself away from his overprotective mother, Don Baker occupies a shabby one-room apartment. He tries to support himself by being a singer-composer.

Along comes Jill Tanner who was married for six days at one time and, consequently, doesn't want any more deep involvements with men. Nevertheless, because she is affectionate and friendly, she falls in love with Don, and this in spite of his blindness. But when he asks her to marry him, she is afraid of getting hurt again and hesitates to say "Yes."

Don tells her that even though she has eyes to see, she, and not he, is the one who is really handicapped, because she is afraid to step out in faith and make another commitment to love someone. His own faith and courage eventually convince Jill to open her eyes and see the freedom from fear she can have as well as the wonderful possibilities of their life together.

Gershe's play about this young man who is blind from birth has some similarities to today's gospel story. A man who was born blind meets Jesus and has his eyes healed. He then becomes a symbol of the struggle between light and darkness, good and evil.

In his commentary on John's gospel, R.H. Lightfoot points out that the light-darkness conflict is introduced in the Prologue: "The Word came to be the light of men, a light shining in the dark, a light that darkness could not overpower" (Jn 1:4-5).

Lightfoot then proceeds to show how this light-darkness conflict is personified and dramatized in the man born blind and the Pharisees in today's gospel story.

On the one hand, the man born blind moves progressively from darkness to light. Initially he refers to Jesus as simply the man who *healed* him. Next, he describes Jesus as a *prophet*. Then during his interrogation he insists that Jesus must be *from God*. Finally, in the last scene, he believes in Jesus as the *Son of Man*.

On the other hand, the Pharisees, who thought they had the light, gradually plunge deeper into darkness. At the first inquiry, they *acknowledge* the miracle but are upset by the violation of the Sabbath. During the second interrogation, they *cast doubt* on the authenticity of the miracle. Finally, during the third questioning, they *threaten* and *maltreat* the man born blind.

Are we like Jill in *Butterflies Are Free* or like the Pharisees in the gospel? We have eyes to see, but are we not sometimes blind and in the dark? We walk in darkness whenever we close our eyes to our fears, insecurities and selfishness, or whenever we refuse to face the truth about our hangups, addictions and greed. We walk in the dark whenever we fail to see the sufferings of the poor, the sick and the abandoned, or whenever we ignore the lonely, the oppressed and the downtrodden.

Would that we were more like the sightless Don Baker in the play or like the man born blind in the gospel, so that we could walk in the light even though we might be enveloped by darkness.

Light shines in us every time we see more than meets the eye, have a vision of our unlimited possibilities, or make commitments with daring and courage. Light shines through us every time we brighten our surroundings or other people's lives. As St. Paul says in the second reading, we are

children of the light whenever we "produce every kind of goodness and justice and truth" (Ep 5:9).
Only Jesus could say, "While I am in the world, I am *the light* of the world." But all of us can say, "While I am in the world, I will not be overpowered by darkness. I will at least be *a light* in the world."

5th Sunday of Lent                                        Ezk 37:12-14   Jn 11:1-45

# DEATH BE NOT PROUD

John Gunther's book *Death Be Not Proud* tells the story of his son's last year of life. At sixteen, when most young people are dreaming about their future, John Gunther Jr. was dying from a brain tumor.
   The boy's quiet courage in his encounter with death prompted critic Judith Crist to write: "His story is a glowing affirmation of the nobility of even the shortest of lives." Book reviewer Walter Duranty of the *New York Herald Tribune* said: "To read *Death Be Not Proud* is to grasp the meaning of man's power to defy Death's hurt; to be filled with confidence and emptied of despair."
   Like John Gunther Jr., Jesus too had something to say about living and dying. But unlike John Gunther Jr., Jesus could make the fantastic claim that he himself is the resurrection and the life, and that whoever believes in him will never die.
   For the last two Sundays we've been hearing Jesus make some startling I AM statements: "I AM the living water . . . I AM the light of the world." Today we hear another strong I AM statement: "I AM the resurrection and the life."
   Christ's assertion is just as relevant for us today as it was for Martha and Mary in the gospel and for the Gunther family, because death is just as destructive in our day as it was in theirs. Close to home we see our dearest relatives die from cancer and our youth killed in car accidents. We read about people in distant parts of the world being wiped out by war, starvation and disease.
   We also experience other forms of death whenever we see marriages end in divorce, religious vocations terminated by departures, and careers

cut short by unemployment. We suffer a kind of death every time our environment gets polluted, parochial schools close from lack of funds, and big cities decay from crime and violence. Indeed, we too need to hear that Jesus is the resurrection and the life.

Because we experience death in so many ways, we can't help but wonder: Is there any meaning to life, or is it just an absurd existence? Is there some glorious destiny for us, or is this all just a futile endeavor?

In today's gospel Jesus claims to answer these questions. In effect he says, "You have a suspicion that life does somehow continue and that death is not the last word. I have come to tell you that your suspicions are correct. Like Lazarus you will rise from the dead. You have an intuition that life, however short, does have meaning and value. I have come to tell you that your intuition is true. If you have faith like Martha and Mary, you will see the glory of God."

As the Mass continues, we reaffirm our faith in our Lord's words. No matter how hopeless our situation may be, with the prophet Ezekiel we believe that out of it the Lord will somehow bring new life. No matter how disillusioned we may be, with St. Paul we trust that he who raised Jesus from the dead will raise us to new life also. No matter how devastating death may seem, with Martha and Mary we make a leap of faith and say: "Lord, I have come to believe that you are the Messiah, the Son of the living God. You are the resurrection and the life."

Palm Sunday                                    Mt 21:1-11   Mt 26:14-27:66

# OBERAMMERGAU

Oberammergau is a small village in the Bavarian Alps that is famous for its Passion Play. This drama enacts the passion of Jesus from his triumphal entry into Jerusalem to his resurrection. It consists of 18 acts; has more than 700 villagers participate in the cast, orchestra and chorus; and takes a morning and an afternoon to perform.

With only three interruptions caused by war, the Oberammergau Passion Play has been staged every ten years since 1634 in fulfillment of a vow made by the villagers for deliverance from a plague.

Although our liturgy here today is not of the same magnitude and prestige as the Passion Play at Oberammergau, and although we are not assembling because of the threat of some plague, what we are doing is a sacramental ritual that should be full of meaning and power for us.

The palms that we blessed and the Passion according to Matthew that we read draw us into the drama of Holy Week, not merely as spectators, but as participants. The palms we hold and take home with us are signs that we are willing to march with Jesus, not only in moments of triumph and glory, as when he entered Jerusalem with the crowd crying, "Hosanna to the Son of David!" but also in moments of suffering and agony, as when he was condemned to death with the crowd crying, "Crucify him!"

On the one hand, it is easy to praise God when we are enjoying success, are feeling healthy, and are surrounded by a loving family and a circle of friends. Nonetheless, even in these favorable circumstances, blessing God is important to make us realize that he is the source of these gifts and that we should use them for his glory.

On the other hand, it is difficult to believe in God when we are discouraged by repeated failure, suffer from sickness and pain, or feel abandoned by everyone. But it is precisely in such moments that we really participate in the passion of Christ. We then know from personal experience why Jesus prayed in the garden, "My Father, if it is possible, let this cup pass me by," or why on the cross he cried out, "My God, my God, why have you forsaken me?"

Moreover, it is also in such moments that we experience the power of Christ's passion—to say "Yes" to the Father's will when our world seems to be collapsing, and to expect that soon we will see the glory of God reveal itself in some way.

Today's reading of the Passion ended on the dismal note of death—Jesus died and his tomb was sealed with a stone. Sometimes that's the way our day ends: on a dismal note, for we still suffer our pain, hurt from our losses, or feel terribly lonely.

However, Passion Sunday is not the last word of the Jesus story. Rather, it is only the first word of a Holy Week that will reach its climax next Easter Sunday. The final word will not be the death of Jesus, but his rising from the dead.

So too, no matter how many of our days seem to end in a depressing way, they are not the last word of our story. Rather, they are only a prelude to triumphs we have yet to experience in this life, and they point to that ultimate victory which will be ours in the next life.

There we will again process with palm branches, not to mark Christ's triumphal entry into the earthly city of Jerusalem, but our own victorious entrance into the heavenly city of Jerusalem.

Easter (A, B, C)  Ac 10:34, 37-43  Mt 28:1-10

## HOLD MY BODY DOWN

The all-black musical *Your Arms Too Short To Box With God* is Vinnette Carrol's vibrant version of what the gospel of Matthew would have been like, if it had been written with a little bit more of that old-time religion. With buoyant negro spirituals and exciting choreography, *Your Arms Too Short To Box With God* celebrates the life, death and resurrection of Christ.

In the final scene of the first act, Jesus has just risen from the tomb and is standing high at the back of the stage in a glow of yellow celestial light. With a thunderous voice the risen Lord sings a song entitled, "Can't No Grave Hold My Body Down."

That song sums up the joyous news of Easter. We hear an angel sing it for Jesus as he greets Mary Magdalene and the other Mary at the tomb: "Can't No Grave Hold My Body Down." You can almost sense its rhythm keeping pace with the two women as they hurry to tell the good news about Jesus to the disciples: "Can't No Grave Hold My Body Down."

Two days before, Christ's enemies had done their worst to him. They had him bound in the garden, scourged at the pillar, crucified on the cross, and pierced with a lance. But neither death nor a stone seal nor an armed guard could contain Christ in the grave. He was raised from the dead by God his Father.

This good news of Christ's resurrection is symbolized by the Easter lilies that decorate our homes and churches. All through the winter these flowers lay buried in the cold, frozen earth. But with the spring sunshine, showers and breezes, these lilies come alive, break through the ground and bloom. No ground can hold these lilies down. No ground can contain their new living blossoms.

What can we learn from the lilies of the field? What can we learn from the musical *Your Arms Too Short To Box With God*? Two things.

First, we can learn something about our own resurrection. Easter is not only a celebration of Christ's rising from the dead, but is also an anticipation of our own rising one day from the dead. Because we already share in the risen life of Christ through baptism, "Can't No Grave Hold My Body Down" either. When we die, our body will decay and disintegrate, but it is not destined to stay that way. By the power of God's grace our bodies will rise again to be clothed with immortality and incorruptibility.

In his book *Hymn of the Universe*, Fr. Teilhard de Chardin says that if we are to be assimilated into God, he must first break down the molecules of our being so as to recast and remold us. It is the function of death to bring about in us this required organic decomposition, so that the divine fire can descend upon us and bring about our transformation. In this way the power of death to cause our dissolution and extinction is harnessed by God to accomplish our resurrection and re-creation.

A second thing we can learn from the lilies and the black musical is what they tell us about our present life. Before we die in the radical sense, we die many times in a lesser sense. Every time we suffer a loss, fail in some enterprise, or are disabled by an illness, we die a little bit. But if we have faith, "Can't No Grave Hold Our Spirit Down." We discover new dreams to pursue, new challenges to take on, and new reasons to try again.

Every time we are overwhelmed by problems, discouraged by disappointments, or beset by worry, we are diminished in some way. But if we really believe that "Can't No Grave Hold Our Spirit Down," we find that the impossible becomes possible and the unreachable becomes reachable. With Christ we rise again!

2nd Sunday of Easter                              Ac 2:42-47   Jn 20:19-31

# TAKE YOUR HANDS

Several years ago a *Joy of Life* program was put on by the University of St. Thomas in Houston. The program featured outstanding people from the Houston area. Some of these celebrities were from television and stage, others from professional football and the opera.

But of all the people who appeared in that *Joy of Life* program the one who stole the show was a 6-year-old mentally deficient girl. When the spotlight focused on her, a sign on her back could be read: "I am retarded, but I am glad I am alive."

What an affirmation of faith on the part of her parents! Their 6-year-old child was retarded, but they were glad she was alive, and they made her feel glad that she was alive. It was an affirmation of faith comparable to Thomas' in the gospel: "My Lord and my God."

In fact, their faith surpassed the faith of Thomas. He believed because he saw the Lord. These parents believed even though they had not seen the Lord. Thomas had to touch our Lord's hands and side before he believed. These parents could touch our Lord only by faith. Every time they held their retarded daughter they believed that they were touching the Christ living in her by baptism.

Their affirmation of faith is what Jesus praised in the gospel when he said: "Blessed are they who have not seen and have believed."

If only we could take Christ's words seriously, there would be no situation in which we could fail to see the risen Lord. Sometimes a family has one of their teenage daughters get pregnant, or one of their sons becomes hooked on drugs. The first reaction of the parents may be anger.

But Jesus seems to be saying that they should take their fingers and feel their daughter's pregnant womb, and take their hands and touch their son's needled arm. "Do not persist in your unbelief, but believe," Jesus says. "Believe that these too are still my disciples, and that I still live in them. Believe that I want, not their rejection, but rather their reconciliation."

Sometimes a family has an alcoholic father or a neurotic mother. The children may feel resentment or hostility towards them. But our Lord seems to be saying: "Take your hand and support my staggering body. Take your fingers and calm my shattered nerves."

So it doesn't matter what the situation may be. With faith we can say with the disciples: "We have seen the Lord. We believe that the Lord is risen and lives in his people."

It doesn't matter whether the issue is infidelity, immigration, abortion, or AIDS. With faith we can hear Christ say: "Don't persist in your unforgiveness, your prejudice, your cruelty, or your fear. Take your hand and find some way to forgive from the heart, to release aliens from oppression, to protect the unborn in the womb, or to minister to a dying AIDS victim."

During the liturgy we profess our faith in the presence of Christ in the

Eucharist. We see only bread, but we say with Thomas: "My Lord and my God." At the end of the liturgy we will be sent to "love and serve the Lord"—to love and serve the Lord in mentally deficient 6-year-old children and in teenage rebels; to love and serve the Lord in alcoholic parents and in senile grandparents.

We are challenged not to persist in our unbelief, but to believe—to believe in the risen Lord, and to believe that he still lives in his people. Do we have enough faith to take our hands and touch him in his people?


3rd Sunday of Easter                                    Ac 2:14, 22-28   Lk 24:13-35

## THE GRASS IS GREENER

In one of the *Peanuts* comic strips, Lucy and Linus are standing before a hill. Lucy says that one day she will go over that hill and find the answer to her dreams. But Linus answers with his usual realism. He says that perhaps there is another little kid on the other side of the hill who thinks that all the answers to life lie on this side of the hill.

The point of this *Peanuts* parable is that life always seems better on the other side of the hill. The grass always looks greener in another field. Might not this parable be applied to the two disciples in the gospel on their way to Emmaus, and in some sense to us?

The two disciples were leaving Jerusalem disappointed because, after all, they had left everything to follow Jesus. Expecting a hundredfold return, they apparently received nothing. They had seen Jesus work miracles, too. Expecting quick success, they were apparently defeated by the disaster of Christ's death.

Indeed, the events that happened in Jerusalem were not quite what the two disciples expected, and so they were on their way to Emmaus in search of the other side of the hill of Calvary. Perhaps there they would find the fulfillment of their dreams for success.

Are we much different from Lucy looking beyond some grassy hill? Are we much different from the two disciples who left Jerusalem for Emmaus? How many times have we had our dreams end in disappointment? How many times have we expected one thing and then experienced something else?

When he became Pope, John Paul II never expected that he would be the target of an assassination attempt. When Frank Borman became president of Eastern Airlines, he never expected the company to suffer financial losses. Such people must feel at times like leaving their Jerusalem to search for an Emmaus.

All of us must feel disappointed sometimes at the unexpected outcomes in our lives. All of us must feel at times like leaving the Jerusalem of our responsibilities to look for an Emmaus with more promise. But today's gospel should open our eyes the way the eyes of the two disciples were opened. It should open our eyes to recognize Christ in the opportunities of the present moment and to see the presence of Christ in the midst of the unexpected.

We don't have to leave the surroundings of our Jerusalem to find Jesus. He is with us when we listen to his word in Scripture or listen to each other. We don't have to search for Jesus in some distant Emmaus. He is with us every time we break bread together at Mass or in our homes.

Consequently, it is foolish to wish that the unexpected in our lives had turned out differently, or to think that we have to go elsewhere to encounter Christ. Why not open our eyes to recognize his presence in our midst before he vanishes from our sight? Why not open our hearts to welcome him in as we discover him in each other?

In his poem "The Kingdom of God," Francis Thompson wrote:

> O world invisible, we view thee.
> O world intangible, we touch thee.
> Does the fish soar to find the ocean,
> The eagle plunge to find the air,
> That we ask of the stars in motion
> If they have rumour of thee there?
> Not where the wheeling systems darken,
> And our benumbed conceiving soars,
> The drift of pinions, could we hearken,
> Beats at our own clay-shuttered doors.

4th Sunday of Easter   Ac 2:14, 36-41   Jn 10:1-10

# GATEWAYS

The United States has two outstanding gates that are known the world over. One is the Golden Gate Bridge in San Francisco, and the other is the stainless steel Gateway Arch in St. Louis. Both gates are marvels in engineering, magnificent in their architecture, and highly symbolic monuments.

The Golden Gate Bridge spans the strait between the Pacific Ocean and San Francisco Bay. It was described by poet Henry May as a "curve of soaring steel, graceful and confident over infinity." The Gateway Arch in St. Louis is considered a symbol of 20th-century steel structures, just as the Eiffel Tower in Paris was considered a symbol of 19th-century iron structures.

If Christ were speaking today he would probably use either of these two gates for his image instead of the sheepgate image of this Sunday's gospel. In another of one of his famous I AM statements he says: "I AM the sheepgate. Whoever enters through me will be safe."

Although we might prefer a more contemporary gate image, we can learn much from our Lord's sheepgate metaphor. A sheepgate allowed a shepherd to lead his flock into a sheepfold or corral, where it would be safe from attacks by predatory animals and secure against marauding thieves. By identifying himself as a figurative sheepgate, Jesus claims that anyone who comes through him will be *safe*. Safe from what?

The first kind of safety we need is safety from harm. Sometimes this may mean protection from harm in our outer world, from accidents, injury or sickness. More often it means safety from harm in our inner world, from discouragement, depression or despair. Even though we may be wounded in our outer world, the Lord will never let us be destroyed in our inner world.

A second kind of safety we can count on is safety from negative influences. There are all kinds of sinister influences in the world trying to rob us of our faith and ideals. For example, corrupt government officials threaten our quest for justice and freedom; greedy investors undermine our desire to share and help the poor; misguided entertainers distort our sense of decency. It is not easy to follow Christ faithfully in a world hostile to gospel values. We need Christ's reassurance that our faith and ideals will ultimately prevail.

A third kind of safety we need is safety from worry, anxiety and self-pity. Excessive concern can drain our energy and immobilize us. If we are too worried about our health, finances or relationships, we can't function productively, advance in personal growth, or deepen our life in the Spirit. Only Christ can make us safe from being dominated by worry, overwhelmed by anxiety, or paralyzed by self-pity. Only Christ can help us to live fully with joy and enthusiasm.

In one of his talks, dream-analyst Robert Johnson tells how he helped a woman who was troubled by demons. He told her to draw a circle every time a demon began to disturb her and to imagine herself inside that circle. According to Jungian psychology, a circle is a primitive symbol of safety. The woman followed Robert Johnson's suggestion, was gradually freed from her demons, and went on to live a healthy life.

Perhaps Christ's gate and sheepfold imagery is another variation of this primitive symbol of the circle of safety, but a variation that brings it to fulfillment. Jesus is not just like a sheepgate or a circle. He *is* the sheepgate. He *is* our safety in any trouble. He *is* our fullness of life.


5th Sunday of Easter                                           Ac 6:1-7   Jn 14:1-12

# DO NOT BE TROUBLED

During the Second World War, Prime Minister Winston Churchill gave some of the most stirring speeches of all times. For example, after England had suffered a demoralizing defeat at Dunkirk, Churchill reminded the House of Commons about their commitment to ultimate victory. He said:

> Victory at all costs, victory in spite of terror, victory however long and hard the road may be, for without victory there is no survival. We shall not flag or fail. We shall go on to the end. We shall fight in France, we shall fight on the seas, we shall fight in the air. We shall defend our island, whatever the cost may be. We shall never surrender.

With words like that, Churchill aroused the hearts of his people to remain undaunted, even though they were on the verge of destruction. He encouraged them not to lose faith, however fierce the fight became.

In today's gospel Jesus gives one of his own stirring speeches. The scene is the Last Supper, his disciples are present, and the time is the eve of his darkest hour, the day of his death. And yet, in spite of knowing that the worst is about to occur, Jesus tells his disciples: "Do not let your hearts be troubled. Have faith in God and faith in me."

These words are some of the most reassuring in the whole Bible. Nonetheless, for many of us these words are not reassuring at all. In fact, they seem unrealistic. How can Jesus tell us not to be troubled? Doesn't he realize all the troubles that afflict us?

On the international scene our security is threatened by the possibility of nuclear war. On the national scene our peace is disrupted by increasing violence and crime. On the urban scene our property is jeopardized by rising costs and unemployment.

In our personal lives we have troubles with our work and troubles with our marriage, troubles with our children and troubles with our parents, troubles with our car and troubles with our health.

We even have imaginary troubles to add to our real ones. We imagine failure and loss, and we become afraid. We imagine criticism and rejection, and we become paralyzed. True, these things may never happen. Still they upset our peace of mind.

Doesn't Jesus realize all the troubles that disturb us? Aren't his words unrealistic? The answer is that Jesus does know about them, and that is why his words are relevant and, indeed, reassuring. Jesus knows about troubles because he himself experienced them.

He had troubles with the Pharisees who twisted his words, troubles with his disciples who understood so little, troubles with Judas who betrayed him, troubles with Peter who denied him, troubles with fear of his impending death.

Yet, in spite of all these troubles, Jesus was able to say with calmness and confidence: "Do not let your hearts be troubled. Have faith in God and faith in me."

The faith Jesus recommends is not an escape from reality. Rather, it is a declaration that even if the worst does happen, we will not be destroyed by it. Even if everything seems to be collapsing, we will not be crushed.

Our faith is an affirmation that even if others leave us, Jesus never will, for he has promised to lead us to the place he has prepared for us, so that where he is, we also may be.

6th Sunday of Easter         Ac 8:5-8, 14-17   Jn 14:15-21

# TRIPLE CROWN WINNERS

Up until 1987 only eleven horses had won the coveted Triple Crown in thoroughbred racing. That is, only eleven horses had finished first in the Kentucky Derby, the Preakness, and the Belmont Stakes. The first two horses to accomplish this extraordinary feat were Sir Barton in 1919 and Gallant Fox in 1930. The last two were Seattle Slew in 1977 and Affirmed in 1978.

What is it that makes some horses winning thoroughbreds? Why is it that some horses have more speed, strength and stamina than other horses? Essentially, of course, these traits have to come from within the horses themselves: from their own inner capacity and from their inherited gene structure.

Still it seems that they also need help from outside. To become champions, they need the help of expert trainers and skillful jockeys to activate and develop their inner powers.

It is the same with us. Born human, we have within us capacities to love, learn, choose, work and so on. But we need the help of parents, teachers and friends to activate and develop these capacities so that we can reach our full human potential.

That is why we need the Holy Spirit and why Jesus promised to send him to us: "I will ask the Father and he will give you another Paraclete—to be with you always; to remain with you and be within you."

According to *Peake's Commentary on the Bible*, the word *paraclete* means one who is called to our side as a *helper*. For example, a helper was often a legal counselor in a court of law. In another sense, the Holy Spirit is a special kind of helper who is always with us to help us activate and develop our inner capacities.

Moreover, the Holy Spirit is given not only to be with us at our side, but also to dwell *within* us. His seven gifts are not some magical cloak we put on our outside, but a new source of life and power that operates from within the very depths of our being.

What are some of the ways in which the Holy Spirit helps us?

First, we become *conquerors*. With the Holy Spirit working within our hearts there is no obstacle we cannot overcome in order to grow and expand—whether that obstacle is fear or laziness, drugs or alcohol, a physical handicap or an emotional disorder.

Second, we become more *creative*. Under the inspiration of the Holy Spirit we discover more beauty and harmony in the universe and are able to express our vision in new works of music, art, literature and science.

Third, we become more *compassionate*. Whenever we encounter hunger, sickness or unemployment, the Holy Spirit prompts us to do something personal to alleviate these pains experienced by other people.

Fourth, we see things with greater *clarity*. The Holy Spirit dwelling within us opens our eyes to see things from God's point of view—the shortness of time and the length of eternity; the wisdom of discipline and the foolishness of selfish indulgence; the value of prayer and the waste of worry.

Praise God for giving us the Holy Spirit to dwell within us as a helper. We may never win things like Triple Crowns or Academy Awards, but with his help we will reach a peak in personal growth and enrich the lives of people around us. We may never be given gold medals at Olympics or honorary degrees at graduations, but we will become more Christ-like as the Holy Spirit transforms us from within.


Ascension                                    Ac 1:1-11   Mt 28:16-20

## STILL WITH US

In his book *He Leadeth Me*, Jesuit priest Walter Ciszek chronicles his spiritual odyssey of twenty-three years in Russia, five of which were spent in the dreaded Lubyanka prison in Moscow and ten of which were spent in the harsh Siberian slave labor camps. Fr. Ciszek was finally released from Russia in 1963 in exchange for two Soviet spies held in the United States. He died in 1984 at age 80.

Fr. Ciszek's book tries to answer the question, "How did you manage to survive in Russia?" He claims that he was able to endure the inhuman conditions in which he found himself because he experienced somehow the presence of God. He never lost his faith that God was with him, even in the worst of circumstances.

Today's gospel must have been especially meaningful to Fr. Ciszek. As Jesus is about to ascend into heaven he speaks his final words to his disciples: "Know that I am with you always, until the end of the world."

In his study of Matthew's gospel, Fr. Donald Senior underlines the significance of the *with you* phrase. The beginning of Matthew's gospel was marked by the revelation that Jesus would be called *Emmanuel*, that is, *God-with-us*. This theme of God's abiding presence in the person of Jesus is now matched at the end of Matthew's gospel by our Lord's own promise: "Know that I am *with you* always, until the end of the world."

This keynote of Matthew's gospel, namely *God-with-us*, explains somewhat why Matthew has no ascension story as such. The evangelists Mark and Luke write specifically that Jesus was taken up to heaven, but not Matthew. Although Matthew sets the scene for the Ascension, he stops short of actually saying that Jesus ascends.

Perhaps this is Matthew's way of stressing the *staying* of Jesus with us, as opposed to his *going away* to heaven. It may be Matthew's way of calling attention to our Lord's new, invisible presence in our midst—a sacramental presence transcending all barriers of time and place, as opposed to his historical, visible presence limited by space and time.

We are dealing here with a paradox, a mystery. In one sense, Jesus has *gone away* by ascending into heaven. But in another sense, he is *still with us* here on earth. Our Lord's *going away*, his Ascension, is most important to us because it confirms his claim to be God's own Son; it completes the cycle of Incarnation-Redemption-Glorification; and it gives us hope of one day following him.

But equally important to us is our Lord's *abiding presence*. Whenever we read his word, break his bread, gather to pray in his name, and minister to the least of his brethren, we experience his *being-with-us*, here and now. Whenever we deny ourselves for him, carry our cross after him, or suffer persecution because of his name, we know that he is *with us* to support, encourage and inspire us.

In the familiar story entitled "Footprints" a man at the end of his life wanted to know why in tough times there was only one set of footprints in the sand. After all, the Lord had promised to walk with him all the way. The Lord replied by telling him that he never left him in times of trial. When the man saw only one set of footprints, it was then that the Lord carried him.

The Lord was with Fr. Ciszek for twenty-three years of hardship in

Russia. The Lord was with the man walking in the sand. May the risen Lord be with us all the days of our life.



7th Sunday of Easter                                             Ac 1:12-14   Jn 17:1-11

# ALFIE

The movie *Alfie* tells the story of a British playboy by the same name. During the film, Alfie has affairs with five women, his "birds" as he calls them. In all of these relationships Alfie avoids getting too deeply involved or attached, even though one of his "birds" gives birth to his child and another gets an abortion. Alfie's philosophy is to take care of yourself first and to live for your own pleasures, even if you have to use or hurt other people in doing so.

But when he is confronted with the possibility of his own death because of an illness, Alfie begins to reflect on the meaning of his life. His questions are summed up in the lyrics of the song Bert Bacharach wrote for the movie: "What's it all about, Alfie? Is it just for the moment we live? What's it all about?"

If we were to ask these questions—not of Alfie the Playboy, but of John the Evangelist—we would get his answer in today's gospel: "Eternal life is this: to *know* the Father as the only true God, and him whom he has sent, Jesus Christ."

This is what life is all about—to *know* the Father and his Son Jesus. Life is not just for the moment—in *knowing* God we already have eternal life. Some of us find John's answer so simple that we don't take it seriously. So we seek the answer elsewhere. For example, Alfie sought the answer in sex; John Belushi sought it in drugs; John DeLorean in financial power.

In a sense John's answer is simple. To live fully, to have eternal life, it is sufficient to *know* God. Yet, in another sense, his answer is most sublime. *The Jerome Biblical Commentary* says that *to know* in the Bible is not just perceiving or being aware of someone. *To know* also implies personal experience, intimacy and commitment. Thus, in Genesis we read that Adam *knew* his wife Eve and she conceived a child.

Contemporary psychiatrist Paul Tournier also talks about this profound kind of knowing in his book *To Understand Each Other*. He says that emotional incompatibility in marriage is a myth. In his opinion, emotional incompatibility is really a failure to get to *know* and understand one's spouse—a failure to spend enough quality time with them, to share their feelings and values, to experience things together, to dream their dreams.

If this kind of knowing is essential between husbands and wives, it is no less so between God and us. To *know* God requires an intimate relationship, a deep union and a radical commitment. It means spending time with him in prayer, listening to his word in Scripture and experiencing his power in the sacraments. To *know* God means discovering his beauty in creation, feeling his presence in people and discerning his hand in what happens to us.

In the musical *The King and I*, there is a song called "Getting to Know You." If we sang that to the Lord we would be putting John's gospel into music: "To *know* you, Lord, is our source of happiness in this life and our destiny in the next life. To *know* you gives meaning to our brief life now and anticipates the fullness of life later."

"What's it all about, Alfie?" "To *know* the Father as the only true God, and him whom he has sent, Jesus Christ."


Pentecost (A, B, C)                                        Ac 2:1-11   Jn 20:19-23

# FIRE

Fire is an awesome element. It can both destroy and create. Under arsonists, fire can burn down homes and villages. Under skilled workers, fire can transform materials into ceramics, steel and glass.

For example, Steuben glass is noted for its distinctive designs, extraordinary clarity and remarkable strength. It took Steuben craftsmen almost a year to complete the massive "Great Ring of Canada" as our nation's gift to Canada on the occasion of its centennial in 1967.

Although many talents were used to fashion that Steuben glass, it would not have been possible without fire. Technicians can put together the right combination of sand, alkalis and oxides, but only fire can transform these ingredients into clear glass. Artists can create a design for the glass, but only fire can give it actual shape and form.

Because fire has such immense power to transform and create new possibilities, it is an apt symbol for the Holy Spirit. Thus, in the first reading from Acts we hear how the Pentecost event was marked by the signs of a strong wind and tongues of fire.

In his commentary *Invitation to Acts*, Fr. Robert Karris writes:

> The Spirit's coming, an interior experience, is described exteriorly "like a powerful wind" and "like tongues of fire." In Jewish tradition wind and fire are symbols of God's presence, as, for example, in God's supreme revelation on Mt. Sinai.

Besides its power to transform, fire has other uses that make it indeed a suitable sign for the Holy Spirit. In cold weather we gather around a campfire or fireplace to get warm; the heat generated by a fire has led to its association with love, affection and passion.

A fire lights up, brightens and illuminates space to dispel darkness. We use fire to purify precious metals like silver and to sterilize wounds in emergencies. Because fire consumes and turns matter into itself, it is put to work to get rid of waste and refuse.

Besides having properties that make it useful, fire has the capacity to arouse certain feelings in us. Fireworks inspire awe, vigil lamps devotion, fireplaces togetherness and bonfires excitement.

There is especially one property of fire associated with the Holy Spirit that seems suggested in the gospel: the power of fire to spread and grow and not be contained. Jesus said to his disciples: "As the Father has sent me, so I send you." Then he breathed on them and said: "Receive the Holy Spirit."

As the fire of the Holy Spirit inflames the hearts of the apostles, it cannot by its very nature be contained. So the Lord is sending them to spread this fire to others, to pass on his Spirit to others.

Pope John Paul II emphasized the importance of spreading the fire of the Holy Spirit when he addressed the youth of Scotland in 1982:

> There is no place in your lives for apathy or indifference to the world around you. Christ counts on you, so that the effects of his Holy Spirit may radiate from you to others and in that way permeate every aspect of the public and the private sector of life.

In his book *Not I, Not I, But the Wind That Blows Through Me*, Peter DeRosa expressed much the same idea this way:

Whoever rights wrongs, feeds the hungry, cares for the dispossessed . . . whoever is sensitive towards the numerous little heartaches people suffer, is an envoy of Christ. And whoever shares in Christ's mission, shares in the Fire of the Spirit. A parent or teacher who helps youngsters to be sensitive to beauty, enables them to love truth, to honor sincerity, is also a Paraclete, a light and fire.

Let us pray again that the Holy Spirit will come to fill our hearts and kindle in us the fire of his love, so that the Lord can send us to spread that fire and renew the face of the earth.


Holy Trinity                                              Ex 34:4-6, 8-9   Jn 3:16-18

# THREE, YET ONE

In his brilliant series *The Ascent of Man*, author Jacob Bronowski devotes an episode to mathematics under the title "The Music of the Spheres." He shows historically how man's ascent in civilization was marked by an increasing understanding of mathematical patterns which he saw reflected in the harmonies of music, for example, or in the motion of the spheres around the sun.

One of the most fascinating geometric discoveries by the early Greeks was the fact that three fixed points, not all on the same line, determine uniquely one and only one triangle, one and only one plane, and one and only one circle. Why this should be, we don't know. All we can do is observe it as a fact and apply it to the real world in art, architecture, engineering and science.

Even more mysterious is our belief that there are *three Persons*, yet *one and only one God*. Why this should be, we don't know. All we can do is accept it as a revealed fact and apply it to our Christian life.

Today's readings are part of this Trinitarian revelation. In Exodus we read about God announcing his name to Moses as Yahweh, and then giving us the meaning of that name as a God who is merciful and gracious. In the second reading, St. Paul concluded his letter to the Corinthians with a Trinitarian farewell: "The grace of our Lord Jesus Christ, and the love of God, and the fellowship of the Holy Spirit be with you all" (2 Cor 13:13).

Finally, in the gospel of John, Jesus tells Nicodemus that God his Father so loved the world that he sent his only Son. Recall that last Sunday on Pentecost we also read in John's gospel that Jesus breathed on his disciples and said: "Receive the Holy Spirit."

In his book *The Theology of the Trinity*, Laurence Cantwell devotes a chapter to interpreting the Trinity in the light of the universal religious sense of mankind.

This sense of religion makes itself felt first in a feeling of awe at finding ourselves in a world we did not make. We see evidence of God's hand in creation, but we don't see God himself. Our awe expresses itself in worship.

Second, a religious sense is felt by an insight into God's presence at the heart of the world. Poetry, music, art and human love awaken in us an awareness of divine presence in our very midst. We perceive that human activity has a divine dimension.

If the first religious sense can be characterized as *vertical*, pointing *beyond the world*, then the second way can be characterized as *horizontal*, pointing the way *within the world*. In the first way we look at God as that mysterious source from which creation came—the *Father* as we would say. In the second way, we see God as a presence within creation—the *Son* as we would say.

There is a third dimension to the ways a religious sense is felt, a *depth* dimension whereby we detect a presence *within ourselves*. Great artists, for example, testify to an inspiration from within their very being which moves them to creative activity. This divine spark within us we call the *Holy Spirit*.

No matter where we look, then—*up* into the universe, *out* into this world, or *inside* our own hearts—we sense the presence of a mysterious God who is *three*, yet *one*.

In every dimension of our existence God reveals himself to us in order to surround us with his light, share with us his life and draw us into his love. May we always praise the Father for creating us, the Son for redeeming us and the Holy Spirit for sanctifying us.

Corpus Christi                                            Dt 8:2-3, 14-16    Jn 6:51-58

# FOOD FOR THE WORLD

The book *No Need for Hunger* is a study published by Jonathan Garst in which he says that we have solved the food problem technologically. It is the political and economic problems which impede the flow of this advanced technology from one country to another. Garst claims that by working together the scientist, industrialist, salesman and farmer could feed the world.

In another study done on food and famine, Professor Dando of the University of North Dakota concluded that while previous famines were the result of natural causes such as drought, famines in the future will be the result of human causes such as politics or economics. At this moment more than two-thirds of the world's population is hungry. Unless we solve the food problem, we will soon be facing famine on a global scale, according to Dando.

Indeed, we need food for our body to live. But as Christians we also need another kind of food for our spirits to live. The food *par excellence* for our spirits is the sacrament of the Eucharist, the food of Jesus himself under the form of bread.

In the gospel Jesus says: "I myself am the living bread come down from heaven. Anyone who feeds on this bread will live forever. The bread I will give is my flesh, for the life of the world."

When we reflect on world hunger it teaches us something about the Eucharist. Without adequate food for our body, we become weak and cannot work; we become easy victims to disease and sickness. Without food we quickly lose interest in anything cultural or spiritual; we lose our freedom and become enslaved by poverty and injustice. In other words, without food we cannot live a full human life and enjoy health, work, learning and freedom.

It is no different in our life of the spirit. Without the food of the Eucharist we become weak and incapable of reaching out to help others; we become easy victims to temptation and depression. Without the bread of life we quickly lose interest in reading Scripture and in praying; we lose our freedom in the Spirit and become enslaved by the materialism of the world. In other words, we need the Eucharist to become fully alive in our life of the spirit.

*A Cycle* 45

In the first reading from Deuteronomy, we heard how God allowed the Israelites to be hungry in the desert and then fed them with manna. He did this to show them that "not by bread alone does man live, but by every word that comes forth from the mouth of God."

In his commentary on today's gospel, Fr. Donald Gelpi says that by eating the food of the Eucharist we show in effect that we no longer draw our life simply from the things of this world—no longer do we live by bread alone, or by beer, or by television, or by cars, or by balanced budgets, but by every word that comes from the mouth of God. And the supreme Word of God became flesh in Jesus, who is now present in the Eucharist.

This is the meaning of the bread of life—a Spirit-filled people of God who feed on the Eucharist in faith as a sign of their total dependence on the Lord as the ultimate source of their life.

Not only that, but it is a people sharing its bread with others—bread for the hungry by helping the poor; bread for the oppressed by fighting for justice; bread for the lonely by offering friendship; bread for the despairing by giving encouragement.

Yes, there is *No Need for Hunger*—physical or spiritual—if only we get our scientists, industrialists, salesmen and farmers working together with the help of our governments; if only we become a Spirit-filled people who feed on the Eucharist and share it with others. Pray that we may truly become a people of faith who live on the real food that is Jesus himself and find ways to fulfill each other's needs.

2nd Sunday of the Year         Is 49:3, 5-6    Jn 1:29-34

## NICKNAMES

Nicknames are popular descriptive titles given to people in addition to or in place of their regular names. For example, Babe Ruth as the Sultan of Swat in baseball, Red Grange as the Galloping Ghost in football, William Cody as Buffalo Bill in cowboy lore, Teddy Roosevelt as the Bull Moose among presidents, and General Patton as Old-Blood-and-Guts in the military.

Nicknames usually capture some key characteristic of a person's identity or give a condensed description of their outstanding qualities. Thus

Ivan the Terrible conjures up images of ferocity and violence, while the Little Flower, Therese of Lisieux, reminds us of gentleness and kindness.

Today's readings give us some biblical nicknames for Jesus.

In the first reading, Isaiah calls him God's *Servant*, and then proceeds to identify his mission. Through his *Servant* the Lord will show his glory, gather Israel back to himself, and reveal his light to all the nations.

In the gospel, John the Baptist dubs Jesus as the *Lamb of God*, and then he, too, goes on to describe the Savior's mission. As the *Lamb of God*, Jesus will take away the sin of the world, baptize with the Holy Spirit and demonstrate that he is in fact God's Chosen One.

In his Pelican commentary on this gospel, John Marsh concludes that in this one word *lamb*, the evangelist has drawn together overtones of meaning from Old Testament prophecy, current Passover practices and the apocalyptic hopes of the times.

First, Old Testament prophecy. In Isaiah 53 the *Servant* is crushed for our sins and is led like a *lamb* to the slaughter. Nevertheless, because of his suffering he will take away the sins of many and win pardon for their offenses.

Second, current Passover practices. Every year the Jews re-enacted the Paschal story of Exodus 12. They slaughtered a year-old male *lamb* without blemish and sprinkled its blood on their doorposts. They then prayed that the Lord would pass over their homes as he destroyed their oppressors.

Third, the *lamb* in apocalyptic literature. In the book of Revelation the lamb is first slain as a victim for our redemption but then becomes a victorious conqueror who takes his seat upon God's throne.

Now that we know where John the Baptist got his nickname for Jesus, so what? Let's face it—the *Lamb of God* is not exactly a popular title suggesting strength, such as Richard the Lionhearted. But if we look more closely, we will see that the title *Lamb of God* does, in fact, stand for courage.

Although the Suffering Servant in Isaiah 53 went in silence to his sacrifice, he also went in *strength* and by his own choice. As followers of Jesus, can we take up our cross freely, with dignity, and in strength?

The paschal lamb was a means of *liberation* for God's Chosen People from the oppression of Egypt. To be a disciple of the Lamb implies that we accept the challenges of liberation—whether from Communism, economic injustice or racial bigotry.

The Lamb of the book of Revelation is a *conquering Lamb*—a Lamb who makes war on poverty and hunger, and who battles against immorality and corruption. We witness to the Lamb every time we fight for human rights, stand up for decency and protest incompetence in government.

The *Lamb of God* is more than a nickname. It is a challenge for us to keep on taking away the sins of the world so that it can truly be baptized with the Holy Spirit.

3rd Sunday of the Year                                Is 8:23-9:3   Mt 4:12-23

# FISHERMEN

In one of the finest films ever made, *The Old Man and the Sea*, Spencer Tracy plays the lead role of an aging fisherman. Based on Ernest Hemingway's novel by the same title, this movie depicts man's struggle against insurmountable odds.

As the Old Man in Hemingway's saga, Spencer Tracy battles for hours to catch a great fish, only to have it attacked by sharks as he tows it toward shore. By the time he reaches shore, only the backbone of the giant fish is left.

The Old Man beaches his skiff, shoulders the mast and trudges up the hill to his shack. He says: "Man is not made for defeat. Man can be destroyed, but not defeated."

Today's gospel begins with the story of some other fishermen. The setting is the Sea of Galilee in the land of Zebulun and Naphtali. The fishermen are Simon Peter and his brother Andrew, and two other brothers, James and John.

Walking along the shore, Jesus calls them to leave their fishing nets and to come after him. He promises to make them fishers of men. They immediately abandon their boats to follow him.

Why would Jesus choose fishermen as his first disciples? It certainly wasn't for their educational background or their training in Scripture. Such men would be found in the synagogues, not by the seashore. It certainly wasn't for their glamour. Glamorous fishermen are only found in ads, drinking Cutty Sark Scotch or using Old Spice After-Shave Lotion.

No, the first disciples were probably chosen because they were like the

Old Man in Hemingway's story. Not pious, but good men down deep. Not easily discouraged, but patient and persevering. Not self-indulgent, but hard working. Not educated, but full of wisdom.

And like the Old Man, they would come to know that "man is not made for defeat." Through their experiences with Jesus, these first disciples would learn that "man can be destroyed, but not defeated."

For the next three years they would observe Jesus teach, preach and heal. They would then see him crucified but rise from the dead and ascend into glory. Indeed, they would come to know through their Jesus-experience that "man can be destroyed, but not defeated."

Moreover, after Pentecost, when they received the power of the Holy Spirit, these fishermen would embark on their own mission to catch men for Christ. They too would heal, preach and share with others their hope of eternal glory.

Although we may not be fishermen like the first disciples or Hemingway's Old Man, we too are called by Jesus to live for him, not just earn a livelihood. We are invited to leave behind our old securities and launch out with him onto a larger sea in life.

In other words, we are called to be witnesses for Jesus and fishers of men and women for him. And we fulfill our ministry whenever we reach out in love to heal others by words of comfort in their times of sorrow or by gestures of encouragement in their moments of crisis.

We witness to Jesus whenever we proclaim the indestructibility of hope by bouncing back from our own losses or by starting anew after a tragedy. We draw others closer to the Lord whenever we pray together as a family or forgive one another's offenses.

To be fishers of men and women is more than a metaphor. It is a mission from, through and in Christ.

4th Sunday of the Year                    Zp 2:3; 3:12-13   Mt 5:1-12

# BE HAPPY

Robert Schuller has become one of the foremost preachers on television and his Crystal Cathedral one of the most familiar churches on the American scene. Much of his popularity stems from his optimistic approach to the gospel message of Jesus, an approach he sums up as "possibility thinking."

Schuller's positive point of view is reflected in his best-selling book *The Be-Happy Attitudes*, a commentary on the eight beatitudes our Lord teaches in today's gospel.

The first beatitude in Matthew's listing is: "Blessed are the *poor in spirit*; the reign of God is theirs." Schuller renders this as: "I need help; I can't do it alone." Certainly material poverty does not make us happy, but poverty of spirit does—that realization of how empty we are before God and how much we need him to fulfill our lives.

The second beatitude is: "Blessed are the *sorrowing*; they shall be consoled." Schuller translates this as: "I may be hurting, but I will bounce back." Sorrow and pain are part of everyone's life. But rather than allow ourselves to be defeated by them, we can, in the words of Schuller, find a way to "turn our scars into stars."

The third beatitude is: "Blessed are the *meek*; they shall inherit the land." Schuller interprets it to mean: "I've got to remain calm, kind and corrected." Meekness does not mean weakness; instead it means blending strength with gentleness and combining courage with calmness.

The fourth beatitude is: "Blessed are they who *hunger and thirst for holiness*; they shall have their fill." Schuller rephrases it as: "I really want to do the right thing." In a consumer-oriented society, our appetites are played upon to want more and more of everything. But happiness can only be found at a deeper level where we hunger and thirst for the things of God—his word, his presence, his peace.

The fifth beatitude is: "Blessed are they who *show mercy*; mercy shall be theirs." Schuller rewrites it as: "I'm going to treat others the way I want them to treat me." This beatitude challenges us to show compassion, understanding and forgiveness to others—for we, too, stand in need of support, affirmation and encouragement from them.

The sixth beatitude is: "Blessed are the *single-hearted*; they shall see God." Schuller restates it as: "I'm going to keep the faith flowing through me all the time." Since the basic meaning of single-hearted is pure, unmixed or unadulterated, we become single-hearted when we commit ourselves completely to God's cause.

The seventh beatitude is: "Blessed are the *peacemakers*; they shall be called children of God." Schull.o takes it to mean: "I'm going to be a bridge builder, a peacemaker.'' We may argue about strategies to follow, but we cannot argue about getting involved in some way in peace and justice issues.

The eighth beatitude is: "Blessed are those *persecuted* for holiness' sake; the reign of God is theirs." Schuller expresses it as: "I'm going to be happy anyway." Although we may not be persecuted for our faith like Christians living under Communism are, we suffer from more subtle forms of attack on our Christian values through the media and advertising. We too need to be just as committed and courageous.

Whether we prefer Matthew's version of our Lord's eight beatitudes or Robert Schuller's formulation is not important. What matters is that we find our happiness through them. Problems and pain are part of everyone's pilgrimage. But by taking a positive approach to them through the *beatitudes* or *be-happy attitudes*, we can truly be happy people.


5th Sunday of the Year                                 Is 58:7-10   Mt 5:13-16

## SALT AND LIGHT

On July 16, 1981 a beautiful 19-year-old girl was killed in an automobile accident near Houston. Her name was Nancy Powell. All who knew Nancy grieved over the tragedy because she was a very special person.

For example, one of her boyfriends wrote:

> Her purity, freshness, enthusiasm, and most of all her ability to love bathed all of us who were around her. She was truly a joy. Nancy's essence was that she saw people for what they really were, but loved them as if they were at their best. Her special kind of love will be a motivator throughout my life.

Another boyfriend from college wrote:

> We all loved Nancy very much and will miss her deeply. I will always be looking for her to come bouncing into the room, bringing with her the love that exemplified her life. Her radiance always seemed to bring out the very best in people. Beneath that carefree personality was a very loving person who always had time to help out.

## A Cycle

Nancy Powell lived only nineteen years, but her memory continues to inspire all who knew her. She was the kind of person Jesus could point to in today's gospel and say: "Do you want to be the salt of the earth and light of the world? Then be like her."

In other words, if we want to add flavor to people's lives and brighten up their existence, then we should speak and act in ways that will have these effects. When people like Nancy Powell come into a room, their presence brings peace and joy. When they leave, life seems more drab and dull. When we are with them, we feel affirmed and energized. When we are separated from them, we feel a little lonely and flat.

When we go to work or come home, do people feel better because we're around, or do they get nervous because they expect trouble? What kind of flavor or light do we bring with us? This is the personal sense in which disciples can be salt and light for Jesus.

Besides adding taste to food, salt also preserves it from spoiling. In a world growing more and more corrupt because of greed, injustice and lust, we are called as disciples to preserve such Christian values as sharing, human rights and decency. In a world decaying because of dishonesty, disloyalty and disrespect, we have to be committed to preserve our Judaeo-Christian traditions of integrity, responsibility and care.

Besides illuminating our homes, lamps are also lit to serve as guides on streets and waterways. In a world darkened by abortion, nuclear arms and ecological pollution, people need us as guides to find solutions compatible with the gospels. In a world dimmed by unemployment, hunger and hostilities, we have to take leadership roles to brighten the world's horizon.

It is an awesome task to transform the social order. But it is a task in which Nancy Powell wanted to share. She was studying to be an elementary school teacher. Like her we should have confidence because it takes only a tiny pinch of salt to have a tremendous effect, and it takes only a tiny flame or light to dispel darkness over a vast area.

All of us can be that kind of salt and that kind of light. Thank God for our high call to be signs of his presence in the world. Praise God for the opportunities we have to give glory to him.

6th Sunday of the Year    Si 15:15-20   Mt 5:17-37

# EMBODY THE LAW

In Gilbert and Sullivan's light opera *Princess Ida*, one of the characters sings: "The law is the true embodiment of everything that's excellent. It has no kind of fault or flaw. And I, my Lords, embody the law."

If we shift from comic opera to serious gospel, this rhyme helps us to understand the Sermon on the Mount. Jesus did not come to abolish the law and the prophets, but to fulfill them.

*Law and prophets* here was a summary description of God's revealed word in Scripture. Being a good Jew, Jesus recognized that they were "the true embodiment of everything that's excellent."

For example, the Ten Commandments embody reverence for God, his name and his Sabbath day. They embody respect for parents, marriage, life, property, human rights and truth.

It is this kind of reverence and respect that Jesus came to fulfill. But he would do so in a new way, with a new teaching and with a new authority.

First, Jesus does it in a *new way* because he embodies in his own being all that is excellent in the law. By word and deed Jesus shows us what it means to respect the weak and protect the poor. Some satire is involved when Gilbert and Sullivan's character sang: "And I embody the law." But with Jesus it becomes a serious statement.

Second, Jesus fulfills the law with a *new teaching*. His demands for discipleship far surpass the demands of Old Testament law. A deeper kind of holiness is expected of his followers. Not only is a crime of violence like murder forbidden, but even the anger that is the root cause of such a criminal act. Not only is the act of adultery to be shunned, but even lustful looks that are the beginnings of adultery. Not only are false oaths to be avoided, but any words that might compromise our honesty.

Indeed, these are new teachings that go beyond the letter of the law to its spirit; that no longer stress legalism, but love; that transform one's attitude from "What should I not do?" into "What more can I do?"

Third, Jesus brings the law to fulfillment with a *new authority*. In a series of six contrasting statements Jesus begins by saying, "You have heard it said of old," and then he finishes with his escalated demands, "But what I say to you is." Can you imagine how shocking this was to his listeners? For them the supreme authority was the revealed word of God in

A Cycle 53

Scripture. They must have thought that Jesus was either mad or a megalomaniac to claim an authority greater than the Scriptures.

It was only after he died and rose again that his claims would be understood. Only then would his disciples see that Jesus did in fact fulfill the law. Only then would they realize that he did embody in himself all that was excellent in the law because he was the Son of God.

As disciples of Jesus, to what extent do we fulfill the law and the prophets? Are we satisfied with a minimal legalism, like going to Mass once a week and not killing our neighbor? Or are we striving for quality and excellence the other six days of the week?

Do our thoughts reflect honesty and integrity? Are our motives lofty and noble? If not, then we're no better than the scribes and Pharisees. Do our words show respect and care? Are we demonstrating by our actions unselfishness and love? If not, then our Christian witness is weak.

We may not be without faults and flaws, but at least we must try to embody God's laws and persevere in our pursuit of excellence.


7th Sunday of the Year                                      Lv 19:1-2, 17-18   Mt 5:38-48

## LOVE YOUR ENEMY

In 1963 a five-week civil rights boycott erupted in Birmingham, Alabama. Under the leadership of Dr. Martin Luther King, Jr., demonstrators used Gandhi's nonviolent tactics to persuade stores to provide full service to black customers. Martin Luther King requested that sit-in volunteers sign a commitment card to pledge themselves, body and soul, to the nonviolent movement, and promise to keep the Ten Commandments which he listed.

Martin Luther King's third commandment required walking and talking in the manner of love, for God is love. His sixth commandment read: "Observe with friend and foe the ordinary rules of courtesy." His eighth commandment demanded that a demonstrator refrain from the violence of fists, tongue or heart.

According to Martin Luther King's Ten Commandments, *love* and *nonviolence* had to be the soul power of the Civil Rights Movement. According to another great master, Jesus Christ, *love* and *nonviolence* have to be the soul power of Christian disciples.

In today's gospel Jesus says: "You have heard the commandment, 'You shall love your countryman, but hate your enemy.' My commandment to you is: love your enemy and pray for your persecutors."

The gospel doesn't describe the crowd's reaction, but we can imagine how startled they were. Surely Jesus must be joking. Love the Roman army which has plundered our farms, desecrated our synagogues, and occupied our land? Love the enemy who has taxed our property, humiliated our leaders, and enslaved our youth?

Indeed, it was a hard saying to hear. Nevertheless, there it is recorded by the evangelist without any qualifications or exceptions. Commentators agree that Christ's command to *love your enemy* is one of his unique and original sayings. It has no parallel in biblical or other Jewish literature of the period.

Why would Jesus make such an incredible statement? Perhaps an answer can be found from the context. This statement is the last of a series of six contrasts Jesus is making between the Old Law and his New Law.

The whole series was introduced in last week's gospel with his principal teaching: "Unless your holiness surpasses that of the scribes and Pharisees, you cannot enter the kingdom." The series is now concluded with the final remark of today's gospel which restates Christ's main point: "In a word, you must be perfect as your heavenly Father is perfect."

That is why we must love our enemy. We have to do more than is humanly expected and imitate our heavenly Father, who loves both the good and the bad without discrimination.

The next question is how such a love is possible. An important distinction is necessary. Love is essentially an act of the *will* and not a *feeling*. So we don't have to *feel* good about our enemies, but we do have to *will* good to them. We don't have to experience nice *feelings* about enemies, but we do have to *will* at least their healing and salvation.

Jesus commands us to love our enemies, not because he approves of their wickedness, but because he loves all his creatures and wants them to be saved, not so much because of what they are now—sinners—but because of what they can become—saints.

On the cross, Jesus showed how far we may have to go in loving our enemies. Through the civil rights demonstrations, Martin Luther King showed the power love has to change the hearts of the enemy.

In the midst of today's crises, Jesus needs new witnesses to this power

A Cycle 55

of love over hate and of forgiveness over animosity. Will we stand up and show that we are Christians by our love for our enemies?

8th Sunday of the Year   Is 49:14-15   Mt 6:24-34

## LILIES OF THE FIELD

In 1963 Sidney Poitier won an Academy Award for his performance in the film *Lilies of the Field*. He played an ex-GI, Homer Smith, who stumbles across five East German refugee nuns in Arizona. The nuns need a maintenance man and Homer Smith needs a job.

But instead of paying Homer for his work, the Mother Superior proposes that he stay on and build a chapel for them. Her dogged determination and absolute trust in God inspire Homer to take on the project. The simple faith of these five nuns to expect from God whatever they need transforms Homer Smith from a skeptic into a believer. He builds their chapel.

The movie's title is taken from today's gospel. The *lilies of the field* are part of the imagery Jesus uses in his parable about not worrying and putting more trust in God.

In his book *Invitation to Matthew*, Fr. Donald Senior comments on today's gospel parable:

> This passage is not an invitation to passivity, nor does it spring from a trivial romanticism about nature and its beauty. These verses are a call to action—action that proceeds from a commitment to the Kingdom. Such commitment frees one to live fully in the present, and not be immobilized or diverted by anxiety about one's future.

In other words, when Jesus says that we should learn from the lilies of the field and from the birds of the sky, he is not saying, "Don't work," but rather, "Don't worry." And when he tells us to let tomorrow take care of itself, he is not telling us, "Don't plan or provide for the future," but rather, "Don't be anxious or uptight about the future."

We know from other parts of the gospel that Jesus encourages hard work and diligence, and he praises wise planning and astuteness regarding the future. His main point of today's parable, however, is "don't worry." He says it five times to make sure we don't miss it.

Instead of worrying he wants us to put our faith in God, to seek first his kingdom and to trust in him more. Work, yes, but not as if God didn't exist or care about us. Provide for the future, yes, but not with excessive concern or anxiety.

We must not allow ourselves to get too melodramatic over this parable. Disciples of Jesus like those five nuns in the movie indeed have a lot of faith and trust, but they also work hard themselves and pray often. Wonderful stories are told about saints like Vincent de Paul and Mother Cabrini and how God rewarded their faith and multiplied their resources. But Vincent de Paul and Mother Cabrini also toiled to the point of exhaustion and prayed when it seemed useless.

Another point of realism about this parable is its stark implication about death. A gracious God feeds his birds, but some birds still freeze to death. A caring God clothes the flowers with splendor, but these same flowers also wither and die. So too, a loving Father knows all our human needs and provides for them, but we still experience pain, suffering and death.

Are these contradictions? No, they are a call to faith—faith in a God who will ultimately give us more than we can see now; faith in a God who will in the end restore more than we've ever lost; faith in a God who will eventually win the victory for us when he raises us from the dead.

The *lilies of the field* then is not some pious parable, but a call to action and a commitment to faith. We are called to work with all our might, but not to worry. We are expected to provide for the future, but without anxiety. We are going to encounter suffering and death, but with faith and trust in the living God.

9th Sunday of the Year                                    Dt 11:18, 26-28   Mt 7:21-27

# LONDON BRIDGE

Little children are still taught the old nursery rhyme "London Bridge." It recalls an historical event that took place in 1014 when the Danes occupied

Britain. To regain London from the Danes, who had their main defense on the bridge, King Aethelred enlisted the help of King Olaf of Norway.

King Olaf had his men row under the bridge, lay cables around its pilings, and then pull them away. Thus London Bridge came falling down, the Danes were defeated, London was regained by King Aethelred, and a nursery rhyme was born.

When a new London Bridge was built it was constructed with "stone so strong" that it would "last for ages long," and not come falling down because of weak wooden pilings being pulled or washed away.

In today's gospel Jesus doesn't talk about bridges falling down, but about houses. However, the basic idea is the same. If we build a house or bridge with a weak foundation instead of setting it solidly on rock, then a storm or a flood or an enemy's attack will make it collapse in ruin.

Our Lord applies the imagery to the two ways we can hear his words. If we *do not* put them into practice, we build on shifting sand. If we *do* put them into practice, we build on solid rock.

In the modern world of mass media we hear and see a lot of messages competing with our Lord's words in the gospel: easy instant gratification as opposed to self-denial and carrying one's cross; stockpiling material things as opposed to being poor in spirit; doing your own thing as opposed to keeping the commandments.

If we buy into the values promoted by the world, then we are laying the foundation of our lives on unstable sand. Eventually our indulgence in sensual kicks will leave us empty; our material things will become boring; and having our own way will only make us more restless.

But if we believe in and live by the gospel values of Jesus, then we are setting our lives on solid rock. No adversity will be able to destroy the fulfillment we find in Christ; no loss will be able to deprive us of the joy we experience through Jesus; no disappointment will be able to shatter the solidarity we have with him.

As it turned out, for 900 years London Bridge did not fall down again, even during World War II. It was dismantled stone by stone and put together again in Lake Havasu in Arizona for tourists in the late 1970's, but it did not fall down again like its predecessor in 1014.

In a similar way, if we truly make Jesus our "rock of safety," as today's Psalm 31 invites us to do, then we will indeed "be stouthearted and take courage" when the rains come and the winds lash out against us.

None of us can be spared from some kind of setbacks and sufferings in this life. To survive the worst we need the solid bedrock of faith in Christ. With the sure anchor of the hope Jesus holds out for us and with the steadfast support of his love, he will always be our "Bridge Over Troubled Waters" and he will always "lead us on."

10th Sunday of the Year                                              Ho 6:3-6   Mt 9:9-13

## SECOND CHANCE

*The Natural* is a movie starring Robert Redford as a baseball player named Roy Hobbs who is blessed with natural talent. An innocent, sunny-faced farm boy, Hobbs gets his first big league tryout when he is 20 years old. He packs his home-made bat with the word "Wonderboy" carved in it, bids farewell to his girl friend and heads off to the majors. But he wastes his chance when he is waylaid by a sinister seductress on the eve of his tryout.

It takes Roy Hobbs fifteen years to work his way back for another chance to play in the big leagues, and to redeem himself both as a baseball player and as a man. Finally, his magic bat leads the New York Knights on a charge out of the cellar to the pennant, and he returns to his childhood sweetheart to begin a new life with her.

*The Natural* may be too melodramatic as a movie, but it does make us feel good to see a hero who had fallen from grace get a second chance and succeed. Perhaps, too, that explains the appeal of today's gospel story about the call of Matthew to be an apostle—he gets a second chance.

Actually Matthew is an anti-hero because he's a hated tax-collector. He was a Jew who sold his services to the Roman conquerors to collect taxes for them from his own countrymen.

In the eyes of a good Jew, Matthew had already made a mess of his life by betraying both his country and his religion. Jesus was well aware of this, and yet he was willing to give Matthew a second chance by inviting him to follow him.

Matthew sensed that something significant was happening. Here was a supreme chance to leave his old life and to start again; a once-in-a-lifetime opportunity to redeem the past and to create a new future. Like Roy Hobbs in the movie, Matthew didn't miss his second chance. He seized the moment and followed Jesus.

*A Cycle* 59

William Barclay observes that Matthew left behind his tax-collector's table but took with him his writing pen to compose a gospel later. He lost a lucrative position but found an apostolic mission. He gave up economic security but gained a destiny.

In a sense we're all second-chance people in the company of Roy Hobbs and Matthew. We've all made mistakes or wasted opportunities in the past. Perhaps it was not continuing our education, or drinking ourself out of a good job, or messing up our marriage.

Whatever it may have been, the Lord gave us a second chance. He saw us for what we were in terms of our past foolishness, but he also saw what we could become in terms of our future possibilities.

It's no different today. Jesus doesn't want us sitting around some table collecting taxes of guilt and self-pity when we make more mistakes. He invites us to leave the table and follow him; he calls us to take new directions with our life and to explore new paths.

Sometimes we find ourselves in awkward or undesirable positions through no fault of our own: an accident may have disabled us; economic misfortunes may have impoverished us; or death may have deprived us of someone very dear to us.

In these circumstances, too, the Lord always finds a way to give us a second chance of some sort. He may invite us to discover a previously undeveloped talent, to take on another challenge, or to make new friends.

Jesus won't let us sit still in such situations. He summons us to new adventures and further growth. He stretches our imagination to look beyond the tables surrounding us and see new visions and new missions.

11th Sunday of the Year               Ex 19:2-6   Mt 9:36-10:8

## GIVE YOUR GIFT

In a 1984 article *Newsweek* described Tom Monaghan as a man who had gone "From Pizza to Pennant." The title had reference, first of all, to his ownership of Domino's Pizza—the second largest pizza chain in the United States—and, secondly, to his ownership of the Detroit Tigers baseball team who roared in '84 to win the World Series.

*Newsweek* went on to say that Monaghan's life had all the stuff of an old Frank Capra movie starring Mickey Rooney as a gutsy kid, because Tom grew up in an orphanage and in a series of foster homes from the time he was four.

With the encouragement of Sr. Mary Berarda, Monaghan learned at the orphanage to have faith in God and in himself to be anything he wanted to be. He worked hard selling vegetables, fish, newspapers—anything to earn a dollar. Eventually he became the self-made millionaire he is today.

Near Ann Arbor in Michigan he is building not only new corporate headquarters for Domino's Pizza, but also an orphanage and a home for the elderly. Tom Monaghan is a devout Catholic who attends Mass daily and takes seriously our Lord's words in today's gospel: "The gift you have received, give as a gift."

The context of the passage in which Jesus spoke those words is the summoning of his twelve apostles and sending them on mission. In doing so he gave them power to expel demons, cure the sick and even raise the dead. However, the special powers they received were not given for their own personal gain. Rather, they were given primarily to benefit others.

It is the same with us. Our talents have been given to us by God as gifts. We may have worked hard to develop these gifts, but originally they were given to us without our deserving them or having any claim on them. We don't *own* the gifts; we are only *trustees* or *stewards* of them. So like the apostles and Tom Monaghan, we are obliged to use these gifts to benefit others.

We are dealing with a paradox here. If we try selfishly to hold on to the gifts for ourselves, they will never achieve their full purpose. But if we try to share them with others, they will reach their perfection.

In the words of the late Oscar Hammerstein:

> A bell is not a bell until you ring it;
> a song is not a song until you sing it;
> and love in your heart wasn't put there to stay;
> love isn't love until you give it away.

We may not have money to give away to worthwhile causes like entrepreneur Tom Monaghan has. But all of us can give words of encouragement to someone the way Sr. Berarda did to Tom. We may not have miraculous powers as the twelve apostles had when Jesus sent them on mission. But all of us have the capacity to comfort, sympathize with and affirm people who are hurting in some way.

Whatever gifts we have—gifts of listening or reassuring; gifts of repairing or building things; gifts of serving or volunteering—these gifts have been freely given by God and should be just as freely given away.

Scientist Albert Einstein once said:

> There is one thing I know, that man is here for the sake of other men. Many times a day I realize how much of my life is built on the labors of my fellowmen, both living and dead. And I must earnestly exert myself in order to give in return as much as I have received.

The Eucharist we celebrate is an apt symbol of giving freely of what we have received. Jesus gives and shares the gift of himself with us so well under the signs of bread and wine that we can't help but be inspired to give and share the gift of ourselves with others.

This, too, is meant when the Lord commanded: "Do this in memory of me—freely have you received, freely give of yourselves the way I did."


12th Sunday of the Year                    Jr 20:10-13   Mt 10:26-33

# DO NOT BE AFRAID

The book *Audacity to Believe* is an autobiography by Dr. Sheila Cassidy. In it she relates how she left England in 1971 to escape the "rat-race" professionalism of British medicine to go to Chile to work among the poorest of the poor.

In 1975 Dr. Cassidy was arrested by the Chilean secret police for having treated the bullet wounds of a revolutionary leader. At an interrogation center she was stripped, tied to a bed, and tortured by electrodes attached to her body. Then she was placed in solitary confinement for three weeks and imprisoned in a detention camp for another five weeks before she was finally released and expelled from the country.

Dr. Cassidy writes:

I did not hate the men who had hurt us . . . The freedom of spirit we enjoyed was something that our captors did not possess. Incredibly, in the midst of fear and loneliness I was filled with joy, for I knew without any vestige of doubt that God was with me, and that nothing they could do to me could change that.

Dr. Sheila Cassidy knows from experience the full meaning of today's Scripture readings. With Jeremiah in the first reading she can proclaim that the Lord was with her like a mighty champion. Her persecutors failed and did not triumph.

She knows that Jesus was speaking the truth when he said in the gospel: "Do not let men intimidate you. Do not be afraid of those who can deprive the body of life but cannot destroy the soul."

Jesus doesn't pretend that we will be exempt from problems, pain or even persecutions. But he does promise to be with us when they do come upon us.

In times of persecution, torture may touch our body but cannot reach our soul. As human beings we are always more than our body. We have a spirit whereby we can know, choose and love. The secret police could inflict pain on Dr. Cassidy's body. But they couldn't force her free will, change her mind or destroy her faith.

The ordeal Sheila Cassidy went through will probably never happen to us. Nonetheless, we have our own difficulties and sufferings to face. And so we, too, need to hear Christ's encouraging words: "Do not be afraid of them." We, too, need to be reminded of Jeremiah's declaration that the Lord will be with us to see us through.

The worst things that can happen to us may deprive us in some physical or emotional way. But they should never destroy our faith, hope or love. Consequently, we may see our car wrecked, our home burned, or our marriage broken up. But none of these things should shatter our faith that God is still with us and cares for us. With him at our side we will find a way to survive these setbacks.

We may suffer the loss of our health, our job, or a loved one through death. But none of these things should topple over our hope that somehow good will come out of it—that in some way we will emerge from the misfortune stronger, wiser or more compassionate.

We may hurt because we're overlooked, unappreciated or misunderstood. But none of these things should lessen our love. Our hearts are too big to allow such hurts to keep us from reaching out to people who may be hurting more than we are.

"Do not be afraid, then," Jesus says, "if trials, sufferings or disappointments beset you. They may hurt you in some way or other, but they should never destroy your spirit or your will to survive."

13th Sunday of the Year                    2 K 4:8-11, 14-16   Mt 10:37-42

# HOSPITALITY

*Leave 'Em Laughing* is a movie made for television about the life and death of Jack Thum, played by Mickey Rooney. Jack Thum was a real-life Chicago clown who devoted his whole life to making kids happy, especially in the hospitals where he entertained them for free. He and his wife Shirlee took off the streets into their home and hearts 37 stray children and raised them as their own.

Near the end of his life Jack Thum found it difficult to be funny because of the pain caused by his terminal cancer. Nevertheless, to make one of the small runaways living with him smile, Jack played his clown role to the end to *leave 'em laughing*.

The script about clown Jack Thum's care for kids seems almost to have been taken literally from our Lord's words in today's gospel: "He who welcomes you welcomes me, and he who welcomes me welcomes him who sent me. I promise you that whoever gives a cup of cold water to one of these lowly ones because he is a disciple will not want for his reward."

The theme of welcoming and showing hospitality to someone appears also in the first reading. There an elderly married couple take into their home the prophet Elisha and his servant Gehazi, and as a result are rewarded with the promise of the birth of their first son.

Welcoming someone into our home or hearts is not an easy thing to do, especially today with so many pressures and tensions in our lives, with so much rivalry and competition in our schools and places of work, and with so much violence and crime in our streets.

In his book *Reaching Out*, Fr. Henri Nouwen discusses this problem and sees the movement from *hostility to hospitality* as one of the three main movements of the spiritual life, the other two being the movement from *loneliness to solitude* and the movement from *illusion to prayer*.

Fr. Nouwen defines hospitality as the creation of a friendly space where a stranger can enter and leave in freedom. The aim of hospitality is not to change people or mold them or convince them about our beliefs, but to provide a comfortable empty space for them to enter and discover their own best selves.

On the one hand, good hosts will be good listeners for their guests, feel their pain, share their struggles and dream their dreams with them. In a word, they will *affirm* their guests.

On the other hand, good hosts will set limits, however flexible, for their guests, confront them if need be and challenge them to further exploration in their journey through life. In a word, they will invite their guests to *grow*.

Whenever parents do these things for their children, or teachers for their students, or people in the helping professions for their patients, we see taking place in a hostile world a significant movement toward hospitality; we see fulfilled our Lord's promise that in welcoming children or students or patients, we welcome the Lord himself into our hearts.

Moreover, when we reach out beyond the ordinary boundaries of our everyday life and welcome the lowly stranger in the streets into our hearts, we see the kingdom of God's love become real.

Showing hospitality in some form or other to the poor and the downtrodden, the refugee and the immigrant, or the unloved and the unwanted, gives them a chance to be free and to find their own destiny. In the words of Fr. Nouwen, we give them a chance "to sing their own songs, speak their own languages, and dance their own dances."

14th Sunday of the Year                                      Zc 9:9-10   Mt 11:25-30

# COME TO ME

In 1903 a poem was composed by Emma Lazarus and inscribed on a tablet in the pedestal of the Statue of Liberty. The poem was entitled "The New Colossus" and is best remembered for the following lines:

## A Cycle

> Keep, ancient lands, your storied pomp! cries she
> With silent lips. Give me your tired, your poor,
> Your huddled masses yearning to breathe free,
> The wretched refuse of your teeming shore.
> Send these, the homeless, tempest-tost to me,
> I lift my lamp beside the golden door!

Up until 1954 the island on which the statue stands was an immigration center. Who can count the number of immigrants who passed through there or tell the stories of new beginnings they found there? Who can measure the inspiration they received from the words written by Emma Lazarus?

Today's gospel gives us another set of inspiring words. Jesus' invitation is similar to the Statue of Liberty's, but infinitely more consoling because it is a divine revelation and not merely a stone inscription.

Jesus says: "Come to me, all you who are weary and find life burdensome, and I will refresh you. Take my yoke upon your shoulders and learn from me, for I am gentle and humble of heart. Your souls will find rest, for my yoke is easy and my burden light."

*The Interpreter's Bible* calls this "The Great Invitation," the very sound of which rings out like cathedral bells. To whom is the invitation given? To *all*, and, in the context of the gospel, this refers to those who are burdened with the works of the Mosaic Law. But *The Interpreter's Bible* goes further when it says:

> Christ set no limits to that blessed *all*. We cannot limit the application. The sad in heart are included, and all who bend beneath time's load.

Experiencing weariness and finding life burdensome is part of the human condition. There is the ordinary fatigue we feel from hard work—the kind nurses and doctors, cooks and secretaries, teachers and entertainers feel after a hectic day on their job.

Then there is the weariness that comes from boredom. We feel a vague, general dissatisfaction with life. Colors look gray, the atmosphere feels heavy and food seems insipid.

An extreme kind of weariness borders on severe depression and suicide. Everything seems tedious, empty and meaningless. One feels like giving up the struggle because it doesn't seem worthwhile any more.

Just as there are different degrees of weariness, so too there are different types of burdens. There is the ordinary burden of responsibility that comes with being a leader, director, parent or teacher.

Then there is the burden of being sick, handicapped, out of work, widowed or divorced. In such circumstances we feel the heavy weight of being restricted—physically, financially or emotionally.

There are also the burdens we sometimes carry in looking after others—perhaps taking care of a retarded child, a crippled spouse or a senile parent.

And yet, no matter what kind of weariness we feel or what kind of burden we bear, Jesus says: "Come to me and I will give you rest. Come to me and I will give you strength. Come to me and I will give you grace."

If only we could believe that, we would feel new energy in our bodies, see new visions in our imaginations, and find new reasons for living. If only we could take Jesus at his word, we would fulfill our responsibilities with joy, fight to overcome difficulties with determination, and take on challenges with courage.

Indeed, we would find that "his yoke is easy and his burden light."

15th Sunday of the Year                                  Is 55:10-11   Mt 13:1-23

## MULTIPLYING GOOD

A Washington, D.C. track observer once described Glenda Moody as: "A very large white woman functioning as a track coach for young black men, and succeeding very well."

Glenda came to Washington, D.C. in 1967 at age 21 to work for the Department of Recreation. She found that the high school runners in the area had no organized competition or place to go during the summer. So with a modest nucleus of three runners she founded the D.C. Striders. Today their membership is well over 200.

More than 175 of Glenda Moody's runners have won full, four-year athletic scholarships worth about one million dollars. Glenda has made quite an impact on these young black men. Besides their track form, she has also shaped their attitudes with her belief in the fatherhood of God, the unique worth of every person and the responsibility of each individual to make this a better world.

## A Cycle

Like many other great coaches, teachers and parents, Glenda Moody's influence for good has multiplied many times over. Her success sounds one of the keynotes of today's gospel parable.

Jesus tells the story of how a sower sowed seeds in different kinds of ground—footpaths, rocky ground, ground covered with thorns, and good ground. The seeds that fell on good ground brought forth grain thirtyfold, sixtyfold and some a hundredfold.

In his Pelican commentary on this parable, J.C. Fenton observes that the quantities of grain production Jesus quotes are far higher than was usual. A little more than sevenfold was considered average, whereas tenfold was considered good. The fantastic numbers Jesus cites emphasize the immense power of his word as it is spoken to us. There is no proportion between what we contribute to God's kingdom and what he accomplishes through us.

We see a multiplication principle at work even in the natural order. For example, Eugene P. Smith, a professor of mathematics at Wayne State University and a past president of the National Council of Teachers of Mathematics, has inspired thousands of mathematics educators and students. His love for mathematics has been multiplied a hundredfold through them and will continue to spread well beyond his lifetime.

The same is true of all great mentors and their love for a certain field: Martha Graham in dancing; Leonard Bernstein in music; Beverly Sills in opera. All of these mentors have had their influence multiplied a hundredfold among their disciples.

Outstanding coaches like Vince Lombardi, poets like Robert Frost and heroines like Helen Keller—all of these have had their vision of life multiplied through the people they've touched in some way.

If this is true of the natural order, how much more true must it be of the order of grace. Who can deny the tremendous good done by the parents of Pope John Paul II and Mother Teresa? Certainly much of that good was done directly by their children, but it would never have happened had not the parents raised those children in a faith-filled family.

We never know, then, how many times even a single act of kindness will be multiplied in God's hands, or how the harvest of a lifetime of dedicated service to some noble cause will be increased a hundredfold by God.

The seed of God's word has immense power to reproduce and bear fruit in our lives. All God asks is that we provide good soil by having faith and trust in him, and he will do the rest—he will take our talents, as he took those of Glenda Moody, and use them to build his kingdom in the hearts of his people.


16th Sunday of the Year     Ws 12:13, 16-19   Mt 13:24-43

# MUSTARD SEEDS

On December 17, 1903, at Kitty Hawk, N.C., Orville and Wilbur Wright made the first powered air flight. Their best attempt measured 852 feet in distance and 59 seconds in time. Since then aviation has made immense progress. The Boeing 747 Jumbo Jet alone stands higher and longer than the first flight by the Wright Brothers. Already we've sent astronauts to the moon, the Mariner spacecraft to planets like Mercury and the Discovery space shuttle on routine flights.

From the simple first flight of the Wright brothers we have developed a spectacular space program. The same has been true in other fields of endeavor. From small beginnings great things have been developed in music, theater, literature and education.

Today's gospel gives two other examples of this axiom and applies it to the growth of God's kingdom. From the small beginning of a mustard seed, a large plant grew. From the tiny yeast mixed in flour, a whole mass of dough expanded.

So too with the kingdom of God. The Church had an insignificant beginning with a man's death on a cross. But because of God's power, its final victory through the resurrection will be a spectacular success.

The Church's mission began in a simple way with the twelve apostles. But because of God's power it has undergone tremendous development over the centuries and its eventual extension will be something awesome.

If we examine our own spiritual growth, we discover a similar phenomenon. Our spiritual life was initiated with a simple sign—a washing with water in the sacrament of baptism. From that moment on we have held within us the very life and power of God himself; we have within us a dynamism to develop and do great things for God.

If we nurture that seed with the bread of the Eucharist and enrich that yeast with the word of Scripture, we cannot help but grow and expand and produce something marvelous for the Lord.

It doesn't matter how limited our talents are. With God's grace, we can use those talents to do tremendous things in the world. Rosa Parks didn't have much talent, but because she insisted on her right to sit anywhere on a public bus, she was instrumental in starting the Civil Rights Movement.

It doesn't matter how small our community of believers is. With God's impetus behind us, we can accomplish mighty works for him. The Ploughshare Seven were a tiny band, but because they demonstrated against the use of nuclear arms, they were a factor in the formation of the bishops' pastoral letter *The Challenge of Peace*.

Nor does it matter how insignificant our ideas or efforts seem to be. With God supporting us, those ideas and efforts will join forces with those of other people to achieve their purpose. In the 1940's Sister Kenny insisted on treating polio patients with movement and therapy, as opposed to putting them in immobilizing splints. As a result of her efforts, the medical treatment of infantile paralysis was revolutionized.

We need never get discouraged, then, by how small the seed of our own resources seems to be. Under God's care that tiny beginning can grow and multiply to produce great things in his kingdom. We need never despair at how weak the yeast of our talents appears. In God's hands that yeast can be transformed and expand to reestablish all things in Christ.

17th Sunday of the Year   1 K 3:5, 7-12   Mt 13:44-46

# TREASURE HUNTS

Most of us have read the story of *Treasure Island*. We are still fascinated by the adventures of such characters as Jim Hawkins, Billy Bones and Long John Silver. Many of us have been fascinated, too, by the movie *Raiders of the Lost Ark* and its sequel *Indiana Jones*. Such movies appeal to our childhood fantasies about treasure hunts.

This is what today's parables appeal to: our capacity to enjoy a search for treasures. One of the parables is about a treasure hidden in a field while the other is about a pearl of great price. The two parables are different in the sense that the treasure is found by chance in a field, whereas the pearl of great price is located after a deliberate search. But their theme is the same: the tremendous joy someone has when he discovers a hidden treasure or a priceless pearl.

This joy is so overpowering that it dominates all his feelings and thoughts. He will give up everything to obtain that treasure or pearl, because what he has now seems valueless compared to what he is able to obtain.

This joy is so overwhelming that it seizes the person completely and penetrates his inmost being. To secure this joy he will make any sacrifice; to possess that treasure or pearl he will pay any price.

So the decisive thing is not what one gives up to obtain the treasure or pearl he finds. Rather, the decisive thing is the reason for doing so—the all-surpassing joy he experiences.

This is the way it should be with the kingdom of God. Our discipleship for Christ should be like the adventure of a treasure hunt. It should not be dull, routine or monotonous. On the contrary, like the adventures of Jim Hawkins or Indiana Jones, it should be mysterious, exciting and full of risks.

We have the good news of God's revelation in the Scriptures. The Bible is like a treasure map showing us how to find the Way, the Truth and the Life. This good news should cause joy in our lives—joy because we have access to the hidden treasure of God's wisdom and knowledge; joy because we seek a crown that is imperishable and unfading; joy because all else seems valueless compared to the riches we find in Christ.

Hearing the good news of the gospel should fill our hearts with such gladness that no price would be too great to pay for it. The joy we find in Christ should be so overwhelming that no sacrifice would be too heroic to make for him. Once we taste the goodness of the Lord, the unreserved surrender of even valuable things for him becomes easy. Once we experience the peace that Jesus alone can give, the renunciation of everything that interferes with it becomes reasonable.

If our discipleship is like the adventure of a treasure hunt, then why do we find it dull and tedious sometimes? Perhaps because we don't have enough faith to see the mystery and excitement that is there.

If hearing the good news should overwhelm us with joy, then why are we so sad and serious sometimes? Perhaps because we don't have enough confidence in the power of God's word to generate joy.

A Cycle                                                              71

If following Christ fulfills our every expectation, then why are we so reluctant sometimes to make sacrifices for him? Perhaps because we don't have enough courage to take such risks for him.

Pray that God may strengthen our faith, our confidence and our courage so that we can undertake our discipleship as an adventure, discover the joy of the good news, and give up whatever is necessary to secure that treasure or pearl we have found hidden in Christ.


18th Sunday of the Year                                    Is 55:1-3   Mt 14:13-21

# HUMAN HUNGERS

In his book *Toma Tells It Straight*, ex-policeman David Toma journals his life story. It takes us through his days as a boxing champion for the Marines, a professional athlete, a Newark cop for 16 years with the Vice, Gambling and Narcotics Squad and an undercover policeman who infiltrated Mafia circles.

On the one hand, Toma's adventures as a cop caused him to be wounded and hospitalized more than 30 times. On the other hand, they also served as the inspiration for the *Baretta* television show.

But there was a time when David Toma was a drug addict. After the death of his five-year-old son, he tried to escape from his feelings of guilt, anger and despair by resorting to tranquilizers.

Eventually he broke his 100 pill-a-day habit. Today he travels the country to talk to teens and parents about the damage which drugs and drink do to us. "Get high on life," Toma says. "God should be number one in your life, and you should be next. Get high on yourself."

David Toma's message about finding fulfillment in God and self instead of in drugs and drink fits in well with today's readings from Scripture.

In the first reading from Isaiah the Lord says: "Why spend your money for what is not bread; your wages for what fails to satisfy? Heed me, and you shall eat well . . . Come to me, that you may have life."

The gospel story dramatizes this teaching through Christ's multiplication of the five loaves and two fish. The people are in a deserted place, a symbol of the emptiness of their lives. They are hungry and thirsty, not only for food and drink for their bodies, but also for nourishment for their spirits.

After the miracle they eat their fill, and there are even twelve baskets of fragments left over. We can't help but recall here one of the eight beatitudes: "They who hunger and thirst for holiness shall have their fill."

In what amounts to a commentary on this gospel, the U.S. Bishops, on the occasion of the 41st International Eucharistic Congress in Philadelphia in 1976, made this statement:

> There is no one of us who does not hunger in many ways: for, besides physical hunger, human beings have deep emotional, intellectual, and spiritual hungers. Pleasure, power or possessions may temporarily quiet the pangs of some hungers. They cannot satisfy us on the deepest levels of our personhood. *Only God can do that.*

In other words, as long as we try to nourish our lives with fame, wealth and amusements, we find that our appetites are never fully satisfied. Some of us, unfortunately, even become enslaved by our appetites and become addicted to alcohol or drugs.

But if we nourish our lives with the bread of life—Jesus Christ—we find our hunger and thirst for higher things satisfied. We discover that we can feel a sort of peace and contentment even with the little we may have; that we can be joyful and glad even when there is some sorrow to bear; that we can experience order and harmony even when things seem chaotic.

As we wait for the Lord to feed us with his Eucharist, pray that we may not waste our time seeking satisfaction in substitutes for the Lord, but instead to find our fulfillment in him; that we may not wander around our deserts hungry and thirsty, but instead to let him fill us with the wine of his word and the bread of his body.

19th Sunday of the Year  1 K 19:9, 11-13   Mt 14:22-33

# WALKING ON WATER

*A Man Called Peter* was a best-selling biography that was later made into a movie. It narrates the life of Peter Marshall, a Scotsman from Glasgow

## A Cycle

whose desire was to be a seaman but whose destiny took him to the U.S. Senate as a chaplain. As a lad, Peter enlisted in the British Navy, but his career lasted only two days when it was discovered that he was only 14 years old. Later, while working as a machinist and teaching Sunday School, Peter felt called to be a minister.

Persuaded by a cousin to come to America, Peter set out in faith to cross the cold waters of the North Atlantic. With little money, no friends and only a job reference, Peter likened himself to other men of faith who ventured into the unknown, men like the patriarch Abraham, the explorer Columbus and the pioneer Brigham Young.

The Lord continued to guide Peter Marshall in surprising ways through the Presbyterian ministry, his marriage to Catherine, his parish assignments and finally to his fame as chaplain to the U.S. Senate.

Peter Marshall died in 1949 when he was only 46, but in that short lifetime he inspired thousands of people by his preaching, his friendliness, and above all by his faith.

Another man called Peter who ventured over water is the subject of today's gospel. Peter the apostle follows in faith the Lord's bidding to walk on water. But when his faith falters, he begins to sink. In desperation he cries out to the Lord to save him. Jesus stretches out his hand to catch Peter, but expresses his disappointment over Peter's lack of faith.

In *The Jerome Biblical Commentary*, scholar John L. McKenzie sees symbolic significance in this gospel story. Chapter 14 starts a section of Matthew called "the ecclesiastical portion." The apostles in the boat personify the Church, to which Jesus is always near even when the situation is threatening.

Moreover, Peter's prominent place in the story, unique to Matthew, increases its symbolic significance. Peter's special position among the apostles begins to build up with this episode. But, to fulfill his role, Peter must have faith.

As long as Peter kept his focus on the Lord, all went well. As soon as he forgot about Jesus and worried about the wind, he began to sink. Perhaps this is what faith means: keeping our focus on the Lord, regardless of the turmoil around us; trusting that he is always near to support us, regardless of the waves of trouble that engulf us.

This kind of faith is more an encounter *with* God than it is a belief *about* God. It is more an experience of the divine *presence* itself, than an acceptance of dogmatic *pronouncements* about it.

Such a faith won't remove all our difficulties. In fact, it might create some new ones. But it will give us the strength we need to cope with them. Such a faith won't be a master key unlocking the answers to all our questions. But it will give us the assurance that Christ holds the key, and that will be enough for us. Such a faith will not eliminate all the darkness that sometimes surrounds us. But it will filter through some light to allow us to recognize Christ's presence in that darkness.

Yes, the Lord is always near, even when we can't see him or feel his presence. But it takes faith to contact him. Peter Marshall had this kind of faith when he voyaged across the Atlantic—a staunch and steadfast faith that saw him through all uncertainty, every unknown and each difficulty.

What kind of faith do we have? Will we sink with Peter the apostle, or sail with Peter Marshall?


20th Sunday of the Year                                          Is 56:1, 6-7    Mt 15:21-28

## PERSISTENCE

The movie *Norma Rae* tells the true story of a woman whose pluck and grit won a fight to establish a workers' union. Played by Sally Field in the film, Norma Rae starts out as an ordinary worker in a southern textile mill. Gradually she becomes angered by the inhuman working conditions that make her mother deaf and are slowly destroying her father.

So she joins forces with a labor union leader to begin organizing the workers. Norma Rae encounters all kinds of resistance from her bosses in the mill, her pastor in the church and her husband at home.

Her supervisors even use her reputation as a woman of easy virtue to intimidate her. Still, Norma Rae stubbornly sticks to her task. Her tenacity triumphs when the workers vote in favor of establishing a union.

Today's gospel relates the story of another determined woman who met a lot of resistance—the Canaanite woman whose daughter was possessed by a demon. At first her cry for mercy was simply snubbed by Jesus. Then the annoyed disciples tried to get rid of her. Finally, Jesus addressed her contemptuously as a dog.

Still, she persists: "Please, Lord, even the dogs eat the scraps that fall from their masters' table." At last the Lord acknowledges her indomitable spirit: "Woman, you have great faith! Your wish will come to pass." That very moment her daughter was healed.

In his commentary *Invitation to Matthew*, Fr. Donald Senior calls attention to the irony of the story. The Canaanite woman asks for a mere crumb from the Lord's table of miracles. Not only does she secure the crumb of healing she sought, but also access through faith to the Lord's messianic banquet.

What the Gentile woman requested and received was magnificent in itself—deliverance for her daughter from a demon. But what she was rewarded with above and beyond any of her wildest dreams was even more magnificent—the privilege to become one of the Lord's chosen people.

Isn't that often what happens to us? The Lord is never outdone in generosity. If we have faith, there is no limit to what he can do for us. Whether we put our faith in some cause as Norma Rae did, or in a person as the Canaanite woman did, Jesus can do marvelous things through us. He can use us to secure justice for the poor, peace between warring parties or freedom for the oppressed.

If we never quit or allow ourselves to get discouraged, there is nothing we cannot accomplish. We might run into strong resistance or be rebuffed, but if we are indomitably persistent, by God's power we will prevail. We might encounter what seem to be insurmountable obstacles or insoluble problems, but if we remain steadfast in our efforts, by God's grace we will ultimately overcome them.

People like Norma Rae and the Canaanite woman pursue their purposes with dead earnestness. They will not take "No" for an answer. Can we do the same for the cause of Christianity?

In our battles against the nuclear arms race, the spread of pornography or legalized abortion, are we ready to accept ridicule, but not give up our resolve? Are we strong enough to suffer temporary setbacks but not surrender the fight? Can we be looked at as fools and still not lose our faith?

21st Sunday of the Year          Is 22:15, 19-23   Mt 16:13-20

# PUBLIC IMAGES

In his book *The Image-Makers*, William Meyers has a chapter on "Pioneers of Persuasion." One of the stories he tells is how ad executive Rosser Reeves used carefully spliced television commercials during the 1952 presidential campaign to sell General Eisenhower to the public "like a tube of toothpaste."

Ever since then, professional image-makers and marketing experts have been employed to package political candidates in a glamorous way so that they will appeal to the voters' emotions. To be successful today, office seekers have to be as concerned about their public image as about the campaign issues. Appearance and performance on television are as important as one's experience and programs.

In the gospel for today, it seems that Jesus too was worried about his public image. "Who do people say that the Son of Man is?" he asks his disciples. In response they give sort of the latest Gallup poll readout of their day: "Some say John the Baptist, others Elijah, still others Jeremiah or one of the prophets."

But as we read further, we see that Jesus is not interested in his popularity rating. He's interested in the more profound question of his essential identity: "Who do you say that I am?"

Moreover, Jesus is not aiming so much at finding out who he is—he knows that already—but at leading his disciples to discover this for themselves. Scripture scholar William Barclay points out how Peter's discovery was that human categories alone were inadequate to identify Jesus. His public image as carpenter, teacher, healer, prophet and leader all failed to measure up to the true meaning of who he was.

It was only by divine revelation and inspiration that Peter could declare the true identity of Jesus: "You are the Messiah, the Son of the living God." To confirm the accuracy of Peter's confession, Jesus made several significant and symbolic statements.

First, he declared Peter blest for responding to the revelation he was given. Second, Jesus conferred a new name on Peter—he will henceforth be called "Rock." Third, he promised to make Peter the foundation on which he would build his Church. Fourth, Jesus gave to Peter the authority and power to heal and forgive.

A Cycle                                77

All this is history now, and yet the question Jesus asked continues. It is one of those classic eternal questions all of us have to confront: "And *you*, who do *you* say that I am?"

It is a personal question that demands a personal response from us. It is a critical question that calls for us to make a commitment one way or the other. It is a decisive question whose answer will determine our entire destiny.

Whether we're in Caesarea Philippi or in Cincinnati, Ohio we can't dodge the issue or avoid the question. If Jesus is truly God's Son, then either we confess that and live accordingly, or else we deny it and do our own thing.

We can't escape the challenge thrown at us. Either we declare his divine identity in human form and follow him, or else we denounce him as a phony and find someone else.

At this very moment, Jesus is questioning us: "And *you*, who do *you* say that I am? Am I just a nice guy who said a lot of nice things, or am I truly a Savior who gives you his peace? Am I just another of many myths, or am I really the Master and Lord who gives meaning to your life?"


22nd Sunday of the Year                          Jr 20:7-9   Mt 16:21-27

## LOSING

In the 1984 Olympics at Los Angeles, 16-year-old Mary Lou Retton became the first American girl to win a gold medal in gymnastics. To accomplish this extraordinary feat, she had to make many sacrifices during her two years of intensive training prior to the Olympics.

While other teenagers were enjoying themselves with a full schedule of dating and dancing, Mary Lou Retton could only participate on a very limited basis. To improve her skills she had to practice long hours in the gym; to nourish her body properly she had to follow a strict diet; and to increase her confidence she had to compete frequently in meets.

But what Mary Lou Retton gave up in terms of good times and junk food was little compared to what she gained in self-satisfaction and public acclaim when she won her Olympic gold medal. What she lost in the usual social life of a teenager she found in the special setting of becoming a champion gymnast—acceptance, camaraderie and respect.

Mary Lou Retton's Olympic experience illustrates somewhat Christ's paradox in today's Scripture: "If a man wishes to come after me, he must deny his very self, take up his cross and follow me. Whoever would save his life will lose it. But whoever loses his life for my sake will find it."

*The Interpreter's Bible* calls attention to the fact that this "losing-finding" saying is recorded six times in the gospels. It is more than a pious proverb. It is a scriptural axiom and a principle for life.

If we worry about keeping our health, we lose it by becoming hypochondriacs. But if we let go of ourselves and burn up our energy in worthwhile activities, we find that we become healthier and happier people in the long run.

Many of us are afraid to start a regular exercise program like jogging because we might lose out on some sleep or else be too tired to do our work. Yet, once we get going on such a regime, we find that we sleep better and that our energy level rises to do our work.

People who smoke cigarettes or drink alcohol often have to give up these habits. But they gain years of added life in place of them. Diabetics have to let go of foods and drinks with high amounts of sugar in them. But they learn to like other foods and drinks and extend their lifespan in exchange.

These common experiences should convince us that often we have to lose something to gain something better. It is no different in our relationship with the Lord.

Instead of hoarding so many clothes in our closets because we're afraid we won't have enough or the best to wear, maybe we should let go of some of these clothes to help the poor. Instead of overindulging in food, drink or sex because we're afraid we won't get enough to satisfy ourselves, maybe we should feed our bodily appetites less and feed our spirits more with prayer and the reading of Scripture.

As Christ himself says in the gospel, we sometimes have to deny ourselves in order to follow him as disciples; we sometimes have to lose certain things in order to find better things.

The Lord will never ask us to let go of everything, but he will require that we often give up some of our time, energy, money and love to a particular cause or to a particular person.

And as we do so, he will show us how we gain peace, joy, fulfillment and satisfaction. Whoever loses his or her life for Jesus' sake will find it.

A Cycle

23rd Sunday of the Year  Ezk 33:7-9  Mt 18:15-20

# PRAYING TOGETHER

In 1868 Susan B. Anthony and her friend Elizabeth Cady Stanton persuaded a Congressman to introduce an amendment to grant voting rights to American women. Although their efforts failed at the time, they began the Women's Suffrage Movement, which gradually gained momentum until the 19th Amendment was finally passed in 1920.

Today we see the results of the revolution Susan and Elizabeth began as more and more women not only decide political elections with their votes, but also participate in them as candidates themselves.

Other examples of two or three people getting together to initiate significant change include: Ralph Nader and consumer advocate groups, and MADD (Mothers Against Drunk Drivers).

Jesus presents his own pressure group version in today's gospel and he does it in the context of prayer: "If two or three of you join your voices on earth to pray for anything whatever, it shall be granted you by my Father in heaven. Where two or three are gathered in my name, there am I in their midst."

Is Jesus playing a numbers game with us? Is he saying that if two or three of us get together to buy a lotto ticket and then pray over it, we will win the big bucks?

Obviously not, although some have tried this as a magic formula. Jesus is using numbers to impress upon us the importance of praying with others, as opposed to praying by ourselves.

Elsewhere Jesus stressed praying in private. In Matthew 6:6 he recommended that we go to our room when we pray, shut the door, and speak to our Father in secret. Here in Matthew 18, Jesus shows that he equally endorses the practice of praying with others.

He himself prayed this way when he took with him on several occasions his three closest disciples, Peter, James and John. Recall the stories of the raising of Jairus' daughter, the transfiguration and the agony in the garden.

Praying with others is so important to Jesus that he attached two promises to it. First, if we join together to ask for anything whatever, it will be given to us. Second, if we gather together in his name, he will be present to us.

The first promise—getting whatever we ask for—must not be taken literally. Otherwise, we reduce God to something like an applause meter—that is, a God who grants requests to one competing group over another depending on which one prays the loudest or the longest.

The promise really centers on God's answer to our prayers, which may be different from our own imagined answer. God's answer may not solve our problem, but it will help us search for a solution. God's answer may not remove all our troubles, but it will renew our strength to deal with them.

The second promise—God being with us in our midst—can be taken literally. Whether we're in a crowd of two or three million people praying with the Pope on some of his papal visits, or in a small group of two or three praying with a grieving family over someone's death, God is present there.

Moreover, where we pray is secondary. Certainly it is inspiring to pray in a beautiful cathedral, temple or shrine, for there God's presence seems to be very powerful. But it is no less a spiritual experience when we gather to pray at the family dinner table before meals, in a schoolroom before catechism class, in a hospital ward before surgery, or on a street after an accident.

Significant changes can take place in the natural order when two or three people get together to achieve some goal. For all the more reason, magnificent things can happen in the spiritual order when two or three people join together in prayer for something.

God's presence is felt in our midst and his power becomes operative in us. What we cannot do alone, we can do together in terms of correction and forgiveness, healing and service, organization and building.

24th Sunday of the Year    Si 27:30-28:7    Mt 18:21-35

# FORGIVENESS

In his book *High Wind at Noon*, author Allen Knight Chalmers narrates the following story about Peer Holm. At one time Holm was a renowned engineer who had built great bridges, railroads and tunnels all over the world. But later, because of failure and sickness, Holm was barely able to eke out a living for his family.

## A Cycle

Holm had a neighbor with a very fierce dog, and he asked the man to do something about the danger it posed. The neighbor got angry and abusive. One day the very thing Holm feared happened. The dog attacked his little daughter and she died from the wounds.

The sheriff shot the dog and all the village people became embittered against the owner. When sowing time came and all the fields were plowed, they refused to sell him grain. Without seed the farmer would go hungry and be reduced to poverty.

However, Peer Holm could not allow this to happen. So early one morning he took his last bushel of barley and sowed his neighbor's field. Later, when the crops grew, it was obvious what had happened. Part of Holm's own field was bare, while his neighbor's field was green.

That kind of forgiveness is not easy to find, yet it is what our Lord expects of us. In today's gospel Jesus tells his own story of forgiveness involving an unjust steward.

The story is occasioned by Peter's questions about the limits we should set on forgiveness: "How often must I forgive my brother? Seven times?" Current rabbinic teaching was that a man must forgive his brother three times. Peter might have thought that he was being generous in stretching the number to seven.

But Jesus would have none of these limitations. By multiplying Peter's proposed number of seven by seventy, Jesus exaggerates and shows how silly it is to count the number of times we forgive someone. Forgiveness must be unlimited.

His parable makes this clear. How can we calculate how often or how much we should forgive others, when all of this is trivial compared to the way Jesus has forgiven us?

We sometimes forget how extravagant God has been with the frequency and the immensity of his forgiveness of us. Perhaps this is because we become preoccupied with the pain other people inflict on us when they wrong us in some way.

Nonetheless, we should never fail to remember our own offenses against God's people and the hurt that we have caused them, and how the Lord has always been lavish with his mercy towards us in spite of our own unworthiness.

Besides remembering our own sinfulness, Jesus insists that we forgive from the heart. "How is this possible?" we might ask. "How can we forgive from the heart someone like a criminal who has terrorized us?"

In his book *Mere Christianity*, C.S. Lewis says that loving our enemies does not mean feeling fond of them or pretending that they are not such bad fellows after all. Loving and forgiving our enemies does mean, however, to wish that they were not bad, to hope that they may be healed and cured, and to will them good.

It was in this spirit that saints like Stephen, Joan of Arc and Thomas More were able to forgive their executioners when they were martyred. It was in this spirit that Jesus himself prayed on the cross: "Father, forgive them, for they do not know what they are doing" (Lk 23:34). It was in this spirit that Peer Holm forgave his neighbor and sowed his field for him.

25th Sunday of the Year                                      Is 55:6-9   Mt 20:1-16

# WORK PARABLE

The 1954 movie *On the Waterfront* is considered a classic in film making. It features Marlon Brando as longshoreman Terry Malloy, who gets locked in a brutal battle with the ruthless labor boss Johnny Friendly, played by Lee J. Cobb.

The issue is the rights of the dock workers. Not only are the longshoremen being exploited by the ship owners, but they are also being shaken down by their own union leaders.

With the help of Fr. Barry (played by Karl Malden) and Edie Doyle (played by Eva Marie Saint) Terry Malloy undergoes a transformation after his brother is murdered by Johnny Friendly's goons.

From being a tough and uncaring street fighter, he becomes a crusader for his fellow workers and testifies for them to the crime commission against their corrupt labor bosses.

Today's gospel also deals with a labor problem. At first it appears that the parable is setting up a model for management and labor relationships. Such is not the case.

The parable by our Lord is more about the generosity of God than about working conditions. The story is more about the supreme goodness of God than about wage settlements.

The punch line in the parable is the statement at the end: "I intend to give this man who was hired last the same pay. I am free to do as I please with my money, am I not? Or are you envious because I am generous?"

In his book *The Parables of Jesus*, Joachim Jeremias says that today's story does not depict reckless, arbitrary action by the owner. Rather, it portrays the behavior of a large-hearted man who is compassionate and full of sympathy for the poor.

According to Jeremias, the owner sees that if he pays the last group for only their one hour of work, they will not have enough to take home to feed their families. So it is out of pity for their poverty that the owner decides to give them a full day's wage.

Of course this shocks our strong sense of justice. Like the workers who labored all day we protest: "It's not fair! We not only worked longer hours, but also harder in the heat. Surely we are entitled to more than the last group."

But if we're disturbed by this double injustice, then we miss the point of the parable. It's a story about God's goodness and not about labor-relation guidelines. Jesus wants to shake us up purposely: "Don't you see? The owner is what God is like—all goodness and compassion, all mercy and generosity."

In one of his talks, Fr. John Shea points out a problem Christ has—he can't count or measure. He makes too much wine at the Cana wedding—more than 100 gallons of it. He multiplies too much bread for the crowd—twelve baskets of food were left over. He forgives way too much—he uses infinity expressions like 70 × 7 times. The numbers he uses in his talent or debt stories are either too small or too big.

This is Jesus' way of showing that when God does things, he does them in a big way—with extravagance and generosity, with flair and foolishness.

Praise God for always giving us more than what we are entitled to; for forgiving us more than we ever deserve; for blessing us with more than we are worthy of.

Pray that we may be more generous with each other—by not just forgiving offenses, but also by forgetting them; by not just fulfilling our duties, but by offering to do more; by not just doing what is expected of us, but also by doing the unexpected that delights people so much.

26th Sunday of the Year    Ezk 18:25-28   Mt 21:28-32

# BROTHERS

Along with *Oedipus Rex* and *Hamlet*, Sigmund Freud considered Dostoevski's *The Brothers Karamazov* one of the three greatest works in world literature. In Freud's interpretation, the three Karamazov brothers symbolize the nature of man.

The eldest son Dmitri is a wild wastrel. He represents man dominated by sensuality. The next son Ivan is a teacher, writer and atheist. He symbolizes the intellectual dimension of man. The young son Alyosha was a novice at a monastery. He stands for the spiritual nature of man.

The three Karamazov brothers were abandoned by their father Fyodor after their mothers died. They reassemble now to do battle with their father and claim what is rightfully theirs. Their conflicts reflect those of Everyman, which occur not only in his soul, but also in his relationship to God.

Today's gospel parable tells another symbolic brother story. The elder son was told by his father to work in the vineyard, said he'd go, but never went. The younger son was also told to work, refused to go, but later regretted it and went.

Jesus doesn't wait for Freud to arrive to interpret his brother story. He analyzes it himself. The younger son represents the tax collectors and prostitutes whose lives have been a "No" to God, but who now repent and enter the kingdom of God. In contrast, the elder son symbolizes the Jewish leaders who professed to be religious, but who did not respond to John the Baptist's call to repentance.

In point of fact, both groups have their faults, but at least the group who turn toward God is to be preferred to the group who turn away from him. The ideal for us is to live in such a way that what we profess and practice, meet and match.

In other words, we must strive to translate our noble promises into noble performances; to carry out our fine words into fine deeds; to extend our saying, "Lord, Lord," into doing the will of our Father in heaven.

According to Fr. Donald Senior's commentary *Invitation to Matthew*, Christ's parable repeats the demand for repentance that is the hallmark of his teachings. On the one hand, the elder son "knows the right answers, but his response is hollow." On the other hand, the sadder-but-wiser reaction of the younger is more sincere: "He repents and proves it by action."

The parable warns us, then, not to get complacent—that is, to be satisfied with professing our faith, and then failing to practice it; with making promises, and then not keeping them; with making a good beginning, and then not persevering.

For example, we must not worship in church on Sunday, and then work dishonestly during the rest of the week; nor pledge our love at a marriage ceremony, and then pursue our own selfish ways the rest of our married lives.

But besides warning us, the parable also gives us hope. We may have been slaves to some sin in the past, but we can free ourselves from its hold. We may have been sensual like Mary Magdalene, greedy like Matthew, or rebellious like Paul, but we don't have to remain that way. We can change our ways.

With the help of God's grace we can bring our passions under the control of reason; make our desire for money meet the demands of generosity; and curb our rebelliousness by the exercise of service.

There is always hope that we can repent of our ways and start all over again. There is always hope that we can turn away from our mistakes in the past and turn to the Lord by taking on a new agenda for action.

27th Sunday of the Year  Is 5:1-7  Mt 21:33-43

# UNCONDITIONAL LOVE

In 1978 a man traveled to Cincinnati to attend the funeral of Max Ellerbusch. Max had been like a father to this man for twenty years. Nothing unusual, except that as a 15-year-old this man had taken his mother's car, and struck and killed Max's 5-year-old son. This was a week before Christmas in 1958.

Soon after the accident, a surprised court heard Max ask that charges be dropped. Instead he wanted to give the death-car driver a job and help toward his education. Max did all that and more, virtually adopting the 15-year-old boy into his family. Max shared his home, time and understanding with the troubled youth.

We might wonder, "How could Max do that? I could never befriend a wild teenager who had just killed my 5-year-old son. Max must have been a little crazy to go out of his way that much to become like a father for that boy.''

But if Max Ellerbusch was a little crazy, so is God. The parable in today's gospel describes God as a landowner who prepared a beautiful vineyard and gave it to his people to tend. However, his people wanted not just their share of the harvest, but the whole thing. They even abused and killed the prophets God sent to help them.

Finally, in a desperate attempt to save his vineyard and his people, God sent his own Son, hoping they would respect and honor him. Nonetheless, they abused and killed him, too, in an effort to seize his inheritance.

"What a silly story," we might say. "No landowner in his right mind would risk sending his own son among rebels who had already murdered his messengers. How crazy can you get? Who can believe in a God so dumb?"

But that is precisely the point of the parable. Where we would cry for vengeance on the tenants, God chose another alternative—the alternative of unconditional love.

God chose to use the tragic death of his own Son to give new life to his people. He chose to outdo the hatred of his people by his generous outpouring of the Holy Spirit upon them. Yes, when his own Son was crucified, God chose the way of unconditional love, and he is still doing it today.

No matter how far we wander away from him like lost sheep, he gently seeks us out and brings us back to himself. No matter how foolish or wasteful we've been with our lives, he is always ready to give us a new start. No matter how hopeless or desperate our situation might become, he has already prepared a way out for us.

Moreover, what God does for us is an example of what we should do for one another. We may not have an opportunity to give unconditional love in a tragic situation like Max Ellerbusch did. Nonetheless, we do have other hurts in our lives that can either cause bitterness and hatred, or become occasions for generous self-giving.

We can love unconditionally: an alcoholic in our family or among our friends; a spouse whose affection has become cold; a teenager who rejects our family values; a neighbor or fellow worker who tells lies about us.

By allowing the example of Max Ellerbusch to inspire us we can feel beyond our own personal wounds, and reach out with compassion to heal the wounds of another who may be hurting more than we. By following God's way of unconditional love, we can use each death of a part of ourselves as a means of passing on new life to another person.

28th Sunday of the Year                                             Is 25:6-10   Mt 22:1-14

## PRIORITIES

William Manchester's book *American Caesar* is about the life of General Douglas MacArthur. Manchester records some of MacArthur's statements to illustrate the sense of urgency and mission that characterized his leadership during World War II. Of Corregidor he said:

> Intrinsically it is but a barren, war-worn rock, hallowed . . . by death and disaster. Yet it symbolizes within itself that priceless, deathless thing, the honor of a nation. Until we lift our flag from its dust, we stand unredeemed before mankind. Until we claim again the ghastly remnants of its last gaunt garrison, we can but stand humble supplicants before God. There lies our Holy Grail.

The Holy Grail image of liberating the Philippine Islands was a driving force in MacArthur's Pacific campaign. This mission was so urgent to him that nothing else mattered and no sacrifice was too costly.

In contrast to the strong sense of urgency that seized MacArthur, our Lord's parable today pictures a negative attitude of complacency. The wedding banquet is a symbol of his kingdom. Everything is ready, but when the time comes for the feast to begin, none of the invited guests are present.

It's not that those invited refused to come; they merely had more important things to do and would come later. Since the wedding banquet was not high on their priority list and would run until well past midnight, the invited guests decided that rather than cancel or postpone their scheduled business, they would attend later.

In their view, the king's wedding banquet could wait a while; whereas in the king's view, this was a party that could not wait. In other words, Jesus is telling us that the kingdom of God is a matter of urgency and top priority; it demands our response here and now, and not at some other place or at some other time.

Unfortunately most of us don't take our Lord's invitation seriously. How many times does he call his people to come to his weekly Eucharistic banquet on Sundays, only to be ignored because there are more important things to do like playing a game of golf, shopping or sleeping a little longer?

How many times does Jesus invite us to become more prayerful people, only to have us turn away to our television sets for the afternoon soap operas or Monday Night football? How often does Jesus invite us to be more helpful to others, only to have us look beyond their needs to our trivial pursuits or vain amusements?

On the one hand, it's sad to see people drift through life because they lack a sense of urgency. This might mean a wasted youth and a lost education, a humdrum marriage and unfulfilled dreams, a middle age of mediocrity and stagnation, or the onset of old age and the realization of not having done anything significant.

On the other hand, it's exciting to experience people such as General MacArthur who have a strong sense of urgency about some Holy Grail in their life. They pursue with passion liberty or learning or love for the Lord. They recognize opportunities that may never come again and reach out for growth and greatness.

The banquet of God's kingdom is ready, the invitations are sent, and an RSVP is attached. The Lord is waiting for our answer.

29th Sunday of the Year                           Is 45:1, 4-6   Mt 22:15-21

## TRIVIAL PURSUIT

One of the more popular games today is called *Trivial Pursuit*. Its variations are many, including *Celebrity Trivia, Scriptural Trivia,* and *Tiger Trivia.*

In today's gospel the Pharisees play their own game of *Trivial Pursuit.* They have in their presence none other than Jesus himself, the long awaited Messiah and the very Son of God. He comes in word and power to teach and heal. He brings the good news of forgiveness and a new creation.

But all of these momentous things pass the Pharisees by, because they are preoccupied with trivia—how they can trap Jesus in his speech and discredit him. "Master," they ask him, "is it lawful to pay tax to the emperor or not?" They purposely put Jesus in a no-win situation.

On the one hand, if he says "Yes," the people will resent him. Nobody likes to pay taxes, let alone to a foreign power occupying their homeland. Moreover, for the Jews there is an added insult since their religion holds that only Yahweh is their King.

On the other hand, if Jesus says "No," the Pharisees will report him to the Roman government as a revolutionary and an insurrectionist. The Romans then might arrest and imprison Jesus.

But Jesus outwits the Pharisees and gives an answer that goes beyond their question. He insists that they not only give to Caesar what is his, but also return to God what belongs to him.

Christ's answer transcends the trivial pursuits of the Pharisees and expresses a profound principle. He points out that we are citizens of two worlds—the world we *see* of body and matter, and the *unseen* world of the spirit.

As such we have duties in both worlds—to *man* and to *God*. Our duties to *man* include not only what we owe to Caesar (what we owe to our government in terms of taxes and allegiance), but also what we owe to others.

This includes what husbands and wives, parents and children, workers and employers, teachers and students, doctors and patients owe to each other.

We can also add here what the rich owe to the poor, the strong to the weak, and the educated to the ignorant.

Perhaps, too, we can say that this includes ourselves. We owe to ourselves, for instance, taking good care of our health, continuing our education to improve our minds, and taking time out for rest and relaxation.

Besides belonging to the world we *see*, we are also citizens of the *unseen* world of the spirit. As such, we owe to *God* praise and thanksgiving, honor and glory. In a word, we owe to God worship because he is all good and the source of all that we are and have.

However, here too we owe something to ourselves in the sense that we should pray, read the Scriptures, and receive the sacraments in order to develop our life of the spirit. In a word, we have to take care of our inner life as much as we do our outer life.

We must not allow ourselves to make the same mistake the Pharisees did. Their trivial pursuits caused them to miss the meaning and the message of Jesus. May we always render what we owe to Caesar and to God by recognizing what is important in both our outer and inner worlds, and by responding to the opportunities and the challenges they present.


30th Sunday of the Year                                Ex 22:20-26    Mt 22:34-40

# LEPER PRIEST

*Father Damien: The Leper Priest* is a movie made for television in which Ken Howard plays the lead role. The program dramatizes the story of Fr. Damien who came from Belgium to the Hawaiian island of Molokai in 1873 to serve the lepers there until he, too, contracted leprosy and died in 1889.

At that time in history, the colony of Molokai was a dumping ground for lepers and it was like a death sentence to be put there. There was little law and order, medical help and supplies were nonexistent, and housing and sanitation were so bad that the island seemed like a sewer.

At first Fr. Damien found the lepers repulsive. But as he suffered with them, struggled with them and served them, he overcame his revulsion toward the lepers and developed deep feelings of love for them.

Fr. Damien dedicated almost two decades of his life to the lepers because he believed that in doing so he was demonstrating both his love for God and his love for neighbor.

According to our Lord's words in Matthew's gospel this is the *greatest* thing we can do with our lives: to *love* the Lord our *God* with our whole heart, mind and soul, and to *love* our *neighbor* as ourselves. "On these two commandments the whole law is based and the prophets as well."

The full significance of Christ's statement stands out when we see that he is putting together two familiar Old Testament texts. He quotes Deuteronomy 6:5 to make his statement about love of God, and then he cites Leviticus 19:18 regarding love of neighbor.

What is new, then, is not the texts themselves, which every good Jew knew, but the way Jesus puts them together for the first time. By tying them together as the *greatest* of the commandments, Jesus gives them equal weight in terms of seriousness and he gives them a new interpretation.

From now on, all good works have value both as acts of love of God and as acts of love of neighbor. The two can no longer be separated, even in the Bible. We can no longer speak of one without the other.

In other words, by linking the two commandments together Jesus makes *explicit* what was only *implicit* in the Old Testament. For example, today's Old Testament reading from Exodus forbids us to exploit the poor and the helpless because the Lord will surely hear their cry.

*Implicit* in this reading is the close connection that exists between what we do to our neighbor whom we see and what we do to God whom we cannot see. Jesus now makes this close connection not only more *explicit*, but goes on to say that it *sums up* the entire teaching of the Old Testament.

Saints like Father Damien of Molokai and Mother Teresa of Calcutta see this connection so clearly that they spend themselves in loving service to the most abandoned people in society as a way of expressing their love for God.

It may not be our call to minister to the most unwanted, like lepers and AIDS victims, war refugees and immigrants, or alcoholics and drug addicts. But it is our call to balance in some suitable way the *vertical* dimension of our relationship with God in prayer with the *horizontal* dimension of our relationship with other people in mutual service.

The praise we give to God with our lips might be followed up by using those same lips to talk to someone who is lonely, to encourage someone who is disheartened, or to cheer up someone who is sad.

The prayer we say with our hands might be followed up by using those same hands to hug our children or spouse, to prepare a meal for our family, or to do some housework for a shut-in neighbor.

May the cross formed by the intersection of a vertical beam with a horizontal one remind us to love God with our whole being and to love our neighbor as ourselves.

31st Sunday of the Year　　　　　　　　　Ml 1:14-2:2, 8-10　Mt 23:1-12

## SERVICE

Helen Hayes is still recognized as the *First Lady of the Theater*. She is a long-standing member of the Theater Hall of Fame, won Academy Awards in 1932 and in 1970, and was named "Woman of the Year" in 1973 by *Ladies Home Journal*.

But besides her professional successes, Helen Hayes is also noted for her humanitarian services. When her only daughter Mary died of polio in 1949 at age 19, Helen Hayes began helping the National Foundation for Infantile Paralysis with their fund raising.

After her husband Charles MacArthur died in 1956, Helen Hayes got involved in helping Fr. William Wasson with his Mexican orphans in Cuernavaca. During the Civil Rights Movement she played a part in the desegregation of theaters in the Washington, D.C. area.

In 1980 a new hospital was dedicated in her name on her 80th birthday in appreciation for her 40 years of volunteer service at the old facility. At the dedication, New York Governor Hugh Carey said: "In her work for the handicapped Helen Hayes has acted out measure for measure one of her most moving performances in the quiet dedicated service of her fellow human beings."

Indeed, Helen Hayes is a prototype of the kind of person Jesus had in mind when he said: "The greatest among you will be the one who serves the rest."

Service was one of the most striking signs of Christ's own life. He healed the sick, restored sight to the blind, and raised the dead to life. At the Last Supper he washed the feet of his disciples, and after his resurrection he prepared a meal for them on the shore while they were fishing. He characterized his own life as one of service when he said: "The Son of Man came not to be served, but to serve."

Service has also been the keynote of other great people in history. The Buddha was once asked how one could experience the ultimate in reality. He answered: "The great gate of charity lies wide open." In other words, the wise man was saying that if we want to find God, then we must go through the gate of charity by serving the needs of our brothers and sisters.

Another example is Marion Hill Preminger, an internationally known actress and hostess. When asked why she gave all that up to work with

Albert Schweitzer in the steaming equatorial jungles, she replied: "Dr. Schweitzer says that there are two classes of people—the helpers and the non-helpers. I want to be a helper."

We too are called to service in some way. If we want to become a great human being and an outstanding Christian, then we must serve the rest.

Our service might take the form of meeting their *physical and material needs* by: washing clothes or cooking meals for our family; lending a tool or doing some repairs for a neighbor down the street; nursing the elderly or babysitting the young.

Our service might take the form of caring for the *emotional and psychological needs* of others by: offering companionship and friendship; speaking words of hope and encouragement; showing acceptance and giving recognition.

Another form of service might be to meet the *spiritual and faith needs* of others by: giving good example and participating in the parish liturgy; living a simple lifestyle to offset materialism; quietly accepting unavoidable sufferings.

During the Eucharist we repeat Christ's words over the bread and wine: "This is my body which is given up for you. This is my blood which is shed for you." These words are a call for us to serve the rest—to give up our body in meeting the needs of others, not as a burden, but as a privilege; to pour out our blood in ministering to those we live and work with, not in a grudging way, but joyously and generously.

The gate to greatness is service, and it is as wide as our heart to pass through.

32nd Sunday of the Year　　　　　　　　　　　　Ws 6:12-16　Mt 25:1-13

# TIMING

General Douglas MacArthur's autobiography, *Reminiscences*, is full of World War II stories. One such story is about Capt. Thomas G. Lanphier, a pilot of the 339th Fighter Squadron who "became the unsung hero of an extraordinary exploit" on April 18, 1943.

The Japanese code had been broken and our Intelligence learned exactly where and when Admiral Yamamoto was going to fly in to one of the Solomon Islands. Yamamoto was the commander-in-chief of the Japanese Combined Fleet.

So eighteen P-38s were sent from Guadalcanal, 400 miles away, to attack Yamamoto. At the exact hour of rendezvous, Yamamoto's squadron appeared and were met by our waiting planes. Sixteen P-38s went after his Zero escorts, while Tom Lanphier and another pilot were assigned to attack the two bombers carrying Yamamoto and his staff.

Yamamoto's pilot used every artifice to escape, but eventually Lanphier's gunfire hit his bomber causing it to explode and crash. Washington lauded Lanphier's feat as one of the most significant strikes of the war but labeled it top secret and forbade its publication until 1945 when Tom was awarded the Navy Cross.

Timing, alertness and readiness were key factors in this air strike which proved to be a turning point in the war. These same themes are found in today's readings, but for different reasons.

In the first reading, Wisdom is readily found by those who keep vigil for her. She hastily makes herself known to the man who watches for her at dawn.

In the gospel parable, the five wise virgins are the ones who took oil as well as their torches. When the groom arrived at midnight they were ready to greet him. Jesus says that the moral of the parable is: "Keep your eyes open, for you know not the day nor the hour when the Lord will come."

We know what a sense of timing and readiness means for battles in war. But what does it mean for us?

First, we are supposed to be alert for Christ's coming at the midnight of our life when we die. The day of our death is not a day of doom. On the contrary, the wedding scene of the gospel shows that it is an event of immense joy.

We are not getting ready for the worst to happen when we die. On the contrary, we are getting ready for the best to happen—the celebration of a wedding where there will be torchlight and warmth and the riches of a banquet.

Second, we are supposed to be alert when Christ comes every day of our lives. He comes to us in the things we do, in what happens to us and in the people we meet. Yet, quite often we are insensitive to his presence.

Shakespeare once wrote that there is a tide in the affairs of our lives that is either accepted or is lost forever. There will be other comings by our

Lord, just as there are other tides. But that particular coming will never happen again. And if we let too many comings of our Lord pass us by, we end up finding that our whole life has passed us by. We end up with no oil in our lamps.

That brings us to our third point. How do we develop a sense of timing so that we know when to respond to the Lord? The answer is by praying. Prayer not only prevents us from becoming too preoccupied with ourselves, but it also opens us up to Christ's presence.

To pray does not mean that we neglect our work or play, but rather that we pause occasionally to pay attention to the Lord. It's similar to a man plowing a field. He keeps his eyes fixed on the furrow, but sometimes looks up to set his eyes on a distant mark to keep the furrow straight, while at other times he pauses to greet a neighbor.

During this liturgy we might ask Christ to give us this spirit of prayer so that we will be alert for his comings in our daily lives and be ready for his final coming at the time of our death.


33rd Sunday of the Year        Pr 31:10-13, 19-20, 30-31    Mt 25:14-30

# TALENTS

Gwen Verdon is one of the most talented dancers of our time. She has won four Tony Awards for her dancing in Broadway musicals, including such shows as *Can-Can, Damn Yankees*, and *Sweet Charity*.

It would seem only natural that Gwen Verdon, the daughter of a dancer, would grow up to be a dancer herself. But it was not that easy. Gwen's childhood was marred by badly bent legs, the result of rickets. Doctors wanted to break and reset her legs, but Gwen's mother wouldn't let them.

Instead Gwen's mother devised a set of exercises for her to straighten out her legs. She made Gwen walk with corrective shoes, write with her toes, and walk in the sand a lot. It worked, and Gwen went on to become a dancing star.

Gwen Verdon is an example of a person who had a special talent that she developed to the fullest. Making maximum use of one's talents is the topic of today's readings from Scripture.

In the first reading from Proverbs, the talented wife brings her husband happiness day by day, makes clothes for her children, and reaches out her hand to the poor. This wife is praised because she makes maximum use of her talents.

In the gospel, a servant is given five talents. Each talent is worth 1000 silver pieces. He invests these and makes another five talents. As a result, his master says: "Well done. Come share my joy." The servant is praised and rewarded because he made maximum use of the talents entrusted to him.

What about us? All of us are blessed with special talents and resources. But do we make maximum use of them? Do we put them at the service of the community, the parish and our family? Or do we hold back and save ourselves for something we may never do?

*Time* is a resource. Some people try to save time and never make that visit to cheer up their aging parents, never make that phone call to show interest in someone who needs it, or never write that letter to encourage someone in difficulty. Other people use their time wisely to prepare good meals for their family's enjoyment, improve their home for their family's comfort, or pray to God for blessings on their family.

*Money* is a resource. Some people hold it back and hoard it for themselves. They are always saving their money for some imaginary rainy day. But that day never comes, except on the day when they die.

Other people spend their money sensibly. Their own personal needs are simple and so they can afford to be generous to others. These are the people who contribute to diocesan fund drives, or who donate food for distribution to needy families.

*Work* and *education* are resources. Some people work and study as if they were saving themselves for something big in the future. No wonder they feel bored and dissatisfied.

Other people work and study with enthusiasm, and so they feel excited and stimulated. They know that it is better to wear out one's talents than to let them rust.

As we continue this Eucharist, pray that like Gwen Verdon we will not save our talents for something we will never do, but use them to the fullest. Pray that like the talented wife in Proverbs we will make maximum use of our talents to bring happiness to other people. Pray that like the servant in the gospel we will not let our talents lie idle, but use them for our own good and God's glory.

A Cycle 97

Christ the King          Ezk 34:11-12, 15-17    Mt 25:31-46

## HALE AND MILLS

In one of the 1984 issues of the Sunday *Parade* magazine there was a feature story about Mother Clara Hale. She was a 79-year-old black woman who had dedicated the last 15 years of her life to nursing children of drug addicts. Since 1969 Clara Hale had cared for over 500 children who were born already addicted to drugs.

About the same time, *The Detroit News* ran an article about another mother, Lynn Mills. Mrs. Mills was 30 years old at the time and was expecting her second child. She is a Pro-Life activist who pickets abortion clinics in Livonia and Redford in Michigan, and who has housed unwed mothers to help them with their babies.

These are but two examples of what today's liturgy is about—proclaiming Christ as King and extending his kingdom on earth.

The biblical image used today to represent Christ as King is that of the Good Shepherd. In the Old Testament reading from Ezekiel we get a picture of what the Good Shepherd does *for us*. In the New Testament reading from Matthew we see the reverse side of the picture, namely, what the Good Shepherd expects *from us*.

On the one hand, Ezekiel has much to say about what the Good Shepherd does *for us*. If we stray from the fold and get lost, he seeks us out and brings us back to the fold. If we get sick or injured, he heals us or binds up our wounds.

In other words, he looks after us with tender care and concern. No wonder we say in the Psalm refrain: "The Lord is my shepherd. There is nothing I shall want" (Psalm 23). Indeed, he leads us to the waters of baptism; anoints us with the oil of confirmation; spreads his banquet table before us in the Eucharist; and guides us in the right paths by his words in Scripture.

Truly there is nothing lacking in the love God has lavished upon us. That is why we have a Thanksgiving holiday about this time of the year: to praise and thank God for his love toward us.

On the other hand, our Lord's parable in the gospel outlines to some extent what the Good Shepherd expects *from us*. If we want to enter his kingdom, we have to give food to the hungry and drink to the thirsty, whether to the poor in Africa or to the street people in our own big cities in America.

If we want to hear his words of welcome, then we in turn have to welcome the stranger and clothe the naked. If we want to be consoled by the Lord, we have to comfort the sick and visit the imprisoned.

To do these things might seem hard at first, but they are the only way we can become fully human. They might seem too demanding, but they are the only way we can fulfill our destiny.

In a parish bulletin one time, there was the following indictment:

> I was hungry and you formed a humanities club and discussed my hunger. I was imprisoned and you crept off quietly to your chapel and prayed for my release. I was naked and in your mind you debated the morality of my appearance. I was sick and you knelt and thanked God for your health. I was homeless and you preached to me of the spiritual shelter of the love of God. I was lonely and you left me alone to go and pray for me. You seem so holy, so close to God. But I'm still very hungry and lonely and cold.

So, if we want to honor Christ as our King, extend his kingdom on earth, and then enter his kingdom in heaven, there is really only one way. Ask Clara Hale and Lynn Mills and they'll tell us what it is: "Do something for the least of Christ's brothers and sisters, for that we will be doing for him."

# B Cycle

1st Sunday of Advent          Is 63:16-17, 19; 64:2-7    Mk 13:33-37

# CREATIVE WAITING

In his book *Man's Search for Meaning*, Jewish psychiatrist Viktor Frankl tells the story of how he survived the atrocities of the concentration camp at Auschwitz. Frankl says that one of the worst sufferings at Auschwitz was waiting: waiting for the war to end; waiting for an uncertain date of release; and waiting for death to end the agony.

This waiting caused some prisoners to lose sight of future goals, to let go of their grip on present realities and to give up the struggle to survive. This same waiting made other prisoners like Frankl accept it as a challenge, as a test of their inner strength and as a chance to discover deeper dimensions of human freedom.

Waiting is one of the large realities of life. Parents wait for their teenagers to come home. Travelers wait for buses and planes. Actors and athletes wait for their chance to perform. Students wait for the results of their examinations.

Waiting is one of the themes of today's liturgy to open the season of Advent.

The first reading from Isaiah expresses our intense desire as we wait for the coming of the Lord: "Oh, that you would rend the heavens and come down . . . No eye has ever seen any God but you doing such deeds for those who wait for him."

In the gospel, Jesus tells us to be vigilant as we wait for his coming. Since he will be away for only a short time, we should do our tasks while he is absent. As he will return at an unknown hour, we should be ready whenever he comes back.

What we wait for during Advent is not the same thing as what the prisoners waited for at Auschwitz. Yet our waiting for Christ at Christmas includes the fulfillment of every other expectation.

Our waiting during Advent is not under the same circumstances as those of Auschwitz. Yet its final outcome is just as crucial as that of the waiting there. It can be self-destructive, or it can be creative.

Our waiting during Advent is self-destructive if we have no future goal to hope for. Then our waiting becomes like that of a prisoner who sees no end to his confinement, an alcoholic who sees no escape from his addiction or an unemployed worker who sees no opportunity for a job.

Our waiting during Advent can be creative if we have a future goal to look forward to, some thing or person to hope in. This, of course, is Christ whose coming we celebrate at Christmas.

Notice that in the gospel only the man at the gate was ordered to watch while waiting for the master's return. The others were left tasks to do while waiting. If our Advent waiting is to be creative, then we have to do something active.

For example, we have to take some initiative to pray so that the Lord can open our eyes to see our need for his coming as Savior. We have to be energetic about using the sacraments so that the Holy Spirit can increase our desire for the coming of Christ and expand our hearts to welcome him. We have to be enthusiastic about social action so that the power of God can become operative in the world and enable us to change conditions like war, poverty and injustice.

If we don't do these things, then our waiting becomes self-destructive. Pride fills the vacuum left by the lack of prayer. Secularism replaces our sense of the sacred that accompanies the sacraments. Selfishness suffocates the ideal of sharing demanded by social action.

Pray that our Advent waiting will not be self-destructive, but creative—that is, characterized by prayer, the sacraments and social action. May the Lord "protect us from all anxiety as we wait in joyful hope for the coming of our Savior, Jesus Christ" at Christmas.

2nd Sunday of Advent                                          Is 40:1-5, 9-11   Mk 1:1-8

# THE DESERT

In the high desert of Crestone, Colorado in the Sangre de Cristo Mountains there is a hermitage called the Spiritual Life Institute. Founded in 1960 by Fr. William McNamara, the Institute is a center for contemplation under the direction of an ecumenical community of men and women.

At the entrance to the Spiritual Life Institute there is a wooden plaque which serves as the *Magna Carta* of their desert experience. On this wooden plaque is a triangle with three words inside—silence, solitude and simplicity—and three words outside—contemplation, communion and celebration.

One of the desert heroes of this Institute is John the Baptist, who is introduced in today's gospel as a "voice in the desert, heralding the Lord's coming." The gospel then goes on to keynote his desert experience as an ideal Advent preparation for Christmas.

John the Baptist stands tall in a long line of biblical desert figures, including men like Moses and Elijah. Later our Lord himself will go out into the desert for 40 days and be tested by Satan.

Several enormous events took place in the desert, events like the revelation of Yahweh's name and the giving of the law. So it is no wonder that the desert experience is put before us in Advent to prepare for the event of Christ's birth.

As Fr. McNamara's plaque points out, the desert affords us three ways to become prayerful people—the ways of *simplicity, silence and solitude*. These three ways can be part of our Advent practices even if we have no actual physical desert nearby. A desert can be *any* place where we can be alone with God to pray—a corner in the backyard, a nook in the basement, or a park bench.

The first desert aid to prayer is *simplicity*. The desert experience invites us to get rid of all the excess baggage that blocks our way to Christ, and to see things as they really are. In the city we tend to become enchanted by what is pretty, plastic or superficial. In the desert we come to grips with what is truly beautiful, real and substantial.

In the city we are under constant pressure to perform, produce and do many things. In the desert we can *simply be* and discover that what we *are* is more important than what we *have* or *do*.

The second desert aid to prayer is *silence*. Incessant noise and flashing lights surround us so much that we are becoming nervous wrecks. The desert provides a setting of stillness to heal our disturbed spirits and a place of quiet to calm our frazzled nerves. In silence we can hear God speak to us.

The famous musician Andre Kostelanetz (1901-1980) once said that we listen too much to television and too little to nature. The wind was one of his favorite sounds, and he considered utter and complete silence like a song without words or music without notes.

The third desert aid to prayer is *solitude*. We cannot allow ourselves to be driven all the time by the herd instinct to escape loneliness. Sometimes we have to stand alone in solitude to discover who we are and who is our God. Only in solitude can we experience the intoxicating presence of God himself.

In his book *Thoughts in Solitude* Thomas Merton says that a solitary does not count himself out from the crowd. On the contrary, he considers himself as more deeply in touch with the crowd. Without some solitude our life is a pretense of togetherness. With solitude our conversations become true communion.

So we don't have to go to a real desert to prepare the way for the Lord's coming at Christmas. But we do have to go into a symbolic desert during Advent through the ways of *simplicity, silence and solitude*, that is, by taking time to simply be, to be quiet and to be alone.

3rd Sunday of Advent                               Is 61:1-2, 10-11   Jn 1:6-8, 19-28

## YOU DO NOT RECOGNIZE

*Valesa—A Nightmare* is a docu-drama which was written in Poland under a pseudonym and then smuggled out of the country. It tells the story of political prisoners like Lech Walesa.

Near the end of the play a prisoner priest, who usually offers a solitary Mass, is joined by the rest of the prisoners at considerable risk to celebrate the Eucharist. At this moment, the play reaches a climax with the deafening scream of crows—a Polish symbol for the Communist military regime under General Jaruzelski.

The cawing of the crows suddenly gives way to the soft chirping of spring birds and the comforting notes of a piano concerto—a symbol of the optimism of the Polish people that one day their quest for religious and political freedom will be realized.

*Valesa—A Nightmare* shows how Christ can come into our lives even in the worst of circumstances. The Lord came to Lech Walesa in a Communist prison through Walesa's faith and prayers, through his Polish culture and pride, through his fellow political prisoners and through the sacrament of the Eucharist.

Christ's coming is one of the themes of today's Advent liturgy. The Jews send a delegation from Jerusalem to ask John the Baptist if he is the long-awaited Messiah who has finally come. "I am not the Messiah," John answers. "But there is one among you whom you do not recognize—

the one who is to *come* after me—the strap of whose sandal I am not worthy to unfasten."

Louis Evely begins his book *That Man Is You* by asking the question: "Would we have recognized Christ?" We might flatter ourselves by saying that if we had lived in Christ's day, we would have loved and followed him.

"Really?" Louis Evely asks rather sarcastically. Then why is it that we do not hear the Lord now when he is waiting every day to speak to us in the gospels? Why do we not see him now when he is present at every moment in one of our neighbors? Why do we not touch him when he is hungry or thirsty in someone near us?

All through the centuries, Jesus has been coming into the lives of his people, and along with his comings John the Baptist's indictment keeps reechoing: "There is one among you whom you do not recognize."

All through history people keep looking for the Lord to come in the guise of some kind of Elijah of their own imagining, and they keep missing his coming right under their noses.

Are we much different today? We may be strictly orthodox in our observance of the laws of the Church or know all the right answers to the questions of the catechism, but do we really know and experience our Lord in a deeply personal way?

Evely says that God continually reaches out toward us, but we resist his coming by hiding behind layers of distractions. Christ wants to speak to us in the silence of prayer, but we drown his voice with noise from our television sets and stereos.

Besides prayer, another way the Lord comes to us is through his word in Scripture. Hearing God's word in the Sunday readings is not like listening to a cassette rerun. No, when God's word is proclaimed it comes alive to question and enlighten our minds, to challenge and test our wills, and to move and inspire our hearts.

Another avenue the Lord uses to come to us is the sacraments, those intense moments of grace and peak experiences of God. If poet Gerard Manley Hopkins could say that "the world is charged with the grandeur of God," what can we say of the sacraments?

There are many other ways in which God comes into our lives. If we made a list of them we would have to include: happenings to us, both good and bad; people we encounter; the beauty of nature; books, plays and movies that have cultural value; and heroes of our day, like Lech Walesa.

The season of Advent is a time for us to get in tune with all these ways in which Christ comes, so that when he comes at Christmas we will be ready to recognize him, regardless of the form in which he chooses to appear.

4th Sunday of Advent                           2 S 7:1-5, 8-11, 16   Lk 1:26-38

# MESSIAH

When George Frederick Handel's oratorio *Messiah* was first performed in Dublin in 1742, one critic wrote: "Words are wanting to express the exquisite delight it afforded to the admiring crowded audience." A more contemporary music critic, Anthony Milner, says that since that time Handel's chorus of praise has never ceased; his *Messiah* still remains the most frequently performed oratorio by any composer.

Today's readings from Scripture may not be as musical as Handel's text, but they have their own way of telling us about the *Messiah*.

The Old Testament reading from the second book of Samuel presents Nathan's prophecy to King David, a prophecy that would stamp indelibly Israel's messianic hopes: "Your house and your kingdom shall endure forever before me; your throne shall stand firm forever."

The New Testament reading from Luke declares how this messianic prophecy is now being realized through Mary. The angel says to Mary: "You shall conceive and bear a son and give him the name Jesus . . . The Lord God will give him the throne of David his father. He will rule over the house of Jacob forever."

The title *Messiah* comes from a Hebrew word meaning "anointed." Originally only the king was anointed and called *messiah*, the way David and Solomon were. The anointing of rulers invested them with Yahweh's authority and wisdom.

After the exile when there were no more Israelite kings, the term *Messiah* was transferred to some ideal, future Savior who would restore God's favor. This *Messiah* would appear at the time of God's definitive intervention, not only to deliver Israel from its trials, but also to establish its political supremacy.

Jesus was born at a time when messianic expectations were high. His whole life would show how he indeed fulfilled these messianic hopes, but without their political and national overtones.

The title *Christ* was a Greek translation for the Hebrew word *Messiah*, meaning "the anointed one." As more and more Gentiles entered the Church, the word *Christ* gradually lost its distinction as a title and became part of our Lord's personal name. "Jesus the Christ" became simply "Jesus Christ."

After a performance one time of his *Messiah*, Handel remarked of his audience, "I should be sorry if I only entertained them. I wished to make them better." In the same way, after this historical and scriptural study, we should be sorry if we have only been enlightened about the meaning of the word *Messiah*. Is our new understanding going to make us better people?

If Jesus as *Messiah* is going to mean anything to us personally, we must acquire some of the attitudes of the Israelites before he was born. First among these would be an awareness of our *need* for a Savior. Without a Savior we are sinners with no escape. But with a Savior we are sinners who are set free.

Another attitude we need is that of *patient waiting*. Somehow through centuries of trials and exile the Israelites were able to wait patiently for the coming *Messiah*. In an age of instant replay, fast food services and quick computer readouts, we find it more and more difficult to wait patiently for those things in life that need more time to unfold, things like learning and loving, or friendship and family. Are we able to wait patiently in our struggles and setbacks for the Messiah to come and deliver us?

Finally, we need Mary's faith-filled attitude of "Let it be." We may not be too convinced of our own greatness, but since God calls us as he did Mary, "Let it be." We may not be free of all fear when we answer God's call, but since his Spirit overshadows us, "Let it be." We may not be too sure about our resources, but since God sends us sometimes to do the impossible anyway, "Let it be."

Christmas — Mass at Dawn (A, B, C)   Is 62:11-12   Lk 2:15-20

# COME TO THE STABLE

"A Legend from Russia" is a poem by Phyllis McGinley about Christmas. The poem begins as the old grandmother, Babushka, is about to retire for the evening:

> When out of the winter's rush and roar
> Came shepherds knocking upon her door.

They tell her of a royal child a virgin just bore and beg the grandmother to come and adore. Babushka is good-hearted, but she likes her comfort, and so her reaction is to go later. "Tomorrow," she mutters. "Wait until then."

But the shepherds come back and knock again. This time they beg only a blanket:

> With comforting gifts, meat or bread,
> And we will carry it in your stead.

Again Babushka answers, "Tomorrow."

And when tomorrow comes, she's as good as her word. She packs a basket of food and gifts:

> A shawl for the lady, soft as June,
> For the Child in the crib a silver spoon,
> Rattles and toys and an ivory game
> . . . but the stable was empty when she came.

Is that sometimes our own story? Not empty stables, but empty lives. We wait too late to tell someone that we love them; too late to mend a quarrel or heal a hurt; too late to show appreciation to our parents or enjoy our children; too late to sense God's presence or receive his graces.

Like Babushka in the story we say, "Tomorrow, not today; another time, not now." We're too busy, or too blind; we like our own comforts too much, and care about others too little. And so opportunities pass us by. We find the stable empty, our lives hollow, our love wasted.

Don't let what happened to Babushka happen to you this Christmas season. Be like the shepherds. Once the angels left them to return to heaven they said: "Let us go to Bethlehem and see what has happened." The shepherds then "hurried away and found Mary and Joseph, and the baby lying in the manger."

The Lord is not going to send us angels and shepherds today to point out his stable. Instead, he gives us other signs of his presence in our midst—one another. But do we see these signs and respond to them "with haste" today—not tomorrow; or at least this month—not next month?

May we go quickly to make peace with that person we've offended; call on the phone that relative who might be lonely; visit that friend who needs our smile; greet that stranger who might be hurting; feed and clothe the poor who are hungry and cold.

If we can hurry on the day after Christmas to the shopping malls for all the sales and bargains, why can't we hurry during the Christmas season to the Christ Child while he is still to be found in the stable of the hearts of his people?

Sydney Harris once wrote:

> The art of living successfully consists of being able to hold two opposite ideas in tension at the same time: first, to make long-term plans as if we were going to live forever; and second, to conduct ourselves daily as if we were going to die tomorrow.

The secret of a merry Christmas, according to the Babushka legend, is to keep two things in balance: first, to make plans and prepare gifts as if we were going to live forever; and second, to serve the Christ in the people around us as if there were no tomorrow.

Holy Family (A, B, C)                                    Si 3:2-6, 12-14   Lk 2:22-40

## STAR TREK

When the movie *Star Trek III* was introduced it became an instant success. Much of its popularity flowed from its science fiction format and its space age technology. But there were other reasons for its success, too. One of these reasons is its human appeal to our deep instincts for family, not only for the natural family as we know it, but also for other family groups—like parishes, civic organizations and work communities.

The Enterprise crew of the Star Trek movies form a family. Capt. Kirk is a father-figure who tries to keep the family clan together. Mr. Spock, Dr. McCoy, Scotty the engineer, and all the crew members belong to the Enterprise family. They are bonded together by more than their common work. They share with one another deep feelings of friendship, commitment and loyalty.

In their own way, today's readings from Scripture also focus on family values.

The first reading from Sirach stresses the honor and respect we owe to our parents and elders. The second reading from Colossians lists the virtues we need for family life—virtues such as kindness, patience and the readiness to forgive (Col 3:12-21).

In Luke's gospel we see Mary and Joseph bringing the child Jesus to the Temple to present him to God and then returning to Nazareth to make their home as a family.

The Scriptures picture the ideals. What a struggle families have in our day to make these ideals real! Jane Howard examined many of these struggles and published her findings in a book called *Families*. She says that even though families today are changing their size, form and purpose, they still remain in one guise or another everybody's most basic hold of reality.

Jane Howard lists ten hallmarks common to good families.

First, they have a hero or heroine in whose achievements they can take pride and whose feats spur them on to greater things.

Second, good families have a switchboard operator, someone who tracks what all the others are doing and keeps them connected with each other.

Third, good families are devoted to each other's well-being but are also interested in other pursuits like sports, symphonies and sightseeing trips.

Fourth, they show hospitality: they are generous with their invitations, urge you to come early and stay late, and treat you like an honored guest.

Fifth, good families deal squarely with black sheep and black clouds; they cherish their eccentrics and confront their misfortunes.

Sixth, they prize rituals: they come together to observe birthdays, remember anniversaries and feast on holidays.

Seventh, good families are affectionate; styles may differ from polite handshakes to hearty hugs, but they say: "You count because you're one of us."

Eighth, they have a sense of place; they love their homeland and hallow the land where they now live, for these are sacred spaces in their history.

Ninth, good families find some way to connect with posterity; the generation gap doesn't exist because communication lines are kept open between the young and the old.

Tenth, they honor and esteem their elders for their wisdom and experience.

Although Jane Howard does not list prayer or forgiveness or self-sacrifice among these hallmarks, it is not difficult to read these Christian values between the lines of her writing.

To sum up, the Star Trek movies, Jane Howard and today's readings all challenge us to minimize in our family life isolation, apathy and lack of commitment, and to maximize relationships, care and loyalty. They challenge us to form homes where members no longer feel alienated, hostile or bitter, but experience loving affirmation, hospitality and kindness.


January 1 — Mary, Mother of God (A, B, C)  Nb 6:22-27  Lk 2:16-21

# NAMES

In his book *The Name Game*, author Christopher Andersen claims that our name can make us a success or a failure, a winner or a loser. Andersen's book is based on the results of polls he took to determine what qualities most Americans associated with various names.

On the one hand, he found that people are most likely to trust and relate to people with common names such as Kathleen (who is viewed as a person "always most sought after") or Edward (who is considered as a "thoughtful person").

On the other hand, it is difficult to imagine someone like General George Patton as a presidential candidate because of his nickname of "Old-Blood-and-Guts."

One of the themes of today's feast of Mary's Motherhood is that of the name given to Mary's son, the name Jesus.

In the first reading from the book of Numbers, we have a *prophecy* of the power of the Lord's name: "So shall they invoke my name upon the Israelites, and I will bless them."

In the gospel, Luke calls our attention to the *fulfillment* of this prophecy: "The name Jesus was given the child, the name the angel had given him before he was conceived."

In his commentary on Luke's gospel, G.B. Caird says: "The name *Jesus* is the Greek equivalent of the Hebrew *Joshua*, which means 'The Lord is salvation.' " This is essentially the same sense used by Matthew in his gospel when he has the angel say to Joseph in a dream: "You shall call his name *Jesus*, for he will *save* his people from their sins" (Mt 1:21).

The Holy Name of Jesus then has a twofold power. It has the power to *save* us, and it has the power to *bless* us. When we call on the name of Jesus, we invoke the very presence and power of Jesus himself. We place ourselves at his feet in the same way as the blind beggar by the roadside or the disciple John at the Last Supper.

The name of Jesus has power to *save* us from selfishness, self-pity and self-doubt. It can save us from envy, hostility and animosity. It can deliver us from discouragement, depression and despair.

The name of Jesus has power to *save* us from wasting our resources when we should be sharing them; from becoming slaves to our appetites when we should be disciplining them; and from worshiping military might when we should be questioning it.

The name of Jesus has power not only to *save* us from whatever might be sinful, but also to *bless* us with special gifts and graces, such as health after a long illness, healing after an injury or a job after unemployment.

Calling on the name of Jesus can bring graces like new strength to go on when we feel like giving up; new experiences of friendship and family when we feel lonely and left out; new visions and challenges to excite us when we feel listless and stagnant.

Jesus himself claims power for his name when he promises that we will expel demons and heal in his name; that he will be present with us whenever two or three gather together in his name; that we will receive whatever we ask for in prayer in his name.

As we begin this new year, may the name of Mary's son Jesus be often on our lips to praise him when we rise in the morning and to thank him when we retire in the evening; to invoke him when we need him to save us and to summon him when we need his blessings.

2nd Sunday after Christmas (A, B, C)         Si 24:1-4, 8-12   Jn 1:1-18

# WORD POWER

In a recent issue of *American Heritage*, critic Jonathan Yardley examined what he considered the top ten books by American authors that shaped our cultural, social and domestic life. These books were written by such familiar authors, for instance, as Dale Carnegie, Horatio Alger, Fannie Farmer, Mark Twain and Dr. Benjamin Spock.

The significant influence their writings had on the American people is an example of the power words have. Words have always stirred our imaginations, aroused our emotions and inspired us to action.

For example, consider the impact of words spoken by orators like Cicero or statesmen like Churchill; lines written by playwrights like Shakespeare or poets like Tennyson; lyrics composed for songs like the French "Marseillaise" or the American "Battle Hymn of the Republic."

Indeed, words come in all kinds of shapes and forms, and they have a tremendous power over us. So it is not surprising that God, too, uses words to reach us.

"In times past, God spoke in fragmentary and varied ways through the prophets; in this, the final age, he has spoken to us through his Son" (Heb 1:1-2).

The gospel of John starts with: "In the beginning was the Word. The Word was in God's presence, and the Word was God . . . The Word became flesh and made his dwelling among us, and we have seen his glory."

These few verses by John summarize and synthesize centuries of both Jewish and Greek thought, for he was writing about the beginnings of Christianity out of a Jewish background for a Greek world.

On the one hand, for the Jews a spoken word was much more than a mere sound. It was considered to have a life and power of its own. At every stage of the creation story in Genesis, we read, "And God said . . ." Thus, God's word is creative and dynamic.

When a Jew gave a blessing or a curse, the word went out and began to act, and nothing could hold it back. That is why Isaac could not recall the blessing he gave mistakenly to Jacob instead of Esau.

Also, in the Jewish mind, the word of God enlightens and guides man, especially through God's revealed word in the law and in the wisdom literature.

On the other hand, for the Greeks the term *logos* or *word* was associated with the mind of God. It denoted God's plan, purpose and pattern for the universe. As part of that universe, man's mind was stamped with the *logos* or *word* of God. It enabled him to reason, think, know and judge.

According to John Marsh in his Pelican commentary:

> In fastening upon the term *word* John had provided himself with a means of effective communication with Jews and Greeks, Christians and pagans, religious and profane alike.

What we celebrate at Christmas then is God's supreme revelation of himself through his Son Jesus—his *Word* becomes flesh, the divine can now be seen in the human, eternity appears in time, and the Creator enters creation.

And so powerful is this *Word* become flesh that in exchange he gives us a share in his divinity and makes it possible for us to enter eternity.

But for this to happen we have to allow the *Word* to penetrate our very being, move our imaginations, and inflame our hearts. We have to let the *Word* made flesh become a creative force within us and a light to guide us.

Only then will the *Word* made flesh sound again through us so that the world will hear the good news of his gospel, be inspired by the story of his life, and sing of his glory.


Epiphany (A, B, C)                                                Is 60:1-6   Mt 2:1-12

# ADVENTURERS

When pilots Dick Rutan and Jeana Yeager made their historic flight in 1986 with their spindly Voyager aircraft, the whole world followed it with excitement. For nine days a sky-watch was kept tracking this first non-stop global flight without refueling.

Adventurers and risk-takers like Dick Rutan and Jeana Yeager have always fascinated us. Marco Polo journeying to India and China, Christopher Columbus coming to America, Admiral Byrd going to the South Pole, our astronauts flying to the moon: such adventurers have always aroused our admiration—and our skepticism.

It was no different at the time of the Magi in today's gospel story. To the cynical observer the Magi must have seemed foolish to go following a star. These astrologers had to be a little crazy to leave the security of their homeland to venture forth into a strange country presided over by a madman like Herod.

When the Magi returned home—much to everybody's surprise—they were probably ridiculed. After all, what did they find in Herod's land? A child and his mother? Was that their big discovery? Were there no children and mothers in their own country? How crazy can you get?

Nonetheless, to a person with the eyes of faith, the Magi had discovered an immense secret. They found not only the secret of the star, but the secret of the whole universe—the secret of God's incredible love for his people. For the child they found was no ordinary child but the very Son of God become man.

And what they brought back from their adventure was not material wealth, or art treasures or scientific technology, but the light, joy and peace that only God can give.

Like adventurers and explorers, all of us are restless in some degree or other. A few of us are more restless than others and so we climb mountains, trek across deserts and fly around the world. But most of us are restless just where we are—at home, on the job or in school.

Regardless of what we seem to pursue in particular—fame or fortune, some sort of record or just plain excitement—what we ultimately seek is human fulfillment, something to give meaning to our existence. Our restlessness is basically a quest for the supreme values of life—the good, the true and the beautiful. What we search for is that which is permanent, indestructible and eternal. In a word, our restlessness is a yearning for perfect union with God.

The Magi found all this in Christ, and so can we. But like them we cannot allow ourselves to become complacent and self-satisfied. In a spirit of adventure we have to take risks sometimes.

We have to be foolish enough sometimes to follow our star. Only then will we come to find the perfect wisdom that is Christ. We have to be daring enough to walk occasionally in the darkness of faith. Only then will we come to see the light that is Christ. We have to be courageous enough to accept ridicule and suffering. Only then will we come to experience the peace and joy of Christ.

Like adventurers Dick Rutan and Jeana Yeager, we can pursue our own dream and stretch our own limits—whether in the ventures of the stock market, the law courts or the labs. But whatever the challenge is that we pursue, that pursuit will be useless unless—like the Magi—we seek and find the one thing necessary: Jesus Christ our Savior.

Baptism of the Lord (A, B, C)   Is 42:1-4, 6-7   Mk 1:7-11

# POWER SOURCE

*The Greatest* is a film about Muhammad Ali's career as a heavyweight boxing champion. It shows not only how he was gifted naturally with agility and strength, but also how he trained extensively with rigorous workouts and diets.

But Muhammad Ali said one time that although all these things helped, the real secret of his power source was a set of inspirational tapes to which he listened. The tapes were recorded speeches of a Black Muslim leader, the honorable Elijah Muhammad. They deal with self-knowledge, freedom and potential.

Muhammad Ali would listen to these tapes when he got up in the morning, when he ate his meals during the day and when he retired at night. He claimed that these inspirational messages gave him the power to fight for his black people, not only for their glory in the ring, but also for their civil rights in the arena of life.

In today's gospel, we have revealed the secret of the power of another man, Jesus Christ. At the very beginning of his gospel, Mark wants there to be no mistake about who Jesus is and what the source of his power is.

The baptism scene Mark draws for us is another epiphany episode following last week's one with the Magi. Three signs accompany our Lord's baptismal experience to reveal who he is.

First, the heavens were opened to symbolize a new divine intervention in human history. Second, the Spirit descended on him like a dove signifying the presence and power of God. Third, a voice was heard designating him as God's beloved and favored Son.

The point we want to emphasize is the second sign, that of the Spirit descending on our Lord. The significance of the Spirit is seen from its many Old Testament appearances. For example, in Genesis the Spirit of God hovered over the waters at the beginning of creation; in today's first reading from Isaiah 42 the Lord's Spirit comes upon Yahweh's chosen servant.

According to the Old Testament, then, the Spirit signifies the special presence and power of God. This special divine presence and power are now revealed in Jesus Christ as he is being baptized, and would continue to be revealed all through his life.

*The Interpreter's Bible* says this about our Lord's baptism:

> The gift of the Holy Spirit is an inner transformation, a power for cleansing and energizing the heart and will, the life of God in the soul of man. It reaches into the secret places of the heart, where the springs of life are coiled, and motive power is generated.

In other words, the Spirit that came down upon Jesus at his baptism empowered him to heal and to teach, to give up his life on the cross and to rise from the dead.

This same Holy Spirit has continued to come down upon Christians through the centuries. His power has enabled martyrs to suffer torture, missionaries to work in foreign lands, married couples to persevere in fidelity and monks to go into the desert.

By baptism we, too, have the Holy Spirit dwelling within us. We know that his power is operative in us whenever we are healed or enlightened, enabled to endure difficulties and disappointments, or strengthened to survive losses and disasters.

Moreover, like Muhammad Ali we have a sort of tape recorder to get us in touch with this source of our power, an in-built tape recorder called prayer. Prayer prepares us to listen to the Holy Spirit, to be inspired by him and to be moved by him to do great things.

1st Sunday of Lent　　　　　　　　　　　　　　Gn 9:8-15　Mk 1:12-15

# TRAINING PERIODS

In the movie *An Officer and a Gentleman*, we are taken inside a boot camp where candidates are trained to be naval flight officers. Actor Richard Gere plays the lead role of a candidate who is so intent on being a flight officer that he endures every test and challenge his tough drill sergeant, played by Lou Gossett, can throw at him.

In the end Richard Gere emerges from the training grounds a changed man. Upon entering boot camp he was very selfish—he cared only about his own success and comforts. But before he left he learned how to reach out and help his classmates, he felt real pain when his close friend committed suicide, and he proved himself to be a true gentleman by marrying his girl friend, played by Debra Winger.

Today we begin the season of Lent, a spiritual boot camp in a sense. Its theme of spiritual training is set forth in the gospel. The Spirit leads Jesus into the desert. There in the wasteland he stays for forty days and is put to the test by Satan.

In his Pelican commentary on the gospel of Mark, Dennis Nineham says that at the time of Jesus it was a common expectation that the Messiah would be God's agent to overthrow Satan and all his evil spirits. In order to do this the Messiah would have to undergo a trial of strength and engage in a tremendous battle of cosmic proportions.

By going into the wilderness, the traditional dwelling place of evil spirits, Jesus signals that this final climactic battle between God and Satan has begun. The presence of the tamed wild beasts and the angels who minister to him suggest that Jesus will emerge the winner—not only at this initial encounter now, but also later in a more decisive way through his resurrection and, finally, in a definitive way at the end of time.

We can see then how the elements of training, discipline and preparation play a prominent role in this temptation story. Since it comes immediately before the very first words Jesus utters in Mark's gospel, it seems as if he wasn't allowed to begin his public ministry until he had finished this testing period.

Our Lord's struggle with Satan still goes on, but now the battleground has shifted from the desert into our own spirits. Christ's victory is guaranteed, but it still has to be worked out in our own lives. That is why we, too, have to go through the periodic training periods of discipline and testing called Lent. In imitation of our Lord we, too, have to get ready to do battle with Satan and his evil spirits.

We consider it criminal to send a soldier to war without basic training, or to send a doctor into an operating room without adequate schooling. And yet we casually assume that we can go up against Satan year after year without taking Lent seriously.

Unless we go into training each year to toughen ourselves, we tend to get soft and self-indulgent. It seems that we have a human tendency to slacken in our efforts and to take the easier way whenever we can.

Lenten disciplines counteract this tendency. The time-proven Lenten disciplines recommended by the Church do not consist of doing calisthenics, eating survival food and enduring simulated stress situations. Rather, the Church's Lenten training program consists of prayer, fasting and almsgiving.

If we are faithful to these disciplines, then we will leave Lent changed for the better, much as Richard Gere changed for the better in the movie *An Officer and a Gentleman*. Moreover, we will emerge better prepared and stronger for our struggles with Satan, much as our Lord was after his forty days in the desert.

2nd Sunday of Lent        Gn 22:1-2, 9, 10-13, 15-18    Mk 9:2-10

# CHARLES RAYBURN

Charles Rayburn has been a victim of cerebral palsy since his birth. His only means of communication is an electric typewriter which he strikes with a stylus attached to a band around his head.

In spite of his palsy, Charles Rayburn has published 37 articles in national magazines. One of his articles appeared in *America* magazine and dealt with the Stations of the Cross.

Charles Rayburn is a living example of today's readings about Isaac and Jesus. These three figures and the three readings are tied together by a triple theme—the theme of sonship, death and deliverance.

In the first reading from Genesis, we heard how Abraham was ready to sacrifice his only son Isaac, but God intervened to deliver Isaac from death and destined him for future glory.

In the second reading, St. Paul says that God did not spare his own Son Jesus, but handed him over to death. Later he raised him from the dead to sit at his right hand (Rm 8:31-34).

Finally, in the gospel transfiguration scene, the Father declares that Jesus is his beloved Son. Afterwards, Jesus orders his disciples not to tell the event to anyone before he has risen from the dead.

All three readings thus have the same triple theme of sonship, death and deliverance. Charles Rayburn is a contemporary counterpart of Isaac and Jesus with respect to these themes.

Because Charles Rayburn is unable to walk, talk or use his hands, he has to die daily to many of his dreams and ambitions. Nonetheless, he still sees himself as a son of a loving Father.

In his meditation on the First Station he writes:

> Jesus is condemned to death. This reminds me of my condemnation to live as an invalid. But, is it a condemnation, or is it a gift from the Father—a gift uniting me more closely to divine love than to worldly pleasure?

When he writes about the Fourteenth Station—Jesus being laid in the tomb—Charles Rayburn sees himself one day being laid in a grave. But this burial will only set the stage for his own deliverance from death, his release from all physical infirmity, and his rising to a life of glory with Jesus.

Three themes—sonship, death and deliverance—characterize the lives of three people: Isaac, Jesus and Charles Rayburn. As we begin the second week of Lent, perhaps we can reflect on how these three themes are part of our own lives.

First, do we realize that we too are favorite sons and daughters of a loving Father? With Christ we have been granted all things. No wonder St. Paul says, "If God is for us, who can be against us?" (Rm 8:31).

Second, do we see some purpose to suffering and death in our lives? To see such a purpose we need faith, and to surrender freely to our Father's mysterious, yet marvelous, plan for us we need the trust of Isaac, Jesus and Charles Rayburn.

Third, are we able to delight in the deliverance that is already ours? Our deliverance may still be incomplete, but it has already begun through the sacraments. We have a sure basis for hope in the sacraments.

Like Christ's transfiguration on the mountain, our own transfiguration in this life may still be imperfect. Nevertheless, it breaks through sometimes with brilliance when we do a noble deed.

Praise the Father for making us his beloved sons and daughters. Ask him to strengthen us in our struggle with suffering and death. Look with hope to our future transfiguration when God will raise us from the dead and take us into glory.

3rd Sunday of Lent     Ex 20:1-17    Jn 2:13-25

## YAMASAKI

Architect Minoru Yamasaki began his career humbly by working his way through college for 17 cents an hour at salmon canneries during the summer. He attained the heights of honor when he designed the World Trade Center in New York in 1976 and made the cover of *Time* magazine.

Minoru Yamasaki's architectural career spanned more than 40 years before he died in 1986. Besides the World Trade Center, he was famous for designing the Lambert-St. Louis Airport Terminal in 1956, the Dhahran Air Terminal in Saudi Arabia in 1961, the McGregor Memorial Conference Center in Detroit in 1968, the Performing Arts Center in Tulsa in 1976, and the Founder's Hall in Japan in 1982, just to name a few.

Now suppose Our Lord were to say to us: "Destroy Yamasaki's works, and in three days I will raise them up." We would probably respond the way the Jews did in today's gospel: "It took Yamasaki more than 40 years to build those structures, and you're going to raise them up in three days!"

In other words, on the material level Christ's claim seems ridiculous and, in a sense, it is. We already know that Jesus rejected working miracles like tossing up skyscrapers just to dazzle us with his power.

But on the symbolic level, Christ's claim makes absolutely good sense. As the evangelist himself notes, Jesus was talking about the temple of his body which was going to be raised up from the dead.

We have here an instance of how Jesus speaks in John's gospel on two different levels. His listeners take the immediate literal meaning of his words, only to miss the symbolic sense our Lord intended.

For example, Jesus speaks to Nicodemus about being born again spiritually, but Nicodemus takes it in the impossible physical sense. Jesus speaks to the Samaritan woman about life-giving water, but she assumes that he is talking about ordinary water.

Times haven't changed much. Too often, we hear the words of Jesus in the gospel and miss their main message. Now into the third week of Lent, we've already heard Christ call us to repentance and conversion. But how many of us have been content with merely window dressing our hearts, instead of changing them from within as to our motives, attitudes and desires?

Today's gospel episode also illustrates how John uses dramatic irony. The setting is the Temple in Jerusalem, and the time is the Passover Feast. It foreshadows another visit to the Temple later for the ultimate Passover— our Lord's crossing over from death to life through his crucifixion and resurrection.

The irony is that now Jesus is the one driving people out of the Temple—the sellers and money changers. Later, he will be the one driven out of the Temple by his enemies, who will then destroy the temple of his body.

Questions confront us at both ends. On the one hand, have we ever "turned our Father's house into a marketplace"? We have if we've made them cozy social clubs instead of centers of Catholic Action, or spiritual drive-ins instead of real communities of love.

On the other hand, have we ever driven the Lord out of the temple of our hearts? We have if we've harbored a grudge against someone, judged them harshly, or ignored their cry for help.

While there is still time left to Lent and to our life, may we listen to our Lord's words more with our hearts than with our ears, lest we miss the meaning he intends for us.

Also, when we look at beautiful structures like Yamasaki's World Trade Center, may we see them as signs of the temple of Christ's body—a body that was destroyed by death on Good Friday, but was raised up in glory on Easter Sunday.

4th Sunday of Lent                  2 Ch 36:14-17, 19-23   Jn 3:14-21

## GOING ON

John Voigt and Jane Fonda play the lead roles in the movie *Coming Home*, which is about an American soldier crippled for life because of the Vietnam War. The film focuses on the psychological as well as the physical ordeals of this paraplegic—how he struggles with the help of a woman to accept his handicap, reconstruct his dreams, and create a future for himself.

This Vietnam War vet's situation is very similar to that of the Jews in the first reading. As a people the Jews had just experienced destruction, death and deportation. However, just when it seemed as if it were all over for them, God inspired King Cyrus of Persia not only to release them from exile, but also to help them rebuild their Temple.

God often sends people to help us through a crisis: parents and children frequently intervene to assist each other; a true friend often comes through when no one else will; sometimes it is the pastor, a teacher or a parishioner who bails us out.

Regardless of who it is that God sends to help us in times of trouble, there is one person he always sends to be at our side—his own Son Jesus. In John's gospel we read that God so loved the world that he sent his only Son, so that whoever believes in him may not die but have eternal life.

The primary meaning, of course, is about life after death. When we die, it will not be the end of our life but only a time for change into a new kind of life—eternal life as opposed to temporal life, immortality as opposed to mortality.

But there is also a secondary meaning to the passage. We have eternal life even now. In a sense, we already share in the life to come; it has already begun for us; we only wait for its full development and completion.

In other words, God is sending his Son to be with us every moment of our lives, and if we really believe in him we will not die, but live; we will not give up in times of crisis, but find a way to survive; we will not be defeated by difficulties, but devise ways to overcome them.

What a source of strength to know that if we believe in Jesus, we will not die, but live! Even though death may separate us from someone dear to us, the Lord will be with us in our loneliness and raise up new relationships to support us.

Even though a tragedy like a fire or a flood may devastate our home, the

Lord will be with us to rebuild what we have lost. Even though a mistake may destroy some of our precious dreams, the Lord will be with us and inspire us to start all over again.

Like the Jews in exile or like that Vietnam vet in *Coming Home*, we endure small deaths in many ways. Nonetheless, we can find new life because of our faith in the Lord Jesus.

Like the psalmist in Psalm 137, we may be despoiled of something or depressed for some reason. Nonetheless, we can sing a new song because we remember that God still loves us and is still sending his Son into the world.

So long as we believe in him we don't have to die by giving up, but can continue to live meaningfully by going on.

5th Sunday of Lent          Jr 31:31-34   Jn 12:20-33

## THE GRAIN OF WHEAT

In the movie *The Poseidon Adventure*, a ship is turned upside down by a tidal wave. Under the leadership of a priest, played by Gene Hackman, a small group of passengers makes an incredible struggle for survival.

Several members of this group die during the adventure, including the priest himself. However, it was his heroism which inspired the passengers who did survive to persevere. His death became the source of their escape to life.

Death leading to life is one of the themes of today's gospel. Jesus says: "Unless the grain of wheat falls to the earth and dies, it remains just a grain of wheat. But if it dies, it produces much fruit."

This paradox of death producing life appears in many ways.

We see it in the history of liberation, for example. The martyrdoms of Joan of Arc in France, Mahatma Gandhi in India and Martin Luther King, Jr. in America were powerful influences in the liberation of their people.

In the history of art, literature and music, some artists have put to death in their works traditional forms of expression to give birth to new ones. Pablo Picasso in painting, Ezra Pound in poetry and Igor Stravinsky in music all created new forms of expression by transcending the classical forms of the past.

In the history of transportation, the passing of some means of conveyance was connected with the discovery of better means. During the industrial era the horse-and-buggy was replaced by the automobile. Today the pollution problem and energy crisis signal the death of the combustion engine. Who knows what automotive engineers will design to replace it?

In the history of the Church, the death of some old structures was necessary to allow the growth of new ones. The Old Testament ritual of circumcision was put to its rest for the Jews who became Christians. The Latin liturgy of the Middle Ages was given its proper burial when Vatican II brought out the vernacular Mass.

In our own personal growth there has to be a dying to some of our old attitudes and forms of behavior before we can assume a new lifestyle. Unless we put to death our self-seeking, we cannot bring life to others by the joy we spread and the hope we inspire. Unless we die to our vain ambition to climb the social ladder, we cannot bring life to others by lifting them out of their poverty and indignity.

As disciples of Jesus, this is how our own sufferings become the source of salvation for others. This is how our grains of wheat die in the ground in order to produce much fruit. This is how we lose our life in this world to preserve it for life eternal.

Death and life are deeply related. Whether it is to liberate nations, enrich culture or improve industry, often something has to die in a sense when something new is created. Whether it is to renew the Church or to renew our own personal life, often something must pass away before new life or new forms can emerge.

As the Mass continues, we pray that our Lenten sacrifices may be a source of salvation for others. As our Lord is lifted up in the Eucharist, we pray that the death of our selfishness may draw us into a deeper life with Christ.


Palm Sunday                                    Mk 11:1-10   Mk 14:1-15:47

## TRIUMPH AND TRAGEDY

In 1978 President Anwar Sadat of Egypt and Prime Minister Menachem Begin shared the Nobel Peace Prize. The award was given to them for their joint efforts to reduce Mideast hostilities by framing and signing the U.S.-mediated Camp David peace accord.

The agreement was an unprecedented move on Sadat's part because he was the first major Arab leader to accept Israel's existence as a sovereign state. Only five years earlier, in 1973, he was hailed as a hero for successfully sending Egyptian troops across the Suez Canal to recapture Israeli-occupied territories. But in 1978 Sadat was called a traitor by Arab radicals.

President Sadat was assassinated by some of these Arab extremists in 1981. Ironically, he was killed while viewing a parade to celebrate the anniversary of the 1973 battle that had made him an Arab hero.

The life and death of Anwar Sadat suggest some striking similarities to the life and death of Jesus, similarities that stand out on Palm Sunday. For both Sadat and Jesus had loyal followers who acclaimed them, but also enemies who eventually killed them. Both men entered their final scene to sounds of triumph, only to depart from it on a note of tragedy.

So as we begin Holy Week with Palm Sunday to commemorate our Lord's passion and death, we see paradoxes at work between *triumph* and *tragedy*, and between *rejoicing* and *rejection*.

During the opening ceremonies centered on Christ's triumphal entry into Jerusalem, *celebration* was the keynote—we blessed palms, processed with them and sang songs to re-enact that event.

During the reading of Mark's version of the Passion, *sadness* was the dominant mood—we were appalled by the treachery of Judas, agonized with Jesus in the garden, wept with Peter over his denials, felt helpless at our Lord's trial, hurt with him as he hung on the cross and mourned with Mary over his burial.

What effect should these two moods of celebration and sadness have on us? One is to reaffirm our *faith* in Jesus. The people didn't ask questions of Jesus like, "Are you the one who is to come?" or "Where did you get all this?" They simply exclaimed their faith in him, "Hosanna!" And they expressed it in action by laying down their cloaks for him.

Another effect Palm Sunday should have on us is to solidify our *hope*. We live in a world where death abounds in the midst of life. Every day our newspapers are filled with fatalities because of abortions, AIDS, drug overdoses, suicides, hunger or war.

Nonetheless, the passion and resurrection of Jesus prove that life will prevail over death. They give us hope that even when death has done its worst, life will win out. So, with hope in our hearts, we will continue to do life-affirming things such as caring for the sick, helping the poor, ministering to the abandoned and working for peace.

Triumph and tragedy marked the lives and deaths of Anwar Sadat and Jesus. In some degree or other they mark the life of every Christian's journey to Jerusalem. But we don't have to just endure the tragic. We can also triumph over it because of our faith and hope in Jesus.

Easter (A, B, C)                                               Ac 10:34, 37-43    Mk 16:1-8

# DO NOT BE AMAZED

*The Fourth Wise Man* is a movie made for television and based on Henry van Dyke's 1895 classic. It begins like a Christmas story but ends as an Easter story. Martin Sheen stars as the fourth wise man, Artaban, who was late for the journey the three wise men made to Bethlehem because he stopped along the way to help someone in trouble.

For the next 33 years, he tries to find the promised Messiah, only to miss him at every turn because he is constantly getting sidetracked to help people. In his last efforts to find Jesus, Artaban arrives late one more time at the crucifixion. Jesus has just died on the cross.

At that moment the earthquake occurs and Artaban is struck by a falling tile. As he lies there dying he is broken-hearted because his quest to find the Messiah was never realized.

Suddenly, the risen Lord appears to him. Jesus tells him that for the past 33 years he had, in fact, been found by the fourth wise man in the person of all the people this wise man had helped. Whatever Artaban had done to the least of the Lord's people, that he had done to Jesus himself.

This Easter story is retold in another form in today's gospel. Instead of three wise men seeking the Lord, with the fourth wise man coming along late, we have three women coming to the tomb, seeking the Lord who has been crucified.

Startled by an angel at the empty tomb, they are the first ones to hear the good news of Easter: "You need not be amazed! You are looking for Jesus of Nazareth, the one who was crucified. He has been raised up. He is not here. He is going ahead of you to Galilee, where you will see him just as he told you."

Like the fourth wise man and the three women, we often go looking for the Lord in the wrong places. We expect to find him in places or people or circumstances where we imagine he should be, but he surprises us when he shows up elsewhere.

How many of us go looking for the risen Lord only among our successes and good times, or among the so-called beautiful people and people of influence—but miss seeing him in our failures and bad times too, or among the unwanted and unloved people around us?

Often we go in search of the Lord at some shrine, church or other place we consider sacred, only to pass him by in the secular places where he can be found too—the marketplace, factories and offices.

Poet William Blake understood this as he envisioned the whole world as a place where God's presence is revealed and can be experienced. He wrote:

> To see a World in a Grain of Sand
> And a Heaven in a Wildflower
> Hold Infinity in the palm of your hand
> And Eternity in an hour.

We should not be amazed, then, to find the risen Lord in the beauty of nature and in the works of his creation. Nor should we be amazed to experience him in strange places, chance meetings or unforeseen events, as long as we're open to his revelations and not limited by our own expectations.

We don't have to journey to Jerusalem or Lourdes to look for Jesus. He's as close as the sounds of our own cities or the silence of the night. We don't have to wander far away to find Jesus. He's as near as our next-door neighbor or the next television newscast.

"You need not be amazed," the angel tells us this Easter Sunday. "The risen Lord you are looking for has gone ahead of you to Galilee—to the Galilees of your homes, and your places of work and play. There you will find him, as he told you, in whatever you do for the least of his people."

2nd Sunday of Easter                                    Ac 4:32-35   Jn 20:19-31

# BE AN INVITER

At a national mathematics teachers conference in Toronto in 1982, psychologist William Purkey of the University of North Carolina gave the keynote address. His talk was entitled *Invitations to Teach By*, but it could have just as easily been entitled *Invitations to Live By*.

Purkey began with a forestry fact. If you plant an acorn correctly and provide it with the right conditions, it will grow into a mighty oak tree with a 100% success rate. Kids are like acorns when they come into a family or enter a school—they have unlimited potential to be a success at a rate of 100%.

And yet, more than one-third of our adult population is in trouble with emotional problems, neuroses, psychosomatic illnesses, depression and so on. That's a psychological statistic.

Why such a poor success rate? Purkey claims that it is because somewhere between childhood and adulthood we were more *disinvited* than *invited* to develop and become great.

When do we *disinvite* people? Every time we demean, ridicule, poke fun at them, hurt their feelings, or make them feel unloved. What effects does disinviting have? It diminishes one's self-image and destroys self-esteem.

The opposite of disinviting people is to *invite* them to learn and to love life. We invite people to greatness by making them feel good about themselves, expressing care for them, and showing we understand and appreciate them.

In his book, *Invitation to Greatness*, Fr. Frank McNulty calls these invitations "ego boosters" and notes their effect:

> Words of praise and appreciation, successful accomplishments and achievements are all great ego boosters, but the most effective of all is *love* . . . People in love help one another reach their full potential.

Jesus was the greatest inviter there ever was. The only ones he disinvited were the Pharisees, and they don't count because they disinvited themselves. Today's gospel gives us a good example of Jesus, the *inviter to greatness*.

If we had made that first appearance to the apostles, what might we have said? "Where were you cowards when I was crucified? Peter, my leader, I told you that you would deny me three times, and damned if you didn't do it. One of you was so scared when they arrested me that you streaked off naked.''

That's what we might have said—disinviting things. But what does Jesus say? "Peace be with you. I know you failed. But that's OK. I'm alive now. Receive the Holy Spirit.'' Everything Jesus says and does is inviting, up-building, encouraging and affirming.

Then there is the Thomas scene. Jesus doesn't destroy his already badly damaged self-image. He doesn't scold Thomas for his stubbornness. Jesus simply and gently invites Thomas to touch his wounded hands and to put his fingers into his pierced side.

Jesus gives Thomas positive affirmation—"Thomas, be a believer." Jesus reasserts his apostleship—"Go and teach the whole world; forgive sins." Jesus enhances Thomas' self-image by what he says and does.

Isn't this the way Jesus deals with us, too? He invites us to believe in him, to love life, and to affirm one another. "Don't be a *disbeliever*," Jesus says. "Be a *believer*. Don't be a *disinviter*. Be an *inviter*."

So Jesus sends us into the world to *invite* people to greatness by welcoming them warmly like guests we're happy to see; by reaching out to do little things for them; by showing sympathy when they fail and adding a word of encouragement to try again; by sharing their dreams and celebrating their successes.

"Don't be a *disinviter*," Jesus says. "Be an *inviter*."


3rd Sunday of Easter                           Ac 3:13-15, 17-19   Lk 24:35-48

## AFTERLIFE

In the movie *Resurrection*, actress Ellen Burstyn stars as Edna Mae McCauley who suffers near-death. As a result of a car crash, Edna Mae apparently dies in a hospital emergency room. After a few moments of frantic effort, the medics succeed in reviving her.

During that interval of apparent death, Edna Mae has a mysterious experience of an afterlife. She is transported through a tunnel of light where she meets family and friends who have already died. When she returns to consciousness, she remembers this peaceful experience very vividly, and she is blessed with the power of healing.

The movie *Resurrection* reflects what researchers like Raymond Moody and Elisabeth Kübler-Ross have learned from people who have had similar near-death experiences. Such glimpses of an afterlife do not prove there is a resurrection after we die. They merely hint at its possibility.

We accept that possibility on faith, especially faith in the resurrection of Jesus. This foundation of our faith is found in today's readings from Scripture.

In the first reading from Acts, Peter says: "You put to death the Author of Life by handing him over to Pilate. But God raised him from the dead, and we are his witnesses."

In the gospel, Jesus appears to his disciples after his resurrection. They thought they were seeing a ghost. "Why are you disturbed? It is really I," Jesus says. "Touch me and see that a ghost does not have flesh and bones as I do." Then he eats some fish to try to convince them.

All of us have an irrepressible instinct that says we are more than a corruptible biological composition; that death is not the end; that somehow life must continue beyond the grave. Christ's resurrection confirms this instinct.

First, it says that life after death is real. Death may be dreadful because it separates us from our loved ones, but Christ's resurrection appearances to his disciples show that death does not end our friendships and human relationships. Rather, it adds a new dimension to them.

Death may be fearful because it is our final experience in this life, but Christ's resurrection shows that death is not ultimate in its finality. Life after death is not just a fantasy. Rather, it is a reality based on faith.

Second, Christ's resurrection says that life after death includes the body. Certainly Jesus' risen body has qualities that our body doesn't have yet. For example, it is incorruptible and can pass through closed doors. His risen body is different, but it is still a body.

In the same way, when we rise from the dead, it won't be as pure spirits. We will rise with our bodies transformed by incorruptibility and glorified by immortality.

What reassuring revelations these are! Because life after death is real, we don't have to be terrified of suffering or death. Our victory over them is already won in Christ. We don't have to be disturbed about losing our family or the results of our work. We expect to regain them in the resurrection.

Because life after death includes the body, we don't have to worry about whether our body now is graceful or crippled, energetic or aging. Every kind of body we can imagine is destined to rise from the dead and be transfigured into glory. Just as the flower and the fragrance are one, so too our body and spirit are one. Death may separate them, but the resurrection will reunite them.

Praise the risen Lord for revealing to us that life after death is both real and physical. Thank the Lord for being present with us today in this breaking of the bread, the pledge of our presence together at the heavenly banquet in the afterlife.


4th Sunday of Easter                                    Ac 4:8-12   Jn 10:11-18

# LAYING DOWN ONE'S LIFE

In San Salvador on March 24, 1980, an assassin killed Archbishop Oscar Romero with a single shot to the heart while he was saying Mass. Only a few moments before, Archbishop Romero had finished a hope-filled homily in which he urged his people to serve one another. Turning to the bread and wine on the altar, he said his last words:

> May this immolated body and this blood sacrificed for mankind, strengthen our body and our blood, so that we can *give ourselves* to suffering and pain like Christ . . . to give people a vision of peace and justice.

Since Archbishop Romero was demanding human rights for his people under oppression, he knew that his life was in danger. Still he persisted in speaking out against tyranny and for freedom. He once told newspapermen that even if his enemies killed him, he would rise again among his people.

Because Archbishop Romero was so devoted to his people in San Salvador and because he died defending their cause, he can truly make his own our Lord's words in today's gospel: "I am the Good Shepherd. The Good Shepherd lays down his life for the sheep . . . I know my sheep and for these sheep I will give my life."

The dominant theme in this passage is that of the Good Shepherd *laying down* his life. No less than five times is this phrase or its equivalent used in our Lord's description of himself. Total commitment and sacrifice are the keynote to Christ's role as the Good Shepherd.

In his book *John: The Different Gospel*, Fr. Michael Taylor underlines the positive dimension of Christ's death. Our Lord's death was not a negative work done by darkness but a free laying down of his own life to demonstrate the depths of his love for us. Fr. Taylor writes:

> The Father did not tell Jesus to get himself killed. He told him to show his people how much he loves them. One shows love by *giving of oneself* and Jesus gave himself fully in death. While darkness conspires to destroy him, a more profound plot is being acted out: God's eternal love incarnated in his Son is being *given up* so that the world might share in it.

In order to share in this kind of love God has for us, we in turn have to love one another, be good shepherds for each other, and lay down our lives for one another. This doesn't mean that we have to be crucified on a cross like Jesus or be assassinated like Archbishop Romero. But it does mean that we have to be deeply concerned about each other and committed to each other's well-being.

Good shepherds who lay down their lives mean husbands and wives who can't do enough for each other to demonstrate their devotion; parents who make countless sacrifices for the good of their children; teachers who spend untold hours instructing weak students; doctors and nurses who work untiringly to show they care for their patients.

Good shepherds who lay down their lives mean employers who share profits with their workers; politicians who unselfishly promote the common good of their voters; parishioners who generously support their parish community.

The paradox is that if we shepherd one another in love, we don't lose anything by laying down our life in service. Rather, we gain it back. We take it up again, as Jesus said in the gospel.

In fact, like Jesus who took up his life again in the resurrection transfigured with glory, we too will take up our life again, transformed and renewed by grace. We will experience a deeper kind of peace, enjoy a stronger sense of satisfaction and find a happiness surpassing all our hopes.

5th Sunday of Easter                              Ac 9:26-31   Jn 15:1-8

# LA DOLCE VITA

In the opening scene of Fellini's film *La Dolce Vita* ("The Sweet Life"), a large statue of Jesus is carried over Rome by a helicopter, followed by a second helicopter bearing a young scandal-sheet writer named Marcello. Among the sights juxtaposed with Jesus and Marcello is a bevy of voluptuous bikini-clad sunbathers.

Critic Bosley Crowther sees in this scene a summary of the film's theme:

> Dignity is transmuted into the sensational. Old values, old disciplines are discarded for the modern, the synthetic, the quick by a society that is sated with pleasure and itself. All of its straining for sensations is exploited for the picture magazines and scandal sheets that merchandise excitement and vicarious thrills for the mob.

The film goes on to follow the escapades of Marcello as he flits from mistress to mistress and from orgy to orgy. Marcello embodies the loneliness, emptiness and boredom of the jet-set crowd with whom he keeps company.

Their decay is symbolized in the last scene in which Marcello and his friends find on a beach a strange fish rotting in the sun. Across the inlet, an innocent girl calls to Marcello. Although she reminds him of the good and simple life he once enjoyed and could recover, he cannot find the courage to react to her invitation.

*La Dolce Vita* illustrates what our Lord meant when he said in today's gospel: "I am the vine and you are the branches. He who lives in me and I in him will produce abundantly . . . A man who does not live in me is like a withered, rejected branch, picked up to be thrown in the fire and burnt."

When Marcello grew up with his family in a small town he led a simple but happy life. But now that he has forsaken their religion and lifestyle for the decadence of the big cities, he finds himself not only unhappy, but also dying intellectually, morally and spiritually.

Indeed, Fellini's imagery of the rotting fish and Christ's metaphor of the withered branch are strong symbols of what happens to us when we separate ourselves from our Lord, his Church and our family.

That's the bad news of today's gospel. The good news is summed up under three points by *Peake's Commentary on the Bible*.

First, it recalls Old Testament descriptions of Israel as a vine to symbolize life and growth in union with God. For example, Hosea 10 pictures Israel as a luxuriant vine.

Second, the commentary reminds us that our Lord's metaphor of the vine is part of his Last Supper discourse. From the synoptics we know that it was then that Jesus identified the cup of wine, which is the fruit of the vine, with his own blood of the new covenant. The Eucharist is the supreme sign of his union with us.

Third, *Peake's Commentary* asserts that the true vine is to be found not in Israel, but in Jesus: "Christ the vine is the means by which men are related to God."

In other words, we cannot belong to God's people unless we abide in Christ. We cannot grow in grace and produce fruit unless we are united to Christ as branches to a vine and are nourished by his Eucharist.

If we live in Christ by prayer and sacrifice, then we can produce much fruit, like curbing violence and bringing back peace on our city streets, counteracting pornography and restoring decency in entertainment, and removing injustices and establishing equal opportunities in the job market.

If we remain in Christ by reading his Word and serving his people, then we can do all things, such as curtailing substance abuse and inspiring a love of learning in our students, diminishing dissension and instilling cooperation in parishes, and curbing quarrels and filling homes with loving concern.

Separated from Jesus, we end up like dead fish or dead wood. United to him as branches to a vine we can be living, growing and fruit-producing people.

6th Sunday of Easter               Ac 10:25-26, 34-35, 44-48   Jn 15:9-17

## NO GREATER LOVE

D-Day, June 6, 1944, will stand forever as a day when one of the most daring deeds ever done for freedom took place. In his book *D-Day with the*

*Screaming Eagles,* George Koskimaki details the heroism of the paratroopers who jumped on that day of destiny.

By spearheading the invasion of Normandy, the paratroopers knew that many of them would die from enemy fire in making their drop—either before they jumped, or in the air, or in their landing, or in the open fields.

Yet, in spite of knowing that many of them would have to sacrifice their lives, these paratroopers went ahead and did their duty—in fear, but with faith in their cause; not wanting to die, but willing to die for the liberation of Europe.

The price paid by these brave men was great. Koskimaki reports that one company jumped with 208 enlisted men and 11 officers, but only 69 enlisted men and 4 officers came back.

In a dramatic way these paratroopers demonstrated the meaning of our Lord's words in today's gospel: "This is my commandment: love one another, as I have loved you. A man can have no greater love than to lay down his life for his friends."

In the *Anchor Bible Commentary* on John's gospel, Fr. Raymond Brown points out that the Greek philosopher Plato said something very similar to what Jesus said: "Only those who love wish to die for others."

But Fr. Brown also adds that the statement Jesus made—fulfilled later in his own death on the cross—left a greater mark on subsequent behavior than Plato's statement did. It has inspired martyrs and soldiers and missionaries in every century since the time of Christ.

If we study the gospel text further, we notice that our Lord's words come as a climax to an impassioned plea about love. He uses the word *love* no less than eight times in sixteen lines of his speech. Nowhere else in the gospels does the theme of love dominate a text so strongly.

Since Jesus is about to die, his words on love become his last legacy to us—a legacy he would act out by laying down his life for us literally on the cross and sacramentally in the Eucharist. Moreover, it is a legacy that leads us to do the same thing—to make love our supreme value and to lay down our lives for one another.

Laying down one's life in love may sometimes involve real death, as it did for the Screaming Eagle paratroopers. But more often it means a lot of little laying downs of our selfishness for the good of someone else, especially when we're not in the mood.

Whether we're in Normandy or Nashville, these laying downs might take the form of giving up some television time to call up someone just to be friendly, or going out of our way to visit someone who is sick, or writing a note of sympathy to someone who is grieving.

We lay down our lives whenever we leave aside our comfort to welcome a guest, or lend a helping hand to a neighbor, or volunteer our services for some parish activity.

There is no greater love we can show to our family or friends than to give something of ourselves, or to share something personally, or to set aside something that is very much a part of our life.

Jesus lives on in our love because he laid down his life on the cross for our salvation. The Screaming Eagles live on in our love because they laid down their lives in defense of our freedom. What kind of legacy will we leave behind us? Is there any cause or any person for whom we are laying down our lives in selfless service and sacrifice?

Ascension                                                         Ac 1:1-11   Mk 16:15-20

# SOLAR POWER

One of the national coordinators of Sun Day held early in May every year is Denis Hayes. He works as a researcher at a Washington, D.C. "think tank" and has written a book about solar energy entitled *Rays of Hope: The Transition to a Post-Petroleum World.*

Hayes claims that we are at the crossroads of making a critical choice for mankind—the choice between going solar or going nuclear. Hayes opts for the sun because it is "the world's only inexhaustible, predictable, egalitarian, non-polluting, safe, terrorist-resistant and free energy source."

We've already learned to use the power of the sun to grow food, make wine and operate greenhouses. All we need to do is develop better technology to harness solar energy to heat our homes, drive our cars and run our industry.

People like Hayes are looking at the sky with its sun as the main source of our future power supply. Today we turn our attention skyward for another reason—to commemorate our Lord's ascension into heaven.

But as we do so the idea of *power* appears again, this time in the three readings from Scripture.

In the first reading from Acts, Jesus makes a promise: "You will receive *power* when the Holy Spirit comes down on you."

In the second reading from Paul's letter to the Ephesians, he asks that we may be enlightened to know "the immeasurable scope of the Lord's *power* in us who believe" (Ep 1:19).

Finally, in the gospel, Mark mentions twice the *signs* which accompanied those who believed. First, in the promise by our Lord before his ascension: "*Signs* like these will accompany those who have professed their faith." Second, in their accomplishment after Christ's ascension: "The Lord continued to confirm the message through the *signs* which accompanied them."

Power, then, seems to be one of the principal effects of our Lord's ascension. We have a paradox here. The Lord Jesus removes his physical presence from our midst; nonetheless, his power remains operative. We can no longer see him with our eyes, yet we can see signs of his presence in people whose lives he inspires. We cannot hear his voice with our ears anymore, but still he heals us by the power of his Word when it is read in Scripture. We cannot feel Christ with our own hands, but he continues to touch us through the power of his sacraments.

Going back to our opening image of the sun, Galileo once said that the sun, with all the planets revolving around it and dependent upon it, can still ripen a bunch of grapes as if it had nothing else in the universe to do.

We might say something similar about our Lord. Even though the whole universe depends on his power just to stay in existence, he bathes each of us with the powerful rays of his love as if he had nothing else to do.

However, we seem to ignore his presence and power most of the time, for we still have children starving, workers unemployed and nations warring.

If only we took Christ's promise seriously and actually expected him to continue working his signs of power through us, then even though we might not be able to drink deadly poison or handle serpents, we would at least be able to make some progress in alleviating famine, creating jobs and establishing peace.

May we take our Lord at his word and go out to proclaim the good news that his power is still operative in us and through us.

7th Sunday of Easter                    Ac 1:15-17, 20-26   Jn 17:11-19

# SENT IN HIS NAME

Judge James L. Ryan and his wife Mary live in the Detroit area and have four adopted children. Formerly of the Michigan Supreme Court and now a federal judge, Justice Ryan has given commencement addresses at the high school graduations of some of his children from Catholic Central and Mercy high schools.

In his addresses, Judge Ryan called on the graduates to recognize and accept their God-given individuality, to refine and enrich that unique identity, and to put their special gifts at the service of humanity. He said:

> We live in a society which desperately needs the comfort of your gentleness, the example of your discipline, the joy of your artistry, and the force of your logic.

The scenes in today's readings have some of the characteristics of commencement exercises.

In the first reading from Acts, Matthias is picked by lot to fill the vacancy left by Judas. We might say that he graduates from the rank of a follower into the select group of the twelve apostolic leaders.

In the gospel, the setting is the Last Supper before Christ's death. Up until now, the apostles have been taught by our Lord. But after his ascension they in turn will have to go out and teach others.

Christ's prayer at the Last Supper sounds very much like a commencement speech: "Father, consecrate them by means of truth . . . As you have sent me into the world, so I have sent them into the world."

Like Matthias and the other apostles, we too are sent into the world. It is for this that we have been consecrated by our baptism and commissioned by our confirmation. Like the graduates of today, we too are sent to face the challenges of the future. It is for this that we are instructed every Sunday by God's word and strengthened by the Eucharist.

What a source of confidence for us! During the Last Supper Jesus knew how weak and frail his apostles were. Yet he made a daring act of faith in their ability to proclaim his gospel.

In the same way, Jesus knows how weak we are. Yet he makes a bold act of faith in us. "I know they can do it, Father," he prays. "Do not take them away from their responsibilities at home or from their opportunities at work. Instead, send them into the world to face today's issues and to transform the universe."

What a magnificent task this is—to be sent into the world to change it! Not to run away from its problems of poverty and oppression, but to plunge into them and improve the lot of God's people. Not to turn away from the world's injustice and violence, but to turn toward them and remove them. Not to turn our backs on its abortions and drug addictions, but to confront them and eliminate them.

Our task is not to condemn the world for its sins, but to save it; not to abandon its people, but to redeem them; not to reject its institutions, but to renew them.

It is for this magnificent task that we are sent into the world—to confront it, to influence it, and to change it for the better.

As Judge Ryan and Jesus have reminded us, our purpose in life is not merely a private affair—our own sanctification; it is also a social matter—the world's transformation.

At the end of this Eucharist, like so many school graduates today, we will be sent into the world—to challenge it and to change it for the better. If Christ believes in us, how can we help but go out with confidence in our own unique individuality and ability? How can we help but begin again, commence with eagerness to do our task?


Pentecost (A, B, C)                                     Ac 2:1-11   Jn 20:19-23

# THE BREATH OF GOD

With the new technology available, modern man tends to analyze things scientifically. For example, he can look at the way we breathe and measure the lung capacity of athletes, astronauts and smokers.

By way of contrast, primitive man tended to view things mythologically. For example, in his book *The Heart of the Hunter*, Laurens van der Post tells how a Bushmen tribe in South Africa associated their breath with the wind. The Bushmen reverenced the wind as the source of life and felt as if they were inside it.

When a Bushman died he relied on the wind to blow away his footprints so that no one would be under the illusion that he was still living. Moreover, the Bushman believed that upon his death he would rejoin the great wind from which he came. In this way he would continue his existence, a sort of immortality.

Today's gospel for Pentecost uses another ancient myth about breath and life. The risen Jesus appears to his disciples in the upper room on the evening of Easter Sunday. After greeting them with words of peace and showing them his hands and side, "He *breathed* on them and said: 'Receive the Holy Spirit.' "

In his commentary on this passage, William Barclay says there is no doubt that when John wrote these verses, he was thinking back to the Old Testament creation stories of man. The Hebrews used the same word to signify both *wind* and *spirit*, and, in their understanding, the *wind* was the *breath of God*.

So in Genesis 2 we read how God first formed man from the clay of the earth, and then *breathed* into him to make him come alive. Also, in Ezekiel 37 we have the prophet's vision of the valley of dead, dry bones. Yahweh commands the *Spirit* to come from the four winds to *breathe* life into those bones.

Consequently, what we have symbolized at Pentecost by the words *breath* and *spirit* is a new creation and a new beginning. That's why we sometimes call the Feast of Pentecost the "birthday of the Church."

Before Pentecost the disciples were huddled together behind closed doors. Paralyzed by fear, confusion and hesitancy, they could only wait and pray. But when the Holy Spirit came on Pentecost, his fire kindled their hearts, and his wind drove them out into the streets to proclaim the good news.

That was the beginning of the Church's mission to make disciples of all nations. What those early disciples began is yet to be finished. That's why we need a new coming of the Holy Spirit in our own day.

In his book *A New Pentecost*, Cardinal Suenens points out that even though we have already received the Spirit in baptism and confirmation, we need a new coming by him in the sense that we need a keener awareness of his presence, a stronger faith in his power and a releasing of his gifts.

In other words, even though the Holy Spirit is always with us, as Jesus promised, he can perform new actions within us and through us—like removing obstacles caused by our sins, taking a deeper possession of our hearts or inspiring us to be more generous.

Our need for a new Pentecost and a new creation by the Holy Spirit is expressed in a version of an ancient Irish hymn by Edwin Hatch:

> O breathe on me, Thou Breath of God,
> Fill me with life anew,
> That I may love what Thou dost love,
> And do what Thou wouldst do.
> O breathe on me, Thou Breath of God,
> Till I am wholly Thine,
> Until this earthly part of me
> Glows with Thy fire divine.

Holy Trinity                         Dt 4:32-34, 39-40   Mt 28:16-20

## FACES OF GOD

In 1961 Dr. Carl R. Rogers published a book called *On Becoming a Person*. Since that time it has come to be recognized as a classic in psychotherapy. Its popularity is due in large part to its positive approach.

While Dr. Rogers does not deny the disorders, maladjustments and neuroses that trouble people, he prefers instead to emphasize the immense potential we have as persons to develop, to adapt and to grow.

According to Dr. Rogers, to "become a person" we have to focus more on our possibilities than on our problems, more on our freedom than on our restrictions, more on our capacity to create than on our past mistakes.

Perhaps we can take our cue from Dr. Rogers in our approach to the mystery of the Holy Trinity. In the Creed we confess that there is *one God*, but *three Persons*. Too often we have negative feelings about our faith in this mystery because we can't adequately comprehend it, let alone explain it.

But if we adopt Dr. Rogers' positive approach on becoming a human person and apply it to our perception of the three divine Persons, then perhaps our attitudes and feelings about this mystery will change for the better.

Scripture certainly does all it can to help us take such a positive approach.

The reading from Deuteronomy doesn't dwell on what we don't know about God. It states quite simply that God is Lord of all, that he created us and that there is no other God.

In the second reading St. Paul refuses to get fixated on our fears and on those things that enslave us. Instead, he gets all excited about how we are led by the Spirit into God's family, into true freedom and ultimate glory (Rm 8:14-17).

Finally, in Matthew's gospel Jesus doesn't make a lengthy speech to the apostles about how they should explain the Trinity. He just tells them to proclaim this teaching and to baptize people in the name of that Trinity.

The sacred authors thus take a very positive approach to the Trinity. A modern spiritual writer who does the same is Romano Guardini. In his book *The Life of Faith*, he views the mystery of the Trinity as revealing to us different *faces of God*.

First, there is the *face* of God as *Father*—the beginning and the end of all, the Creator, the Ruler. He is not only the God we obey through the Commandments, but also the God we address as "Our Father." He is not only the God to whom Jesus referred in the parables, but also the God about whom Jesus could say, "The Father and I are one."

Second, there is the *face* of God as *Son*. Jesus is the only-begotten Son of God, the divine Word of God who took on our human nature. On the one hand, Jesus shows us the God who heals us and forgives us. On the other hand, he shows us the God who challenges us to higher things and sends us out to do his work.

Third, there is the *face* of God as *Spirit*. He is the Comforter who is always with us, the Paraclete who teaches us. The Spirit is the very breath of God giving us new life, the love of God poured out into our hearts and the power of God enabling us to become his witnesses.

As we profess our faith today in the trinity of Persons in the one God, may we also pray to them to help us become the kind of person we are meant to be—a true child of God our Father, a living image of Jesus his Son and a consecrated temple of the Holy Spirit.

Corpus Christi                                    Ex 24:3-8  Mk 14:12-16, 22-26

# EUCHARISTIC FAITH

In New York City in 1985, Brigitte Gerney got pinned beneath a fallen construction crane. For six torturous hours, paramedics struggled frantically to keep her alive until she could be rescued.

During that ordeal Brigitte was given not only blood transfusions, fluids and painkillers, but also the Eucharist which she specifically asked for. Brigitte was then taken to a hospital where doctors operated on her for another five hours.

The crane accident was only the most recent of a whole series of mishaps Brigitte had suffered. During the previous fifteen years, her first child had drowned accidentally at age 18 months, her husband died of cancer, her father was killed in an automobile accident, she had two operations to remove cancer and she had suffered multiple injuries in a cable car crash in Switzerland in 1982.

And yet, after all that, Brigitte Gerney did not curse Christ when she was under the crane. She asked for him in the Eucharist. She did not blame God for her bad luck. She asked her rescuers to pray with her. No wonder Dr. Tom Fahey, Jr. said of her: "She has an indomitable spirit and a strong faith in God."

Do we have that kind of faith? Do we believe that strongly in Christ's presence in the Eucharist? On this Feast of Corpus Christi we have an opportunity to reaffirm our faith in the Eucharist. Today we can take our stand with the people of Exodus and accept God's covenant with us: "Lord, all you've said at the Last Supper about the Eucharist, we will believe. All you have commanded about it, we will do."

During the Exodus journey God gave the Israelites manna from heaven to feed them. On the strength of that food they were able to travel forty years through the desert.

During her excruciating ordeal Brigitte Gerney requested and received the Eucharist. On the strength of that bread she was able to survive the six hours she was pinned under the crane and another five hours of surgery.

During our own personal journey through life we sometimes have to cross deserts, encounter accidents, endure disappointments or suffer tragedies. By ourselves we could never survive. Left to our own strength we would give up. That is why we need the Eucharist and the strength that comes from this bread to energize our spirits. This is why we need God's special presence and power.

In Mark's gospel we read how our Lord *left* the upper room and *walked out* to the Mount of Olives. What he *left* was the Last Supper during which he instituted the sacrament of the Eucharist. His *walking out* to the Mount of Olives was also something very sacramental and symbolic. Jesus was showing that he was ready for his rendezvous with destiny and that he was resolved to lay down his life for us on the cross.

May this often be our own experience after celebrating the Eucharist. *Coming in* we may be afraid of what we have to face in the future. But when we *leave*, may we be ready and resolved to take up our cross. *Coming in* we may have serious doubts about how to deal with certain difficulties. But when we *leave*, may we be filled with determination to do what God expects of us.

Do we believe that this is possible? Brigitte Gerney did. Otherwise how can we explain her indomitable spirit in the face of all the tragedies she experienced?

As we continue this Eucharistic celebration, pray for Brigitte's kind of faith in the Eucharist: a faith which firmly believes that Christ is always *present* in the Eucharist, regardless of how *absent* he may seem to be at times; a faith which believes that Christ's *power* is always available to us, regardless of how *helpless* we may feel at times; a faith which enables us to *walk* with our Lord to our own Mount of Olives and to *rise* with him in glory.

2nd Sunday of the Year                                     1 S 3:3-10, 19    Jn 1:35-42

# NAME CHANGES

Can you identify Marion Morrison, Roy Fitzgerald or Ramon Estevez? Maybe not, but they are actually John Wayne, Rock Hudson and Martin Sheen. Do you recognize such names as Frances Gumm, Norma Jean Baker or Betty Pepske? Perhaps not, but they really belong to Judy Garland, Marilyn Monroe and Lauren Bacall.

It is a common practice among entertainers to change their names in order to create a certain kind of image, to establish a new identity or to promote their publicity.

A change in name occurs sometimes in Scripture, and today's gospel gives us a classic example. After Andrew gets acquainted with Jesus, he hurries to bring his brother Simon to our Lord. Jesus looks at Simon and says: "You are Simon, son of John. Your name shall be Cephas (which means Peter)."

Later we learn that *Peter* means *rock*, and that it is upon this *rock* that Jesus will build his Church. Thus *Simon* is given the new name *Peter* to signify his role as the *rock* of Christ's foundation of the Church.

Name changing happens more than once in the Bible. We recall God giving Abram the new name of Abraham and Jacob the title Israel in the Old Testament, or Saul becoming Paul in the New Testament.

To the ancient mind, one's name was synonymous with one's character and personality. Names were carefully chosen because they signified the ideals a person was to live by and the destiny he or she was to pursue. So when a name was changed it meant that someone was taking on a whole new existence as it were, a new character or career or calling.

In the case of Simon's name being converted to Peter, it was Jesus' way of emphasizing Simon's transition from an old order to a new order—from fisherman to apostle and from follower to leader. It was our Lord's way of affirming his faith in Peter as his chief apostle, even though he knew that Peter would one day deny him.

The new name Peter bore would be a constant challenge to him to live up to its meaning and truly become a *rock* on whom others could lean and depend in times of crisis.

We've lost much of this ancient understanding of the symbolism of one's name. Most of us don't even know the source or meaning of our first name. Do you know yours? Mine is *Albert*. It is Teutonic in origin and means "illustrious through nobility."

While my name may not be literally true in my case, it should nonetheless serve as an inspiration and challenge to me. It should evoke ideals and qualities for which I should strive.

We've also drifted away from the Christian custom of naming our children after the saints. As a result, devotion to the saints has understandably fallen off. Not too many of us look to the saints as heroes and heroines to imitate or as role models to follow.

While having a Christian first name may be important, it is more important to never forget that God formed us and calls us by name to be his (Is 43:1); that Jesus no longer calls us servants but friends (Jn 15:15); that our names are written in the Book of Life (Rv 21:27).

If we remember these things about our name—whatever it may be— then we will realize better our dignity as disciples, give more direction to our lives and attain our destiny as saints.

3rd Sunday of the Year                                    Jon 3:1-5, 10   Mk 1:14-20

# COURAGE TO CHANGE

In November of 1984 on one of his PBS *Late Night America* shows, Dennis Wholey confessed that he was an alcoholic. He went on to describe a book he had put together entitled *The Courage to Change: Personal Conversations about Alcoholism with Dennis Wholey.*

The book contains frank and revealing conversations with a wide variety of celebrity alcoholics such as rock singer Grace Slick, baseball player Bob Welch, actor Jason Robards, comedian Shecky Greene and Catholic priest Vaughan Quinn.

Also, there are heartfelt conversations with Rod Steiger and Jerry Falwell, who are children of alcoholics; and Sybil Carter, whose husband Billy is an alcoholic.

Four years earlier, Dennis Wholey confronted his own problem with alcohol and now is on a mission with his book to help other victims of what is sometimes called "the most treatable untreated disease in this country."

Dennis Wholey's message about *The Courage to Change* matches our Lord's message in Mark's gospel: "This is the time of fulfillment. The kingdom of God is at hand. Repent, and believe the good news."

The Greek word for *repent* is *metanoia* and it literally means "to change one's mind." It implies a coming to one's senses with a corresponding change in conduct. As used in the gospel, *metanoia* means to turn away from sin and to turn towards God. In a word, *repent* means to experience a conversion.

This is precisely what recovered alcoholics like Dennis Wholey have done—they have turned away from their past lifestyle of drinking and have turned toward a new pattern of behavior. Their old agenda of indulgence in alcohol has been replaced by a new agenda of abstinence.

Alcohol may or may not be one of our weaknesses. In either case, since we are all sinners, we have other weaknesses to contend with. Christ's call to conversion exempts no one. All of us stand in need of turning more and more away from selfishness and laziness, or from pride and stubbornness, or from greed and possessiveness.

Who of us can say that we have no sins of omission to repent of? Sins like neglecting hospitality and courtesy, or failing to return something borrowed or to say thanks for a favor, or avoiding responsibility and prayer.

But turning away is only half of the conversion process. The other half is to turn towards something better to bring us closer to God, to believe in the good news, as it were.

The easiest way to root out a bad habit is to reinforce a good one—like developing discipline to displace our laziness, sharing more to stem our selfishness, or taking time to pray to cut down on our television viewing.

To believe in the good news challenges us to get involved in a noble cause, like the pro-life program, the war on poverty, nuclear disarmament or the anti-apartheid movement.

Indeed, as Dennis Wholey points out in his book, it takes courage to change, whether personally in our battle with something like alcohol, or socially in our struggle with something like injustice. But change is possible, as his own conversion shows. For some of us, change is imperative if we're ever going to hear the good news.

Moreover, the time is *now*, not later, according to our Lord. The kingdom is *here*, not some place else. Like the four disciples called in the gospel, we have to act *at once*, or it may be too late.

4th Sunday of the Year                                      Dt 18:15-20   Mk 1:21-28

# TEACHING WITH AUTHORITY

In one of its issues *Newsweek* addressed in depth the Women's Liberation Movement. It observed that once the revolution was declared, the nation was flooded with books on the subject.

Some books, like those written by Nancy Woloch and Phyllis Schlafly, were serious studies of the significance of the movement. Other books, like those authored by Betty Friedan and Gloria Steinem, were more strident and dogmatic.

The latter illustrate what often happens in a movement—self-styled prophets emerge who presume to speak with full authority. And so we have had such figures as Hugh Hefner as the spokesman for the Playboy Philosophy, guru Timothy Leary for the LSD cult and the militant Malcolm X for the Black Power movement.

History shows that many of these movements die out and that their prophets fade away. But there is one movement that endures, one prophet who lives forever. The movement is Christianity and the prophet is Jesus Christ.

This is what today's readings from Scripture proclaim.

In the first reading from Deuteronomy, God speaks to Moses: "I will raise up a prophet like you from among your kinsmen. I will put my words into his mouth. To him you shall listen."

This Old Testament promise is fulfilled with the appearance of Jesus. In Mark's gospel we see people spellbound by Christ's teachings because he taught with authority; we see demons obey his command because he was the Holy One of God.

Unlike so many self-styled prophets today who only pretend to speak with full *authority*, Jesus truly speaks with full authority because it was given to him by his Father. "For I have not spoken on my own authority," Jesus says in John 12. "But he who sent me, the Father, has commanded me what I should say."

Unlike so many false prophets today who distort the *truth*, Jesus teaches nothing but the truth. As he replied to Pilate in John 18: "This is why I was born and why I have come into the world—to bear witness to the truth."

Unlike today's self-appointed teachers who enslave us to sex, drugs or violence, Jesus leads us to *freedom*. He declares in John 8: "If you abide in my word, you shall know the truth, and the truth shall make you free."

Unlike today's prophets who make empty promises of finding *fulfillment*, Jesus himself is the source of our fulfillment. As he told the Samaritan woman at the well in John 4: "He who drinks of this water will thirst again. But anyone who drinks of the water that I will give shall never thirst."

Unlike today's false teachers who have only a phony kind of *power*, Jesus gives us a share in the very power of his Spirit. He announces in John 14: "He who believes in me will do the works I do, and greater far than these he will do."

During this Eucharist, Christ comes into our midst to teach us through the readings of Scripture. Like the prophet Moses, he comes to speak the words of God to us, not about trivial things but about ultimate issues like truth, freedom and fulfillment. Jesus comes to teach us, not with empty promises but with full authority and power.

Pray that we may not harden our hearts and stifle his voice. Pray that we may listen to his words and not to the lies of today's false prophets.


5th Sunday of the Year                                    Jb 7:1-7   Mk 1:29-39

# DO WHAT JESUS DID

*The Day the Bubble Burst* is a movie which focuses on the day the Stock Market crashed in 1929 and the banks closed. That day ushered in the Depression Era of lost fortunes, unemployment and soup lines.

But it was not only an era of economic depression. It was also an era of human despair. Thousands of people committed suicide or went insane when they lost all of their savings and had no other resources on which to depend.

Job, too, lost all his wealth, property and even his family. He too knew the feelings of misery, hopelessness and depression. That is why in today's first reading he describes his days as drudgery and his nights as dragging on, and he envisions his life as ending soon without hope.

But it isn't only people of the Great Depression who experienced what Job felt. We see people all around us today who are discouraged because they can't find work; helpless because their disability benefits are drastically reduced; frustrated because their food stamps run out; hopeless because their welfare assistance doesn't match their cost of living.

If we're comfortable, healthy and secure, it's difficult for us to identify with Job or to understand people who suffer like him. Nonetheless, we cannot ignore the depths of human misery that surround us or pretend not to see the poverty of two-thirds of the world's population.

Many a crime or incident of terrorism is a cry of protest against such suffering. They are acts of outrage against the injustice and poverty that destroy the human spirit.

How do we alleviate the misery of today's Jobs? It would be simple if some great world leader arose who could bridge the gap between the "haves" and the "have nots." It would be nice if our governments could supply all the welfare and security we need.

But such solutions are naive and unrealistic. We can't sit back and wait for others to minister to the Jobs of today. We have to get personally involved ourselves.

We see such personal involvement in today's gospel. Jesus personally helped Simon's ill mother-in-law. He cured the sick people who were brought to him. He expelled demons from the possessed he encountered. He went out to preach the good news of hope to the poor.

What Jesus did must be the keynote of our own ministry to the Jobs of today. Where we find sickness we can offer assistance in some form. Where we find possession by drugs or drink we can support programs that help those so afflicted. Where we find depression we can share the good news of hope that can be recovered through prayer.

Sometimes we can help people cope with their difficulties by words or gestures of encouragement. At other times we can help people through their pain by just being present and sympathetic. Whatever we have to say or do to minister to someone who is hurting should be of supreme importance to us.

Such a person may know a day when his bubble burst because he lost his job, his health or a loved one. But he should never know a day or a night without a friend, because he should always be able to depend on our being there the way Jesus would be present—to touch, to listen, to love.

6th Sunday of the Year　　　　　　　　　　　Lv 13:1-2, 44-46　Mk 1:40-45

# FAITH HEALING

In his book *The Spirit of Synergy: God's Power and You*, Methodist minister Robert Keck tells how he was racked with pain and confined to a wheelchair by the age of forty. In search of a non-chemical way to manage his pain, Keck explored Christian faith healing, psychic healing, acupuncture, biofeedback and medical hypnosis.

Quite suddenly, 80% of his pain disappeared and has not returned. Keck believes that his healing happened when all his research formed a momentary *gestalt*—that is, a unified peak experience. This was his discovery of *synergy*, a way of using all the resources of body, mind and spirit for healing and pursuing wholeness.

In his holistic approach to health, Robert Keck uses meditative prayer to tap the resources of altered states of consciousness where God's activity frequently takes place. Keck's contention is that if God can speak to us through dreams, why not let him heal us through meditative prayer if he so wills?

Healing and wholeness are treated in today's readings from Scripture.

The first reading sets the stage for the healing Jesus does in the gospel. There, the book of Leviticus tells us how lepers had to keep their sores exposed and isolate themselves from the rest of the community.

In the gospel we see the other side of the story of leprosy. A leper comes to Jesus and asks to be cured. Jesus stretches out his hand, touches the leper, and says: "I do will it. Be cured." The leper was instantly healed.

Modern medicine can control leprosy today, but has yet to find cures for our own dreaded diseases of cancer and AIDS. Nonetheless, Christ sometimes cures even victims of these illnesses when it is his will and we approach him in faith.

We go to doctors in hospitals as we should, but do we ever consider going also to Jesus in prayer? We put our faith in contemporary medical practices, but do we also put our faith in Christ's sacraments?

Even if Jesus does not heal us physically, he can always heal us spiritually. Today's Psalm 32 proclaims how we can turn to the Lord in time of trouble and be filled with the joy of salvation; how we can confess our sins and have our guilt taken away.

Moreover, Christ can also heal us psychologically. He can transform our despair into hope, fear into courage and anger into acceptance. Our physical sufferings may not diminish, but we will have Jesus to support us as we endure them. Our pain may find no relief, but Jesus will be present to reassure us as we put up with it.

During this Eucharist we have an opportunity to remember and pray for the sick, especially for the sick members of our own family and parish. As we come to Christ in Communion may it be with the faith of the leper in the gospel, an expectant faith in our Lord's power to heal all our ills whether they be physical, spiritual or psychological.

"Lord, if you will to do so, you can heal us." Let Jesus touch us and say, "I do will it. Be cured."

7th Sunday of the Year                                      Is 43:18-25   Mk 2:1-12

## FELLOWSHIP AND FORGIVENESS

After Frank Tanana graduated from Detroit Catholic Central in 1971, he went on to pitch for the Angels, Red Sox, Rangers and his hometown Tigers. At the height of his career, the fire-balling left-hander "lived a pretty wild life" as he chased after cars, women and booze. But he still wasn't happy.

Then in 1978 Frank Tanana injured his throwing arm and found his baseball career jeopardized. He did some serious soul-searching, and through the help of a Bible-reading teammate, John Werhas, he changed his life.

"I repented of my sins," Tanana said, "and asked the Lord into my heart." Since that time, his priorities have been firmly set in the order of God, family and baseball, and he leaves his future in the hands of God.

Tanana's story of finding the Lord and forgiveness through adversity and the fellowship of others is similar to today's gospel story. A paralyzed man is brought on a mat by four friends and lowered through a roof into the presence of Jesus.

"When Jesus saw their faith, he said to the paralyzed man, 'My son, your sins are forgiven.' " He then told the paralyzed man to stand up, pick up his mat and go home.

There is something unusual about this incident. Most miracle stories in the gospels occur because of the faith of the one who is helped. Such was the case of the Canaanite woman, for example, or the blind man Bartimaeus.

In fact, later in chapter 6 of Mark's gospel we will see that Jesus is unable to work any miracles in his own hometown of Nazareth, precisely because of their lack of faith.

But in today's story we seem to have a miracle occurring almost independently of the man being cured. *His* sins are forgiven and *he* is cured, but specifically because of *the faith of his friends*.

In his book *Invitation to Mark*, Rev. Paul Achtemeier makes some comments about this point:

> Faith is ascribed to the four who brought the paralytic man, and it describes a way of understanding Jesus that translated itself into action. These four let nothing hinder them from bringing the paralytic to Jesus. That is what faith means in this story.

What we have here then is a form of faith we sometimes forget about, and yet one which plays an important role in our lives. When *my* faith is weak, I need *your* faith to support me. When *your* faith is weak, you need *my* faith to support you.

Wasn't St. Monica's faith instrumental in the conversion of her son, St. Augustine? Wasn't St. Therese of Lisieux's faith a factor in the work of many foreign missionaries? Wasn't St. Isaac Jogues' faith the seed for the conversion of the very Indians who tortured him?

We never know what far-reaching effects our faith will have on others. But we do know from this gospel story that Jesus uses the faith of other people to touch the life of an individual whose faith may be weak.

This happened to pitcher Frank Tanana. God used the faith of his teammate John Werhas to move Tanana's heart to repentance and conversion. Tanana, in turn, is now being used by the Lord to touch other people's hearts.

All of us have received similar graces because of the faith of "four friends"—whether these friends were our parents, our teachers, our co-workers or our companions. But how often are we one of "four friends" to others? How often is our faith a source of grace for them when they are in doubt or distress?

Maybe today the Lord is telling us, not to pick up our own mat, but to pick up with faith someone else's mat and carry him or her into his presence.

*B Cycle* 155

8th Sunday of the Year  Ho 2:16-17, 21-22  Mk 2:18-22

# LOVE IS FOREVER

Ricardo Montalban is best known for his television series *Fantasy Island*, his commercials for Chrysler cars and for movies like *Star Trek II: The Wrath of Khan*. He and his wife Georgiana Young (Loretta's youngest sister) have been married since 1944 and have four children.

When asked how they have managed to stay married so long in show business, where temptations abound and divorces are commonplace, Ricardo Montalban said:

> It's a question of commitment. Our commitment is all the more serious because we are both Catholics. When Georgiana and I were married we said, "for better or worse, until death do us part." We're not going to make a mockery of those words. That was the cement which kept us together through the very difficult vocation of marriage.

The theme of marriage connects today's reading from Hosea with the gospel from Mark.

In the Old Testament reading from Hosea, the Lord says: "I will espouse you to me forever. . . . I will espouse you in love and mercy. . . . I will espouse you in fidelity."

In the gospel, Jesus used wedding imagery to describe his presence among his disciples as a groom among his guests. His wedding is a time to celebrate, not fast.

Since a marriage metaphor is used to probe the mystery of our relationship with God, what can we learn from it?

First, since our union with God is symbolized by the union between a husband and a wife, it must be marked by *love*. In the theoretical order, love is defined as selflessness as opposed to selfishness. Genuine love does not seek its own pleasure, but the good and well-being of the other.

In the practical order, married love is often depicted by cartoons like the *Love Is* series. In one episode, there was a picture of the husband with this caption underneath: "Love is keeping calm when she plugs up the plumbing."

How much does God love us? "God so loved the world that he gave us his only Son" (Jn 3:16).

Second, just as *fidelity* is a sign of the relationship between a married couple, so too it must be a sign of our relationship with God. Good examples of fidelity can be found among the wives of the returning POW's from the Vietnam War. Even though they were separated from their husbands for as many as eight years, these wives still remained true to their men.

And how faithful is the Lord to us? Even when we ignore him or run away from him or sin against him, he always remains faithful to us. No wonder St. Paul wrote: "It is precisely in this that God proves his love for us—that while we were sinners, Christ died for us" (Rm 5:8).

Third, since permanence is a characteristic of a good marriage, our relationship with God should be *forever*. Despite the rise in divorce rates, permanence in marriage still remains a very much admired ideal. We don't celebrate divorces, but we do celebrate wedding anniversaries.

In spite of today's widespread rapid changes, we still have a deep human need for values that will last. A marriage promise to love and honor someone all the days of our life is precisely such a value.

That is the way God wants to make his covenant with us. He says through the prophet Jeremiah: "I have loved you with an everlasting love" (Jr 31:3).

As we continue this Eucharistic banquet, we should realize that it is a wedding feast. Pray that we may respond to the Lord with a *love* that is selfless, with a *fidelity* that holds firm in bad times, and with a commitment that will last *forever*.

We don't have to go to *Fantasy Island* to find these ideals. We can find them right here in our everyday relationships with each other and with the Lord.

9th Sunday of the Year                                  Dt 5:12-15   Mk 2:23-28

# LAW

In Robert Bolt's play *A Man for All Seasons*, St. Thomas More shows great respect for the laws of England. When his friend William Roper would cut down every law in England to get at the Devil, More asks Roper where he would hide after the last law was cut down and the Devil turned on him.

More says: "This country's planted thick with laws . . . and if you cut them down . . . d'you really think you would stand upright to the winds that would blow through them?"

Thomas More died a martyr in 1535 defending the laws of the Church. He gave up his life out of respect for the legitimate laws of his land.

By way of contrast, the Austrian peasant Franz Jägerstätter died a martyr in 1943 because he defied the laws of his land. Franz was beheaded by the Nazis because he repeatedly refused to take the military oath and serve in what he considered to be an unjust war.

Today's readings also show two contrasting stances with respect to the law.

On the one hand, the first reading from Deuteronomy urges us to: "Take care to keep holy the sabbath day as the Lord, your God, has commanded you."

On the other hand, in the gospel we see the disciples of Jesus violating the law of the sabbath. As they walked with Jesus through standing grain on the sabbath, they plucked off heads of grain to eat because they were hungry.

Jesus justifies their behavior by claiming: "The sabbath was made for man, not man for the sabbath."

These readings are put together not to confuse us, but to clarify our attitude towards law. In his Pelican commentary on Mark's gospel, Dr. Dennis Nineham points out that in exceptional cases laws might rightly be regarded as subordinate to human needs.

Nineham says that laws are formed for man's good, and if the good of man can be really furthered by violating them, then a lower law is broken in order to keep a higher one.

It seems, then, that we have to keep two things in balance. One is our need of laws, both church laws and civic laws, in order to safeguard the common good of society. The other is our freedom from the law when a higher purpose comes into play.

Thomas More had a deep appreciation for our need of laws. Properly enacted laws guarantee our rights, protect our property and promote peace. Such laws deserve our respect and obedience, even at the cost of some personal sacrifice at times for the sake of society's greater good.

Franz Jägerstätter typifies our freedom from the law. Sometimes following a particular law may actually interfere with the overall purpose of laws in general. Franz found this to be true of the Nazis' military service laws. So rather than obey them and be implicated in unjustly taking the lives of others like the Jews, he rebelled against them in order to follow the higher laws of God in the Bible.

Although we may never have to make a life-death decision about keeping or not keeping some law, it is important to reflect on our attitude towards law. Too often we can obey or disobey laws for the wrong reasons, or we can use laws to avoid taking personal responsibility for our actions, or we can hide behind laws to cover up embarrassing situations we'd rather not face.

Christian discipleship demands that we take a mature stance toward laws. We have to see laws as Jesus saw them—as made to serve our needs in community. When laws do this, they require our respect and obedience.

But when a particular law defeats the end of some higher law, we have to exercise our intelligence and sound judgment and seek the greater good.

Of necessity our following of Jesus will always involve some rules and regulations and laws. Of more importance, however, is the way we use our own creativity, imagination and enthusiasm to do what is good, life-giving and loving.


10th Sunday of the Year                     Gn 3:9-15   Mk 3:20-35

# THE KARATE KID

*The Karate Kid* is a movie about a young teenage boy named Danny and the close relationship he develops with an elderly karate expert named Mr. Miyagi. In order to learn this ancient martial art from the old man, the boy has to do what his mentor demands of him—like washing Mr. Miyagi's car a certain way, or practicing how to balance himself on one foot.

A bond develops between the two that transcends their differences in age and culture, and Danny ends up not only learning about karate from Mr. Miyagi, but also a lot about life.

In today's gospel we see another example of the close connection that exists between a master and his disciple. Jesus says that anyone who does the will of God his Father becomes not only his disciple, but also his brother and sister and mother.

What is the will of God? Simply speaking, the will of God is what he wants for our fulfillment and happiness. It is his plan to help us achieve our ultimate purpose in life.

On the one hand, whatever fits in with his designs for us can be called the will of God. This would include getting what we need for our physical, emotional and spiritual well-being.

On the other hand, whatever interferes with his plans for us is not part of the will of God. This would include anything that deprives us of our basic necessities, impedes our growth as persons or harms us spiritually.

There are three questions to address concerning the will of God.

First, are the "bad things that happen to good people" part of God's will? By "bad things" we mean those inexplicable accidents, tragedies and misfortunes that sometimes occur.

No, they are not part of God's will since they produce so much pain and sorrow for us. Nonetheless, even though they are evils, they can still be used by God to bring about some good that does fit into his plan for us.

Second, how do we reconcile human freedom with the demands of God's will? We can distinguish some things as already determined by God's will from other things yet to be determined.

As to the things already determined by God's will, we don't have any choice about them. They would include non-negotiables like being born, being redeemed and being destined to die one day.

As to the things yet to be determined, we do have a say. By exercising our free will we cooperate with God in creating what his will is for us. This would include things like vocation decisions, career choices and lifestyle preferences.

Third, how do we handle conflicts between God's will and our will? We can take our cue from the Karate Kid. He didn't like doing everything Mr. Miyagi demanded of him. However, by doing them anyway, not only did he become skilled in karate, but he also learned about wisdom and spiritual values.

In the same way, as disciples of the Lord we sometimes have to surrender with faith our own desires to his demands. But in doing so, what we gain far surpasses what we give up. We may have to forego smoking or drinking, but we will find better health along the way. We may have to let go of some of our luxuries, but we will experience a solidarity with the poor and the joy of sharing.

Doing God's will can never diminish or impoverish us. On the contrary, it will enlarge and enrich us. Doing God's will may be difficult at times. Nonetheless, it will draw us into a deeper relationship with Jesus as his disciples and as his brothers and sisters.

11th Sunday of the Year　　　　　　　　　　　　Ezk 17:22-24　Mk 4:26-34

## SEEDS

In December of 1955 a Negro seamstress by the name of Rosa Parks stepped into a crowded segregated bus in Montgomery, Alabama and sat in an empty seat reserved for whites. When the bus driver ordered Rosa Parks to move, she said, "No." She was then arrested, handcuffed and jailed.

This incident triggered the Civil Rights Movement. Under the leadership of Ralph Abernathy and Martin Luther King, Jr., a bus boycott and other nonviolent demonstrations were organized that eventually led to the abolition of racial segregation laws in transportation, housing, schools, restaurants and other areas.

When Rosa Parks said a simple "No" to a startled bus driver, she started something far more significant than anyone could possibly have imagined in 1955. At a Freedom Festival in 1965 she was introduced as the First Lady of the Civil Rights Movement.

In tribute to Rosa Parks, Eve Merriam composed the following poetic verse:

> Where is tomorrow born?
> How does a future start?
> On a winter's working day.
> In a Negro woman's heart.

This story about Rosa Parks and the plight of her Negro people is very similar to the situation of God's people in today's readings. Both the Old Testament prophet Ezekiel and the New Testament evangelist Mark are writing for a persecuted community, a people who are outnumbered and oppressed by their pagan neighbors.

Ezekiel and Mark are writing to reassure them, to reaffirm their faith in God's power to take their tender shoot and make it grow into a mighty tree, to take their tiny seed and make it grow into a rich harvest of wheat.

Times are not that much different today. We too find ourselves outnumbered on certain issues like abortion and divorce. We too are ridiculed for our stand about decency in public entertainment and about nuclear disarmament. Like the Old Testament Jews in exile and the early Christians in Rome, we too need to be reassured, to be reaffirmed in our faith in God's power to take our tiny efforts and make them grow into a mighty movement.

All God requires of us is that we trust in him and try. He will work out the rest quietly but relentlessly, so that selfishness will surrender to sharing, evil will give way to goodness and hate will yield to love.

If we have patience and hope, then eventually the harvest of what we've planted will make its appearance: nations will be reconciled, communism overcome and human rights restored; the vulnerable innocent will be protected, the unwanted cared for and the hungry given food.

No matter how small our efforts may be to promote Christian causes, God will multiply them with his hidden power to bring about magnificent results. He did it for Ezekiel and Mark and Rosa Parks. He can do it again through us.

We may not necessarily see these results in our own lifetime, but Christ's parables are a promise that they will happen in his own time.

> Where will tomorrow's trees come from?
> From the shoots we plant today.
> Where will tomorrow's justice and peace get their start?
> From the seeds we sow with our hearts.

12th Sunday of the Year         Jb 38:1, 8-11    Mk 4:35-41

## STORMS

Every now and then we witness a mighty upheaval of the forces of nature causing tremendous destruction of lives and property. For example, hurricane Camille in 1969 demolished our Gulf Coast, a mighty typhoon in 1970 swept devastating tidal waves over Bangladesh killing over 200,000 people, and the volcanic eruption of Mount St. Helens in 1980 resulted in untold damage.

From the more distant past, we can still recall the hurricane that struck Galveston, Texas in 1900 with incredible ferocity and the San Francisco earthquake of 1906 that toppled buildings like toys.

Although we have learned to harness some of the forces of nature in a limited way with modern science and technology, it seems that there will always be some forces beyond our control and subject only to the control of God himself.

Today's readings from Scripture are a sober reminder of this. The Old Testament reading from Job and the New Testament reading from Mark are bracketed together by the word *who*.

In the first reading from Job, the setting is that of a storm. The passage begins with the Lord's question to Job: "*Who* shut the sea within doors? *Who* set limits to it?"

The gospel scene is also set in a storm. After Jesus is awakened he quiets the storm and the disciples ask: "*Who* can this be that the wind and the waves obey him?"

The *who question* in both readings is one of those larger-than-life questions like "Who am I?" and "Where am I going?" The *who question* compels us to confront the existential questions of "Who is Jesus?" and "Who is God?"

To answer these questions we have to go back to the creation story of Genesis. According to ancient mythical stories of the Near East, creation resulted when God subdued the forces of chaotic waters and set bounds to them.

In his book *Invitation to Mark*, Rev. Paul Achtemeier writes:

> Behind our miracle story there lurks an awareness that only God has power to order and sustain his creation. The disciples' final question shows that, despite their lack of confidence in Jesus' care for them, they recognize this point—namely, that Jesus here does what the Old Testament knew God alone could do. God's power is now at work in Jesus.

Artists have often used the image of the boat in today's gospel to symbolize the Church. Since the parish and individual families within the parish are the Church in miniature, the boat is also an apt symbol to represent us. Many times storms toss us around like tiny corks on the ocean, causing us to cry out in fear: "Lord, don't you care? Doesn't it matter to you that we are going to drown?"

Sometimes a storm arises because of a severe alcohol or drug problem, or because of an overwhelming economic or health crisis. We feel that our boat is at the breaking point and that we're going under.

But if we have faith in the Lord's power to control these seemingly uncontrollable forces in our lives, we can ride out the storm and reach that farther shore.

At other times a storm may arise because of an inexplicable feeling of discouragement or depression, or because we feel unappreciated or lonely. But if our faith in the Lord's presence is strong enough, we can make it through that storm and regain our equilibrium.

*Who* controls our destiny? The Lord Jesus does, if only we let him steady our hands and steer our ship.


13th Sunday of the Year           Ws 1:13-15; 2:23-24   Mk 5:21-43

# DEATH

Before he died of cancer in 1974, Stewart Alsop wrote a book called *Stay of Execution*. In this book the one-time columnist for *Newsweek* revealed his thoughts and feelings about his impending death.

Stewart Alsop observed that there comes a time when "a dying man needs to die just as a sleepy man needs to fall asleep." Because he was a man of faith and wisdom, he was able to anticipate his death as a deliverance from suffering, both for himself and for his family.

Stewart Alsop's attitude was not one of stoic fatalism but of Christian optimism. He understood that we will all come to a point in our lives when peaceful surrender to death makes more sense than stubbornly struggling on.

Today's readings deal with the topic of death.

The Old Testament reading from Wisdom tells us: "God did not make death; he does not rejoice in the destruction of the living. For he fashioned all things that they might exist. He formed man to be imperishable."

In the gospel story by Mark we hear the report that Jairus' daughter is dead. Undaunted by this report, Jesus goes and takes her hand and says: "Little girl, get up." She stands up immediately.

On the one hand, we note that these readings do not deny the destroying power of death. But on the other hand, they also declare that in the end death will be defeated by life.

Implicit in these readings is a hint of the day of our own resurrection, when we too will *get up* from our sleep of death and our imperishable nature will be fully revealed. Then will the saying of today's Psalm 30 be true: "Our mourning will be changed into dancing and we will forever give thanks to the Lord."

Nevertheless, the thought of death still arouses a lot of dread in us and depresses us. Otherwise why would we spend billions on such things as cancer research and cryogenics? Is it not perhaps because we dread the idea of being a victim of cancer ourselves? Or because we naively hope that some scientific technique will be discovered that will preserve us from the decay of death?

How do we deal with death personally? Perhaps some of us try to escape from death, at least for the moment. We delude ourselves into thinking that we can defeat death, at least temporarily, by distracting ourselves with drugs, sex or excitement.

Some, however, try to accept death philosophically. This is the method of serious thinkers like Dr. Rollo May. In his best-selling book *Love and Will*, he claims that death is not opposed to life, but is essential for its growth and maturity. The specter of death can make us live with greater urgency and intensity.

Then there are some of us who are able to face death with faith in Jesus Christ. Ultimately it is our faith in the resurrection of the body that enables us to defeat death decisively.

Ours is the faith of the poet Francis Thompson when he wrote in "The Hound of Heaven" that God is our Father and death is only the shade of his hand outstretched caressingly.

Ours is a faith which allows us to read the gospel story about Jairus' daughter not as a mere remembrance of a past historical happening, but as a proclamation and promise of our own rising from the dead by the hand of Jesus.

B Cycle                                           165

14th Sunday of the Year                              Ezk 2:2-5   Mk 6:1-6

# PROPHETS

One of the better known songs of Simon and Garfunkel is "The Sounds of Silence." In it they sing about words glowing in neon signs and messages written on subway walls.

According to Simon and Garfunkel, advertising and graffiti are some of today's prophets, except their sounds are those of silence. They are prophets in the sense that they speak to us about the signs of the times, the values we hold and the goals we seek.

Prophets are the subject of today's readings.

In the first reading, God sends his prophet Ezekiel to speak to the Israelites. "They are obstinate of heart," says the Lord. "But whether they heed or resist, they shall know that a prophet has been among them."

In the gospel, Jesus speaks to his own townspeople, but they lack faith to listen to him seriously. They find him too much for them, causing Jesus to say: "No prophet is without honor except in his own house."

Two themes seem to emerge from these readings. One is the theme of prophets, the other is the theme of our response to them.

*Who are God's prophets today?* First and foremost it is still the Lord Jesus himself, the Word Incarnate. Through his presence in the readings of Scripture he still speaks to us the good news of the gospel. Through his presence in the sacraments he still touches us with his power and healing.

Next there are the people through whom Christ speaks: men such as Bishop Desmond Tutu who questions us about racism, and women such as Mother Teresa of Calcutta who challenges us to care for the poor. Jesus uses charismatic people such as these to inspire us to do noble deeds, even heroic deeds at times.

Some prophets may irritate us because we don't like their lifestyle. For example, free-wheeling rock stars such as Bob Geldof upset some people even though their Live Aid Concert raised money for the starving in Africa.

We should not be surprised at the people God picks to be his prophets. Some of them we will like, others we will dislike. The important thing is to be sensitive to the message the Lord speaks through them about injustice and oppression, or about poverty and hunger.

That brings us to the second theme: *How do we respond to God's prophets?* Too often we are like the Israelites in the Old Testament times of

Ezekiel—we are stubborn of heart. For instance, we pay attention to prophets during an economic recession, but when prosperity returns we forget about their call to a life of simplicity and resume our mad pursuit of affluence.

Often God sends prophets to us to speak about matters of supreme importance, such as the threat of nuclear war. But we are too immersed in superfluous matters, such as whether or not our second car should have air conditioning. Prophets come asking ultimate questions about life and death. But we're too "hung up" with trivial questions, such as how much to pay for a videocassette recorder.

No wonder there is so little peace, justice and happiness in our society. We shut our ears to what God is saying to us through his prophets. No wonder Jesus can work no miracles through us. We find him and his prophets too much for us. We lack faith.

May Jesus open our hearts to hear what his prophets are saying to us—sometimes to provoke and rebuke us, at other times to inspire and encourage us. May he also increase our faith so that we can respond to his prophetic message and allow him to work his miracles through us.

15th Sunday of the Year                         Am 7:12-15   Mk 6:7-13

# TRAVELING LIGHTLY

In his book *The Conquest of Mexico*, author William Prescott tells of the escape of Cortez and his men from Mexico City. It was the year 1520 and the city was surrounded by a marshy lake. To escape over the causeway it was necessary to abandon the vast store of gold they had taken from the Aztecs.

"Take what you want," Cortez told his men. "But do not overload yourselves. He travels safest who travels lightest."

But some of the Spanish soldiers greedily loaded themselves up with all the gold they could carry, and when they had to swim a short distance because of a breach in the causeway, they were too weighed down by the gold and drowned.

Cortez's instructions to his soldiers are reminiscent of our Lord's to his apostles. He tells them in today's gospel to take nothing on their journey but a walking stick—no food, no traveling bag, not even a coin in their belts.

In the Pelican commentary on Mark's gospel, Dennis Nineham points out that since the coming of the kingdom was considered imminent, missionaries like the apostles had to travel lightly if they were going to spread the news of the kingdom in time.

Moreover, if they provided against every anticipated emergency with spare money and extra tunics, they would lose some of their credibility and authenticity when they announced the nearness of God's kingdom.

Since most of us are never going to be missionaries traveling off to foreign lands, and since the end-of-the world threat has lost most of its zing even in a nuclear age, what message might the Lord be giving us today?

Perhaps the answer lies in a key distinction between values and strategies. A gospel value is a life-principle or guide to good living. Examples might include faith in God as a loving Father and loving our neighbor as ourselves.

A strategy is a method we choose to achieve that value or to make it real in our lives. Examples would include praying to God in order to acknowledge him as our loving Father and helping our neighbor rebuild something of his that was destroyed by an accident.

The value Jesus holds out to us in today's gospel is the value of *traveling lightly* through life by living more simply. Or, to put it another way, it's the value of not making too much of material things so that they get in the way of our reaching out to God in trust or to our neighbor in service.

What strategies should we use to achieve this value? The strategies suggested by our Lord certainly do not make sense today. Imagine Lee Iacocca traveling to an automobile seminar with a walking stick instead of a briefcase!

So when Jesus instructs us to *travel lightly* as we journey through life, he's not telling us that we have to get rid of our cars, empty our freezers, clean out our closets or cut up our credit cards.

But he is telling us not to let our material goods make us forget our dependence on God or harden our hearts to the poor. He is urging us not to become selfish with what we have so that we become insensitive to the injustice and oppression that surround us.

We might recall here the words of St. Basil:

The bread that you store up belongs to the hungry;
the clothes that lie in your chest belong to the needy;
and the money you have hidden in the ground belongs to the poor.

Cortez, Jesus and Basil were right—we travel the safest if we travel the lightest. We gain more by giving than by getting.

16th Sunday of the Year                               Jr 23:1-6   Mk 6:30-34

## TAKE TIME TO REST

Peter Ustinov almost defies description if you try to categorize him in a career. Perhaps he is best known as a Hollywood actor who has won two Academy Awards for his roles in the movies *Spartacus* and *Topkapi*, but he also has won three Emmys and a Grammy.

In addition, Peter Ustinov is an accomplished producer, director and playwright, as well as a successful humorist, musician, author and goodwill ambassador for the United Nations.

Nonetheless, when his activities become too much for him, Peter Ustinov retreats to his home in Switzerland. There he likes to simply sit in his vineyard and rest a little.

Jesus and his apostles also had busy schedules, something we see in today's gospel. As they went about teaching and ministering, people often came in such great numbers that they didn't even have time to eat.

So Jesus invites his apostles to: "Come by yourselves to an out-of-the-way place and rest a while." Much like Peter Ustinov going off to his vineyard in Switzerland, they went off in a boat by themselves to a deserted place to rest and relax a little.

Jesus' invitation to find a quiet place and rest a while is one of those timeless statements so often found in Scripture. It is an invitation he extends in every age to every one of us.

We live in a fast-paced society. We've become used to such terms as rapid transit, instant video replay and fast-food restaurants. We're familiar with such phenomena as super-moms, job burnout and information overload.

*B Cycle* 169

Some of us get so caught up in the rhythm of this fast-paced society, that we have trouble at times turning off the motor of our emotions racing inside us. We rush about frantically doing so many things and get the adrenalin flowing so rapidly, that we have difficulty calming ourselves down.

It's no wonder then that we have so many people who can't sleep restfully at night without a tranquilizer, or who can't cope with the stress of modern living without developing all sorts of psychosomatic illnesses.

Our Lord's invitation to rest is not just a pious gesture given only to a chosen few, but an indispensable call to all of us to find some much needed silence and solitude.

Our desert place could be anywhere we can get in touch with the presence and peace of God—a waiting room in a doctor's or dentist's office; a seat on a bus or in our car when traveling; a supermarket checkout line or a line in a post office.

Any place where we can tune out the world's noise and turn to the Lord within us can be a place of rest for us. There we can relax our bodies and ease our minds; we can sit or stand still and listen to the Lord; we can discover deep within us new resources of strength and energy.

Unless we take time off to rest as Christ and his disciples did, our activity will be without direction, our work will become a drudgery and our life will lose its meaning.

We need a place and time to lay our worries before the Lord and let his Spirit heal us, a place and time to sort out our experiences and see things with greater clarity.

Peter Ustinov has his vineyard in Switzerland. Jesus had his desert places. Where do we find some silence and solitude in order to rest a while with the Lord and to be renewed by him?

17th Sunday of the Year         2 K 4:42-44   Jn 6:1-15

## FIVE LOAVES AND TWO FISH

The Episcopal Church of the Redeemer in Houston has become famous for its Spirit-filled people. Under the leadership of Rev. Graham Pulkingham and Rev. Jeff Schiffmeyer, the church has revitalized both itself and its surrounding neighborhood.

This charismatic community has more than 350 of its parishioners gathered together in 40 households sharing their resources and lives. Its neighborhood outreach programs include a community center, a coffee house, a health clinic and a literacy course.

When Fr. Schiffmeyer first came to the Episcopal Church of the Redeemer, he worried about how they could take care of all the people who came to them: alcoholics and drug addicts looking for healing; the blind and handicapped seeking support; clergy and religious in search of a deeper experience of the Holy Spirit.

He asked the Lord how they were going to minister to all these people. His answer came in today's reading from John. In it Fr. Schiffmeyer saw himself asking questions like those Jesus asked: "Where shall we get bread for these people to eat? Where shall we get all the other things they need?"

Fr. Schiffmeyer also saw that, like the apostles, his people's resources were very limited in terms of finances, talent and time. Figuratively speaking, all they had were five barley loaves and two dried fish.

But as he read further, Fr. Schiffmeyer also realized that Jesus was instructing him the same way he instructed his disciples: "Have the people sit down. Let me bless your five loaves and two fish. Distribute them to the crowd and they will have more than enough to satisfy their needs."

In other words, the Lord was telling Fr. Schiffmeyer to trust in him to provide whatever he needed. And the Lord has been faithful to his promise. He never sends to the pastor more people than his parishioners can minister to at any one time, always provides enough financial support for them to carry out their projects, and gives them sufficient time to renew themselves through rest, prayer and song.

Indeed, the Lord Jesus has multiplied their bread and fish. And he does the same for us. Sometimes we too feel overwhelmed as the Lord sends all kinds of people to us: an unloved teenager, an aging parent, a frustrated friend, a depressed neighbor. We look at our resources and cry out: "Lord, I don't have enough time for them; I don't know how to help them. Where shall I go to get what they need?"

But Jesus says: "Trust in me. Just give me your five loaves and two fish, and I will multiply them for you." And somehow he does.

Scripture commentator William Barclay says that the little boy with his five loaves and two fish did not have much to offer, and yet out of what he had, Jesus found the materials for a miracle. Barclay writes:

> The fact of life is that Jesus needs what we can bring him. We may not have much to bring but he needs what we have. Little is always much in the hands of Christ.

Understood this way, the miracle of the multiplication of loaves and fish has meaning for today. The miracle continues through us every time we give ourselves in faith to the Lord.

He takes our limited resources, blesses them, multiplies them and distributes them to his people, and, paradoxically, we find that we still have more than enough left over for ourselves—either in psychic satisfaction, a sense of fulfillment or inner peace.

The right question to ask of the Lord is not, "Where shall we find this or that?" Instead, we should ask, "What is it I have that you want to multiply?"

18th Sunday of the Year  Ex 16:2-4, 12-15  Jn 6:24-35

## BREAD

Dr. Robert Haas is a nutrition consultant for a dozen professional athletes, including tennis star Martina Navratilova. His book *Eat to Win: The Sports Nutrition Bible*, stresses complex carbohydrates and downplays protein and fats.

Dr. Haas says that 60-80% of an athlete's diet should consist of complex carbohydrate foods such as cereals, fresh fruits, vegetables, spaghetti and whole-grain breads. The advantage of complex carbohydrates is that they decrease toxic wastes which make us sluggish and increase our available energy level. Marathon runners use these foods to load up with glycogen for stamina at the end of a race.

Whole-grain breads are one of the key components in such a diet. Bread also plays an important role in the way God nourishes his people.

In today's first reading from Exodus, the Israelites grumble in the desert because of their hunger. So God rains down bread from heaven for them in the form of manna.

In John's gospel, Jesus identifies himself as the real heavenly bread: "I myself am the bread of life. No one who comes to me shall ever be hungry. No one who believes in me shall thirst again."

The Exodus text and John's gospel are related to each other as type and anti-type. Jesus is the new heavenly bread sent by God—a bread that is imperishable, is all-satisfying and gives eternal life.

From her reflections on the Eucharist, Sr. John Vianney Vranak gives us the following insights. The Latin root for bread is *pan*. We still remember the famous Latin hymn by St. Thomas Aquinas, *Panis Angelicus* (Bread of Angels). In the Slavic languages the word *pan* means Lord. For example, in Polish we say *Pan Jezus* for Lord Jesus.

Pursuing the word further into its Greek origins, *pan* means all or every. For example, we are familiar with such words as panacea for cure-all, Pan-Am Airlines or Panasonic radios. Still another meaning for the word *pan* comes from its French connection. The French word for bread is *pain*, a direct derivative of the Latin *pan*, but with a new dimension added because of our English word "pain" meaning suffering or hurt.

All these connotations of the word *pan* converge in the Eucharist in a marvelous manner. Jesus gives himself to us under the form of *bread*. The bread of angels becomes the bread of man. Jesus is our *Lord*, the one sent by God, the one on whom the Father has set his seal.

In the Eucharist we find *all* fulfillment. Whoever believes in the Lord will never be hungry or thirsty again. Jesus paid the price of *pain* when he gave his life for us on the cross. The Eucharist is the memorial of his passion.

No wonder we praise God in Psalm 147 for "filling us with the best of wheat." No wonder the hymn, "Gift of Finest Wheat," has become so popular since its composition in 1976 for the International Eucharistic Congress.

Sr. John Vianney points out that while the word *finest* ordinarily means "the best quality," it can also mean "most pulverized." Both senses are true of the Eucharist. The pulverizing of the grains of wheat to make quality bread is a symbol of the suffering Jesus experienced in his passion.

In this context, we can't help but recall the following statement by St. Ignatius of Antioch before he was martyred by wild beasts: "I am the wheat of God. I must be ground under their teeth in order to become a bread worthy of Jesus Christ."

According to modern nutritionists like Dr. Haas, we need daily bread to keep us healthy, active and strong. We also need the bread of the Eucharist to nourish our spirits, strengthen us in times of trial and fulfill all our deepest yearnings.

19th Sunday of the Year                                         1 K 19:4-8   Jn 6:41-51

## LIVING BREAD

In the movie *E.T.* there are a couple of scenes involving food. Early in the film the young boy leaves some M&M candy for E.T.—a symbolic gesture of his willingness to be friends with E.T. In another scene, while the young boy's family is away from home, E.T. raids the refrigerator to find some food and drink.

These scenes in *E.T.* are not only heartwarming and humorous, but they also emphasize how food and drink are an absolute necessity for life—whether we are human or extra-terrestrial in our life form.

Food and drink are a theme in today's readings.

In the first reading from the book of Kings, Elijah is given food and drink by an angel. Strengthened by that nourishment he is able to walk for forty days and forty nights to the Mountain of God, Horeb.

In the gospel, Jesus claims that he himself is the bread of life come down from heaven. If anyone eats of this bread he will never die. The bread he gives is his own flesh for the life of the world.

Almost as if to make sure we don't miss the connection between his bread and life, Jesus uses the words *life* or *living* five times in the last five verses. Do we fully realize what a fantastic claim he is making?

If we eat the bread of his Eucharist we shall never die, but live forever. We won't be strengthened just to travel forty days and nights like Elijah did. We will be able to walk with the Lord forever. We won't be kept alive just to complete a football training camp for a month or to finish a vacation trip somewhere. We will live forever.

If only we would taste and see for ourselves the goodness of the Lord in the bread of the Eucharist, then we would experience all the blessings promised in today's Psalm 34: we would be delivered from all our fears, especially our fear of death; we would be saved from all our distresses, whether mental worries or physical ailments; we would be made radiant with joy, especially when we love and serve one another.

These blessings are not something we have to wait for until we reach heaven. As the bread of life, Jesus comes down from heaven to us here and now. He is the living bread to be eaten now, not preserved in a freezer for the future.

Notice that Jesus does not say: "He who believes in me *will* receive eternal life." Rather, he says: "He who believes in me *has* eternal life." In other words, by eating his Eucharistic bread we are already in possession of eternal life. Our life in heaven is already begun here on earth.

Does this sound too good to be true? Can Jesus really do this for us? The answers are in the gospel. Jesus says: "Stop your wondering; let me firmly assure you—*I am* the bread of life."

There is no reason then for us to get discouraged and pray for death as Elijah did. Christ commands us to get up and eat and continue our journey—whether it means staying on our job, in school or with our marriage partner.

There is no reason for us to be frustrated, trying foolishly to find fulfillment in things like drugs or drink or sex or money. Jesus is the bread of life—not life in a superficial sense, but life in its deepest sense; not life that is passing, but life that lasts forever.

Thank the Lord for giving us his own flesh to be our bread of life. May his example inspire us to give ourselves too for the life of the world, to be ourselves the bread that others can feed on to find the fullness of life.

20th Sunday of the Year                    Pr 9:1-6   Jn 6:51-58

## THE GOOD LIFE

The world of advertising often appeals to our basic human needs for food and drink. Television commercials like Wendy's "Where's the beef?" cater to our hunger for food. Magazine ads with slogans like Coca-Cola's "It's the real thing" claim that their drink will satisfy our thirst.

The whole express purpose of advertisers is to sell us the *good life* by promising that their products will satisfy our every desire. We might say that today's readings make their own sales pitch for the *good life*, except that they speak about life in a higher sense.

In the first reading from Proverbs, Wisdom invites us to come to her table where we can eat her food and drink her wine. She calls us to forsake foolishness that we may live and advance in the way of understanding.

In the gospel, Jesus says that he himself gives life to the world. His flesh is real food and his blood is real drink. Anyone who eats his flesh and drinks his blood will live forever.

In his Pelican commentary on this text, John Marsh underlines the meaning of the adjective *real* in the phrases *real food* and *real drink*:

> These are what satisfy those hungers and thirst from which men suffer in distinction from all other earthly creatures. Man's genuine nourishment lies in them; without them the really "human" person dies, even though he continues to live in the flesh, but with them he lives the life that is really life both here in the course of history and in that which lies beyond history in the world to come.

We can better appreciate Marsh's insight if we compare some of the extravagant claims of advertisers to satisfy our needs for this life with the claims of Christ to give us life in a higher sense.

Since we have a need for the pleasures of oral gratification, many of us want to have our "Winstons taste good like a cigarette should." But there are also spiritual delights which today's Psalm 34 addresses when it says: "Taste and see the goodness of the Lord."

From time to time we have a need to escape from boredom and monotony. So to answer our need we have airline ads like United's beckoning us to "Fly away in our friendly skies."

Yet when we are weary, only the Lord can really refresh us in the fullest sense: "Come to me, all you who labor and are overburdened, and I will give you rest" (Mt 11:28).

We naturally seek security and protection for ourselves and our families. So insurance companies like Prudential propose to give us a "Piece of the Rock" of security.

Nonetheless, only Jesus can promise and guarantee us eternal life: "The man who feeds on this bread shall live forever."

It seems that no matter what our basic needs are, advertisers claim they have the product or service to provide for them. Yet, contrary to their claims, what they offer is not the *real thing* at all, but only an illusion, a fantasy, a substitute. To verify this, for example, a male customer need only compare his car on a cold winter morning with the television model accompanied by a warm female.

Advertisers shout about the essentials of life, but offer things that are merely superficial. It is only Christ who can show us how to *really* live and to live more abundantly.

What Jesus gives in the Eucharist is not an illusion. It is real food and real drink. What Jesus gives is not something superficial. It is his own body and his own blood. What Jesus gives is not a temporary gratification. It is a life that will last forever.


21st Sunday of the Year                           Jos 24:1-2, 15-18   Jn 6:60-69

## COMMITMENTS

The movie *Lady Sings the Blues* tells the life story of singer Billie Holliday. To play the role of Billie Holliday, singer Diana Ross spent almost nine months reading clippings about Billie, sifting through pictures of her and listening over and over again to her recorded songs. Diana Ross also researched Billie's era of fame, the 1930's and 1940's, and the drug addiction that tragically ended her career.

Diana Ross said:

> I was committed to doing a good job on the film because so many people loved and admired Billie Holliday. So I spent a lot of time listening and kind of feeling her music. I tried very hard to know her as much as I could, so I could let it come out in the songs I sang.

Diana Ross' motion picture debut in *Lady Sings the Blues* was a huge success, not only because of the powerful story it told about Billie Holliday, but also because of Diana Ross' commitment to honor a singer she admired very much.

Commitment is one of the subjects of today's readings.

In the first reading, Joshua and his people commit themselves to serve the Lord their God, for he it is who delivered them from slavery.

In the gospel, Jesus questions his disciples about their commitment to him: "Do you too want to leave me?" Simon Peter answers: "Lord, to whom shall we go? You have the words of eternal life. We are convinced that you are God's holy one.''

What does commitment mean to us in an age of rapid electronic change?

First, consider how a commitment is based on a promise to do something in the future. Even though we cannot foresee the inevitable difficulties that will arise, we promise to find, if possible, solutions to them. By our promise we forbid ourselves to take the easy way out when a crisis comes up.

For example, in marriage there will be unavoidable conflicts which a couple cannot anticipate. Nonetheless, their public commitment to each other is a declaration of their determination to overcome these conflicts as they arise.

Second, a commitment is made to persons and not to institutions. It is a relationship established with real people and not with abstract organizations. Thus a teacher says to his students or an employer to his workers: "You can count on me when troubles arise. You can trust in me in spite of the uncertainties of the future."

In other words, a bond of justice is established with others, and we no longer have the right to consider our actions only our own. They belong also to others to whom we are committed.

Third, a commitment requires a response on our part. It is easy to make a promise in a moment of enthusiasm. It is difficult to carry it out when a crisis comes up.

Yet, if our commitment is to have any meaning, we must respond to the crisis with determination, creativity and generosity. A commitment demands that we discover, insofar as it is possible, a solution to the difficulties. Otherwise we stay in a state of narcissism.

As William James said: "A mature individual commits himself to something larger than the service of his own little ego." In other words, commitments carry us out of the vicious circle of self-seeking into the service of people who need our love.

Diana Ross made a commitment to honor Billie Holliday in the movie *Lady Sings the Blues*, and so she did all the hard work necessary to live up to that commitment.

Joshua in the Old Testament and the apostles in the New Testament made a commitment to follow the Lord, and so they were ready to make the sacrifices necessary to carry out their promises.

How committed are we to the Lord? How far are we willing to go with him?

22nd Sunday of the Year	Dt 4:1-8   Mk 7:1-8, 14-15, 21-23

# LOVE IN ACTION

In Albert Camus' novel *The Fall*, the central figure is a nameless lawyer who tells his life story to a stranger he meets in a Dutch bar. The anonymous lawyer relates how he had always prided himself on being a selfless servant of humanity, a noble man of virtue and generosity.

But then one dark rainy midnight, something happened to shatter his self-righteous image. As he was walking home over a bridge, he passed by a slim young woman leaning over the rail and staring into the river. Stirred by the sight of her, he hesitated a moment, and then walked on.

After crossing the bridge he heard a body striking the water, a cry repeated several times, and then the midnight silence again. He wanted to do something to save her, but he stood there motionless for a while and then went home.

This nameless lawyer in Camus' story reminds us in some ways of the Pharisees in today's gospel. The Pharisees were experts in the law and prided themselves on their scrupulous observance of it. And yet Jesus castigates them for their hypocrisy by quoting the prophet Isaiah: "This people pays me lip service but their heart is far from me."

The lawyer in Camus' story also comes under the judgment of James in the second reading (Jm 1:17-27). He had listened to God's word about loving one's neighbor, but was unable to act on it. He had deceived himself into thinking that he was a selfless servant.

In contrast to the nameless lawyer in Camus' story, there are two lawyers in the Detroit area, namely, Jim Raftery and Phil Tanian, who have heard "the silent screams" of the unborn and have gone out of their way to defend the rights of the unborn against abortion. These men have heard God's word through the cry of the poor and have acted on it.

Today we are the ones crossing over the bridge to encounter the living word of God in Scripture—his commandments, his law, his precepts. If all we do is listen to the word without letting it penetrate our hearts and move us to action, then we are no better than the Pharisees in the gospel or the lawyer in Camus' story.

This does not mean that we have to run around rescuing everyone about to commit suicide or every child about to be aborted. But it does mean that we recognize and respond to opportunities to help people whom we meet

B Cycle                                                                179

on our particular bridge—the unemployed neighbor, the troubled teenager or the neglected shut-in.

As we cross our bridges, we cannot pretend that we do not see the oppressed in Central America, the hungry in India or the victims of racism in South Africa. As the reading from Deuteronomy says, we have to "give evidence of our intelligence and wisdom to the nations." In other words, we have to show concern for them and support programs that will aid them.

Someone once wrote: "Do not display your religion in a window of pretense. The real test is to keep a large stock in your soul."

It doesn't matter what image we use—the window and the stockroom, listening and doing, or lips and heart—the Scriptures confront us today to urge us to consider how we keep our Lord's commandments.

Are we content like the Pharisees or Camus' lawyer to merely observe in them what we find convenient, self-serving and safe? Or are we willing, like Jim Raftery and Phil Tanian, to tackle the main issues of the commandments, take on responsibility and assume some risks?

The choice is ours. Will we tiptoe through life merely paying lip service to God and man, or will we step out and put our whole heart into what we do for God and man?


23rd Sunday of the Year                                Is 35:4-7   Mk 7:31-37

## THE TOUCH OF HIS HAND

There is a poem by Myra Brooks Welch called "The Touch of the Master's Hand." In this poem she tells the story of an old dusty violin being auctioned. The violin is about to be sold for a mere $3 when a gray-haired man steps forward, picks it up, dusts if off and begins to play.

The man plays such sweet music on the violin that when he finishes, the bidding jumps into the thousands of dollars. What changed its value? What transformed the old dusty violin into a precious instrument? *The touch of the Master's hand.*

This is one of the themes of today's readings.

In the first reading from Isaiah, *the touch of the Master's hand* transforms the land and the lives of the Jews in exile. The burning sands of the desert become springs of water. The frightened become strong, the blind see, the deaf hear, the dumb sing and the lame leap.

In the gospel, *the touch of the Master's hand* is none other than the touch of Jesus himself. A deaf and dumb man is brought to him. Jesus puts his finger into the man's ears and touches his tongue with spittle. Immediately the man is able to hear and to speak.

This same touch of our divine Master's hand continues to transform our lives today. Our brothers and sisters are the people who bring us into the presence of Christ so that his power can operate on us. The sacraments are extensions of Christ's hands reaching out to touch and heal us. Scripture is the extension of his words of encouragement to us.

Consider some of the ways Christ heals our infirmities. How many times do we close our eyes in blindness to the hunger of people in Africa, to the plight of earthquake victims in Mexico, or to the injustice among the migrant farm workers in the United States?

How many times do we turn a deaf ear to the cries of frustration from people victimized by inflation, to the cries of loneliness from teenagers hooked on drugs, or to the cries of hurt from people we have injured?

How many times do we keep our tongue silent when we should speak boldly in defense of the unborn and the handicapped, of honesty in government and business, and of chastity in entertainment?

But by the touch of his hand Jesus opens our eyes, unstops our ears and loosens our tongues. He changes our hearts so that we can be more sensitive to the needs of others.

Under his transforming power we become his instruments to accomplish the marvelous works described in today's Psalm 146: to secure justice for the oppressed, give food to the hungry and set captives free.

Christ not only touches us with his hands but also uses our hands to touch others: to sustain the fatherless and the widow, protect the stranger and raise up those that are bowed down.

During this Eucharist, thank the Lord for making the prophetic vision of Isaiah a reality for us. Praise him for translating these poetic verses of Myra Brooks Welch into a personal experience for us:

> And many a man with life out of tune,
> And battered and scarred with sin,
> Is auctioned cheap, to a thoughtless crowd,
> Much like the old violin.

*B Cycle* 181

> But the Master comes, and the foolish crowd
> Never can understand
> The worth of a soul, and the change that's wrought
> By the Touch of the Master's Hand.

24th Sunday of the Year                                         Is 50:4-9   Mk 8:27-35

## RUNNING BRAVE

The film *Running Brave* traces the life of Billy Mills from the time he was a little boy on an Indian reservation until the time he stunned the world by winning the 10,000 meter race at the 1964 Olympics in Tokyo.

On the one hand, the word *running* in the title can be taken as a verb indicating action. The word *brave* then becomes an adverb indicating how the running was done. In this sense, *Running Brave* tells the story of how Billy Mills used running to overcome obstacles of prejudice, homesickness and discouragement.

On the other hand, the word *running* can be considered an adjective modifying the noun *brave*. Here the emphasis is on his Sioux Indian ancestry. He was a brave who also liked to run.

In either sense, the film *Running Brave* shows what determination can achieve in spite of seemingly insurmountable obstacles. To prove that he was not the "quitter" he had been labeled and to win his gold medal, Billy Mills had to run the race in borrowed shoes and he had to come from behind after being bumped off the track.

Today's readings show us another man whose determination overcame what seemed to be insurmountable obstacles.

In the first reading, the prophet Isaiah tells us how to recognize the Messiah. In spite of his sufferings, the Messiah will be the one who *will not turn back* from his course. Instead, he will set his face like flint and go on to achieve his purpose.

In the gospel, Jesus is identified as the Messiah. Even though his journey to Jerusalem will lead him to suffering and death, and even though Peter tries to talk him out of going there, Jesus *refuses to turn back* and resolves to go through with his Father's plan.

We have here a picture of a man who knows what awaits him—a

painful death—and yet will not allow himself to be deterred from his set path. Jesus can already see before him the cross on Calvary, and yet he will not let himself quit his messianic task.

To be a disciple of Jesus, then, means that we cannot allow ourselves to quit whenever some cross confronts us. Instead, as Jesus says, we have to take up that cross and resolutely follow in his steps.

Whether our cross is unfair treatment by others, loneliness or discouragement—a cross Billy Mills had to carry when he was a college student—or whether it is the loss of our health, our job or someone we love—a cross we read about in the papers every day—if we are to be truly Christian, then we cannot allow ourselves to quit carrying that cross.

Instead, we have to believe that God is near to uphold us and is indeed our help, and that we will not only survive, but we will also overcome and triumph. After all, we have our Lord's own promise that even though we may lose something—perhaps even our life—in the end we will save it, provided we are faithful and don't give up.

Jesus himself had to lose his life and die, but three days later he overcame the grave and rose from the dead.

There is a popular Protestant hymn that summarizes what it means to be a determined and resolute Christian. A couple of its verses read:

> The cross before me, the world behind me.
> No turning back, no turning back.
> Though none go with me, still I will follow.
> No turning back, no turning back.

25th Sunday of the Year  Ws 2:12, 17-20  Mk 9:30-37

## MORTALITY

Dr. Leon Kass is a University of Chicago philosopher, biologist and medical doctor. In his book *Toward a More Natural Science: Biology and Human Affairs*, Dr. Kass has an essay about mortality making life matter. Since contemporary science continually seeks to control aging and prolong life, Dr. Kass asks an intriguing question. Suppose science could defeat death and extend life indefinitely. What would we lose?

Dr. Kass examines Homer's immortals and finds them to be merely spectators of the great moral dramas of life. Indeed, Homer's immortals are beautiful and youthful, but they are also shallow and frivolous. Since they never have to face death, they miss meeting some of life's supreme challenges.

In contrast, the limits of time imposed by mortality make us take life more seriously. The sense of not having enough time is a spur to selecting the more important things in life.

Realizing that we don't have forever, we are less likely to waste so much of our time on passing trivia. Instead, we will use more of our time to pursue the enduring transcendentals of goodness, beauty and truth.

Mortality also gives us a sense of urgency. When we have too much time on our hands, we tend to put off doing what is difficult. But if we know that we have only a limited measure of time left, we tend to work more energetically. Mortality is a great motivator for achievement.

Maybe our Lord's sense of his own mortality is what was on his mind in today's gospel. For the second time in Mark's gospel he predicts his passion, death and resurrection. And again his disciples fail to understand.

The contrast is inescapable.

On the one hand, the disciples seem to think that they have a lot of time left with our Lord and that he will be around for many years. Consequently, they are preoccupied with trivia—they spend hours arguing among themselves about who is the most important.

On the other hand, Jesus knows that his time on earth is rapidly running out and that he will soon have to leave his disciples. Consequently, he is preoccupied with teaching them about what really matters in life. Last week it was about taking up one's cross with courage and not compromising one's ideals. This week it is about humility, selfless sacrifice and seeing the Lord's presence in people.

Knowing that one day we are going to die, then, should not depress us. On the contrary, it should spur us on to use wisely what little time we have left. What unattained objectives do we have that we should still pursue? What postponed visits do we still have to make? What good deeds have we delayed doing that we should accomplish?

Realizing our mortality should not make us sad but more selective. Of all the things we can do with our time, what are really the most important ones? Is it something to do with our self-improvement, self-image or health? Or perhaps with our family, friends or fellow workers? Or possibly with God in terms of reconciliation or prayer?

Why waste our precious little time on trivia, when we can spend it on things that really matter?
There is a rhyme which reads:

>He slept beneath the moon,
>He basked beneath the sun;
>He lived a life of going-to-do,
>And died with nothing done.

Like our Lord before us, we are going to die and leave this life. Do we understand this? Do we feel impelled to do something worthwhile with the little time we have left?

26th Sunday of the Year        Nb 11:25-29   Mk 9:38-43, 45, 47-48

# NAME POWER

The power of a name to sell is seen in the world of marketing. If a bottle of wine has the reputable name of Ernest and Julio Gallo on its label, it will sell. If bottles of beer have the long respected Stroh's signature, they will sell.

The power of a name to attract is seen in the way names of celebrities are used. If Lee Iacocca's name appears on a book cover, it will grab our attention. If Bruce Springsteen's name is on a marquee, it will draw a crowd.

A name also has power to influence. If you get the right name on a letter of reference, you might get a job you're seeking. If you have the right names to promote some cause, your movement has a better chance to succeed.

The power of the name of Jesus comes up in today's gospel. John complains to Jesus that someone not of their group was using our Lord's name to expel demons. Instead of backing up John's efforts to stop this man, Jesus seems to approve of such people working miracles in his name, as long as they are doing good works.

In his commentary on Mark's gospel, William Barclay points out that in the time of Jesus everyone believed that demons were the cause of all their physical and mental illnesses. A common way to exorcise demons was to use the name of a more powerful spirit. This ancient belief continues in our own day.

In the movie, *The Exorcist*, the priest called in to expel the demon from the young girl uses the name of Jesus. Healers like Kathryn Kuhlman, Oral Roberts and Fr. Ralph DiOrio use the name of Jesus when they pray over people.

Yet, in spite of these contemporary Christian expressions of an ancient religious belief, most of us suffer from a failure in confidence in the power of the name of Jesus. While unbelievers are not ashamed to misuse the name of Jesus in expressions of slang, vulgarity or cursing, believers hesitate to call on the name of Jesus in times of temptation, trial or necessity.

We seem to have lost our nerve, or perhaps even our faith. What we need is a revival of the ancient Christian custom of invoking the name of Jesus in prayer. We need to recall what some of the early Fathers of the Church wrote about the power of that name.

For example, in his classic sermon on the Holy Name, St. Bernard compared the name of Jesus to oil. He wrote:

> Oil gives light, nourishes, and anoints. Oil feeds the flame, sustains the body, and eases pain. It is light, food, and medicine. The same may be said of the name of Jesus. It throws light on what is preached, it nourishes our thoughts, and it heals the troubled.

If names like Gallo Wines and Stroh's Beer move us to buy products, then why shouldn't the name of Jesus move us to fight racism and defend human rights, or to resist tyranny and support freedom?

If the names of Lee Iacocca and Bruce Springsteen have such power over us, then why shouldn't the name of Jesus make a stronger impact on our lives—in what we think, in what we say, in what we do?

Invoking the name of Jesus is not a magical trick, and yet miracles have happened in that name. Using the name of Jesus is not a superstitious practice, but rather a sacramental which brings us God's grace.

Perhaps our Lord's message today is: "Don't stop using my name to do good. Use it more so that its power can become more operative in your life."

27th Sunday of the Year                                           Gn 2:18-24   Mk 10:2-16

# MARRIAGE MODEL

*The Rules of Marriage* is a made-for-TV movie featuring Elliott Gould as Mike and Elizabeth Montgomery as Joan. After fifteen years of marriage and two children, Mike and Joan begin the painful process of getting a divorce. The film focuses not so much on adultery as the immediate cause of the divorce, but more on the husband-wife relationship and attitudes that gradually led to this event.

As Mike and Joan initiate the divorce proceedings, they begin to see how they treated each other as objects instead of as persons. He treated her as a dutiful housekeeper and as a showpiece at parties. She treated him as a mere bread-winner and as a sex partner.

Both had unreasonable expectations of each other and placed impossible burdens on each other. Never able to really accept each other as they were, they demanded more and more of each other without giving more and more of themselves.

How their story ended we will see later. For now, let us look at what today's readings have to say about marriage.

In the first reading from Genesis, we heard the creation story of man and woman. Since its literary form is that of religious myth, many of its details are not important in themselves, but only as *imagery* to make a point, teach a lesson or reveal a truth.

Thus it is not Adam's sightseeing of the animals at God's zoo that is significant, but the fact that men and women need each other as suitable partners without whom they are in some sense incomplete and suffer from loneliness.

It is not the Genesis rib sculpturing that should concern us, but rather the view that men and women share equally the same human nature symbolized by the bone and flesh.

Nor is the physical problem of how two bodies can occupy one space an issue, but rather how some men and women are destined to live together so closely in a relationship we call marriage that they can be *said* to form one body.

From this marriage model in Genesis, we move to the gospel where Jesus is questioned about divorce. Jesus goes beyond the permissive stance assumed by Moses at one point in history to what God intended from the very beginning of time as the ideal marriage relationship.

There is no compromise on what Jesus holds out as the ultimate and ideal goal of marriage—two people should become one flesh; what God has joined let no man separate; whoever divorces and remarries commits adultery.

Ideally, then, a marriage should be marked by *unity*—a total sharing of body, mind and spirit; and it should be a *permanent* relationship—till death do us part.

But we don't live in an ideal world. We live in a real world where too often selfishness overpowers love, taking dominates giving, and some marriages end in divorce. What does Jesus have to say about that?

To answer this, recall how Jesus condemned adultery, but forgave the woman caught in adultery; how he showed compassion toward the Samaritan woman at the well who had lived with five husbands; and how he gave Peter a new start after Peter had denied him and run away.

Do we continue to strive for ideal marriages? Yes, with all our resources. Do we condemn divorced people whose marriage fell short of the ideal? No, we condemn divorce but not the divorcee. We deal with the divorcee the way Jesus would—by balancing law with love, firmness with forgiveness and principles with practice.

How did the movie *The Rules of Marriage* end? To save their marriage Mike and Joan agreed on one rule between them—*to feel safe*. It was their way of saying that they would be more open and honest and show more understanding and trust. They would begin again to make the ideal real by becoming two in one flesh.

28th Sunday of the Year                                     Ws 7:7-11   Mk 10:17-30

## SELL WHAT YOU HAVE

Jean Vanier is internationally recognized as a humanitarian because of his care for the retarded. The son of a former Governor General of Canada, he served for a while as an officer in the Canadian Navy and later taught at the University of St. Michael's College in Toronto.

But then he left behind all his family wealth and comfortable lifestyle to establish a family-type home for the retarded which he named *L'Arche*. His hope was that it would be an *Ark* of refuge for the retarded in a hostile world. Under Jean Vanier's inspiration, homes similar to *L'Arche* have sprung up all over the world.

Jean Vanier is a modern-day St. Francis of Assisi who has taken literally our Lord's words in today's gospel: "There is one thing more you must do. Go and sell what you have and give to the poor. You will then have treasure in heaven. After that come and follow me."

Unlike the young man in the gospel to whom Jesus spoke, Jean Vanier did not go away sad. On the contrary, he has found immense happiness through his life of simplicity in living with the retarded.

In his talks, Jean Vanier loves to tell how the retarded have taught him to rediscover the joy of ordinary things like playing games together, and to appreciate more the present moment instead of worrying about the future.

In putting aside everything to follow Jesus among the retarded, Jean Vanier has personally experienced what Jesus meant when he promised to give a hundredfold to his disciples even in this life: an inner peace in contrast to the anxiety and restlessness of the world; a deep feeling of fulfillment in the midst of so many lives empty of meaning; an interior joy which seems to escape those who frantically chase after cheap thrills.

The existential questions confronting us in today's gospel are: What must we do to follow Jesus? What is the one thing more the Lord is asking of us?

For most of us, the answer is obviously not to give away everything we have to the poor. But it might be to continue our support of relief funds, mission work and the Catholic Services Appeal. For most of us, the agenda will not include leaving our home and family. But it might mean keeping up our efforts to provide homes for refugees, employment for the jobless and protection for the defenseless.

In other words, the gospel is challenging us to re-examine our values. Have material riches replaced spiritual ones in our homes? Has the television set pushed out all prayer time in our lives? Have excess use of alcohol and cigarettes desensitized us to the movements of God in our spirits?

The primary purpose of the gospel is not to make us feel guilty about what we have, but to lead us to reflect seriously on what our priorities are.

For example, do we have to let go of some of our work and outside involvements in order to spend more time with our family? Do we have to sacrifice some of the luxuries we surround ourselves with, in order to open our hearts more to the plight of the poor? Do we have to turn off some of the noise of today's tapes and records in order to hear the sound of God's voice?

Indeed, how hard it is for the rich to enter the kingdom of God. Why not simplify our lives somewhat to free ourselves to follow the Lord more easily, more closely and, yes, more joyously?

Why go away sad today because we won't let go of the one thing more the Lord wants from us? Why not go away happy like Jean Vanier, believing that no matter how much we let go for the Lord, he will always give us back a hundredfold?

29th Sunday of the Year        Is 53:10-11    Mk 10:35-45

## TRUE GREATNESS

Nobel prizes are awarded every year in literature, economics and science. People who have made outstanding contributions in these fields are given due recognition for their achieved greatness.

Excellence is recognized in the sports world, too. For example, when Pete Rose surpassed Ty Cobb's record number of hits in 1985, he assured himself a place in baseball's Hall of Fame.

We all aspire to greatness in some form or other. It is a desire which our Lord addresses in today's gospel.

The brothers James and John approach Jesus with their own idea of greatness—to sit at his right hand and his left when he comes into his kingdom, a sort of instant-success notion of greatness.

But Jesus has other ideas about greatness. Greatness begins with a cup of suffering and a baptism of pain. Greatness is achieved through service.

We have here another reversal of values for which Jesus is famous. "The first shall be last," "He who loses his life shall save it," and "He who humbles himself shall be exalted" are other examples of how Jesus often reverses our values.

Greatness through suffering and service is not exactly a popular notion today. Greatness through making a lot of money or by drawing huge crowds at a rock concert seems to be today's standard.

But if we look deeper into enduring examples of greatness, we see that the Lord is right. Alexander the Great was a remarkable leader because he stood by his men in battle. Albert the Great was an intellectual giant because he disciplined himself for study. Beethoven was a master composer because he struggled long hours to get the right note. Martin Luther was a great reformer because he persisted in spite of opposition.

True greatness was achieved by these men because they were willing to make sacrifices to realize their vision. They attained their goals because they were able to endure disappointments along the way.

So if we are aspiring to greatness in some area, we have to be able to suffer sometimes, put up with pain, whether physical or emotional, and overcome obstacles. Moreover, if we aspire to higher forms of greatness in terms of what makes us truly human and holy, then we have to be willing to serve others and even to lay down our lives for them.

The word *serve* might bother us a little because we commonly associate it with activity that is menial or demeaning. But the sense in which our Lord uses the term *service* includes any act that is noble and unselfish, any gesture that affirms and encourages someone, and any deed that is done with kindness and generosity.

Understood this way, people who are achieving greatness in God's eyes are: parents who raise their children according to Christian values; teachers who inspire students to high ideals; doctors and nurses who heal and care for the sick; volunteers who visit shut-ins; neighbors whom we can call in any emergency.

In closing, we might say that James and John were acting like wimps when they went after an easy, suffering-free, false kind of greatness. Pray that we might be real men and real women who aspire to genuine greatness—a greatness that has a God-magnitude about it—the giving of service and even our lives for others.

30th Sunday of the Year                                    Jr 31:7-9   Mk 10:46-52

# TRANSFORMATIONS

The musical *Les Misérables* is based on the epic novel by Victor Hugo and dramatizes the adventures of Jean Valjean. After serving nineteen years in prison for stealing some bread to help his sister's starving child, Jean Valjean is paroled.

Unable to find work, Valjean steals from a priest, who in turn lies to save him from being sent back to prison. Given a second chance, Jean Valjean undergoes a moral and social transformation: he takes a new name, becomes wealthy, befriends a dying prostitute, raises her orphan and twice risks everything he's gained to save others.

What the Lord did through the priest for Jean Valjean is similar to what he did for Bartimaeus in the gospel. Both Valjean and Bartimaeus were nobodies—social outcasts. But when Jesus entered their lives, they became somebodies—his disciples.

Mark's story about Bartimaeus is like a dramatic one-act play with seven scenes, namely, the seven verses.

In the first verse, Jesus is leaving Jericho for his final journey to Jerusalem, where he will die. There is an immediate contrast between the sizable crowd tagging along behind Jesus and the isolated blind beggar sitting by the road.

In the second verse, Bartimaeus hears that Jesus of Nazareth, the miracle worker, is passing by. Realizing that this was the chance of a lifetime, he cries out for help.

In the third verse, the people callously rebuke him for bothering the Master and for making himself a public nuisance. But Bartimaeus refuses to be intimidated by them and he shouts after Jesus all the louder.

In the fourth verse, Jesus stops and calls for him. Here Jesus is on his way to die, and yet he stops to help a nobody. Perhaps Jesus takes time to stop to show that this blind beggar is really a somebody, a person worthy of our respect and care.

Do we stop sometimes when we are doing what seems so urgent to assist somebody who is hurting? Or who just needs a little attention? Or who only wants to be appreciated?

In the fifth verse, Bartimaeus responds to our Lord's call with abandon and enthusiasm. He doesn't pile up his cloak neatly—he throws it away! He doesn't get up hesitantly—he jumps with joy!

Compare that with our own response to the Lord. Too often our response is lazy and lethargic instead of being done with energy and alacrity, or with expectation and anticipation.

In the sixth verse, Jesus asks Bartimaeus: "What do you want me to do for you?" It is a key question that is asked of all of us whenever we approach Jesus in prayer. May our answer always be: "Lord, that we may see in areas where we are blind because of selfishness; or hear where we are deaf to the cries of pain around us."

Finally, in the seventh verse, Jesus confirms the blind man's faith with a cure. But instead of going his own way as Jesus instructed, Bartimaeus follows Jesus up the road. What a challenge to us!

When we receive a gift from the Lord, do we go our own way and use it only for ourselves? Or do we sometimes go up the road with Jesus to share it with other people who may need more help than we do?

Many are the times Jesus has stopped to take notice of us and to transform us. When we were nobodies, he made us somebodies. When we were sick spiritually, he made us whole. When we were down, he lifted us up.

Can we in turn stop more often to ask people: "What can I do for you? How can I be of help?"

31st Sunday of the Year                                      Dt 6:2-6   Mk 12:28-34

## WHOLE BEING

Alexander Blake's book *The Nureyev Image* describes how totally committed Rudolf Nureyev is to dancing. According to Nureyev himself, ballet has become his whole life, his only "avenue of fulfillment."

Blake writes the following about Nureyev's dedication to his art:

> For its sake he has fought and sweated, suffered, quarreled, insulted and borne insults, schemed, dreamed and made bitter sacrifices. It takes priority in his life over everything and everybody; his loyalty to it is unquestioning. It is both the means of his living and the end.

The way Rudolf Nureyev loves dancing and dedicates his whole life to it gives us an inkling of what today's readings teach about how we should love God: "You shall love the Lord, your God, with all your heart, and with all your soul, and with all your strength."

This text from Deuteronomy is quoted by our Lord in Mark's gospel. It is called the *shema*, the Hebrew imperative meaning "hear," or "pay attention." The *shema* constitutes the basic creed of Judaism. It is recited every day by pious Jews and it is their last utterance when they die.

By quoting the *shema* Jesus declares that it is also the foundation of his own faith and devotion. But then Jesus goes beyond the *shema*. He combines it with Leviticus 19:18—the verse about loving one's neighbor as oneself.

Both commandments were basic to Judaism. Was their combination into a single moral principle original with Jesus? The answer is not important. What is important is that Jesus incorporated the two commandments into his own life and taught his disciples to do the same. For Jesus there can be no true love of God unless it expresses itself in love of neighbor.

But today's texts tell us not only that we should love both God and neighbor, they also tell us *how*. We must love God with our *whole being*—heart, mind, soul and strength. We must love our neighbor *as ourself*.

Rudolf Nureyev loves dancing with his *whole being*. He rises in the morning with ballet dancing on his mind and he retires at night the same way. He spends six or seven hours a day practicing his routines because he loves what he is doing. For Nureyev dancing is not a duty; it is his destiny.

The same is true of other people who love what they are doing with their *whole being*. Master artists, dedicated scientists, great actors and actresses, outstanding statesmen and stateswomen—all love their careers with their whole heart, their whole soul, and with all their strength.

Should we do less in our love for God? Should we love God less when he is the source of all our talents and resources? Should we be less excited about the Creator of the order and beauty of the universe?

If we love God with our *whole being*, then we will worship him even while we work; pray to him whenever we have an opportunity; read his word as well as the newspaper; listen to his voice just as much as we listen to our radios or television sets.

From loving God with our *whole being* will follow loving our neighbor *as ourselves*. We will look on their needs, feel their hurts and identify with their dreams as if they were our own.

By reaching out to love our neighbor *as ourselves* we will find that the kingdom of God is very near and experience what someone wrote:

I went to the mountains to seek wisdom, but did not find it.
I went to the sea to seek peace, but did not find it.
I went to the temple to seek God, but did not find him.
I went to serve my neighbor, and I found all three.

32nd Sunday of the Year     1 K 17:10-16   Mk 12:38-44

## WIDOWS

The movie *Places in the Heart* features actress Sally Field as a widow named Edna. The setting is Waxahachie, Texas during the post-Depression era of the 1930's.

After seventeen years of marriage, Edna suddenly finds herself a widow when her husband, the town sheriff, is killed by a drunk. She now has to figure out a way to save her family and farm.

To keep the bank at bay, she is forced to take in a blind boarder named Will. To raise enough cotton to support herself, she hires a black sharecropper named Moze. Together with Edna's two children, this team struggles with frontier fortitude against chiseling cotton buyers, a stubborn soil, the ravages of a tornado and human frailty.

By the end of the film, the heartbreaks and triumphs they share forge their makeshift group into a real family.

A widow also plays a significant role in two of today's readings from Scripture.

In the Old Testament story we read about a widow who shared with Elijah the little food she had left, food she prepared with her last bit of flour and oil.

The gospel scene sets the spotlight on another widow. Unaware that she is being observed by Jesus, she puts two small coins into the temple treasury. She gave from her want, from all that she had to live on.

All three widows in our stories come from different periods of time. Yet they have in common their poverty, their faith and their willingness to share. Each of these widows could have found many reasons to excuse herself from sharing the little she had, excuses like "We don't have anything to spare," or "Let others give who can afford it."

But they refused to resort to these excuses and risked stepping out in faith. As a consequence, what they actually accomplished was out of all proportion to what it actually cost them.

By sharing her home with a blind boarder and a black sharecropper, Edna not only saved her farm but gained a new family. By feeding Elijah with some of the food from her last meal, the widow learned that her jar of flour would never go empty, nor her jug of oil run dry. By giving away her last two coins in the temple, the widow in the gospel "pulled off" the biggest financial transaction in history—not in the eyes of the *Wall Street Journal*, but certainly in the eyes of God.

For in the final analysis what counts in the eyes of God is not the size of what we give, but how much it costs us in terms of sacrifice. Generosity is not to be measured absolutely by the amount we give, but relatively according to what we have left.

This is not to say that Jesus discourages giving out of our surplus and abundance. There is a need for that. But it is to say that true generosity comes from the heart when we share with others in our poverty. True giving takes a lot of faith, like that of the three widows.

For it takes faith to share material things when we have little for ourselves, or to volunteer our services when we don't have enough time. It takes faith to listen to others when we don't have the energy, or to inspire joy in others when our own hearts feel empty.

What do we gain when we give in faith? Perhaps the answer lies in this verse:

> And you can't give a rose
> All fragrant with dew
> Without part of its fragrance
> Remaining with you.

33rd Sunday of the Year  Dn 12:1-3  Mk 13:24-32

## TOUGH TIMES

Television celebrity Sid Caesar has written his autobiography under the title *Where Have I Been?* In this book Sid Caesar reveals how he was a heavy drinker during his glory days on television, and how he later became a drunk walking around in a stupor for almost twenty years.

Finally, in 1978 he looked in a mirror and asked, "Sidney, do you want to live, or do you want to die?" He wanted to live and so he "quit drinking and popping pills." Sid Caesar writes further:

> I didn't realize it during those twenty years of drinking, but I had stopped appreciating my wife Florence, and I couldn't even talk to my children. Our family is a lot closer now. I know that you can't take twenty years of hollering and screaming and drinking and make up for it in a couple of years, but I'm trying very hard.

Sid Caesar's recovery from alcoholism has renewed his life. Before, he was destroying his life and family with drinking and drugs. Now, he is reconstructing his life and his relationship with his wife and children.

Sid Caesar's experiences illustrate today's readings from the prophet Daniel and the evangelist Mark. They are telling us that no matter how badly things are going, God will somehow intervene in our history to complete his victory; someday our dead will rise to live forever; one day our heroes will shine like the stars; then we will see the Son of Man coming in the clouds with great power and glory.

In his book *Rediscovering the Parables*, Joachim Jeremias underscores the sign of our Lord's coming, namely, the fig tree sprouting its leaves. In Palestine the fig tree is different from other trees because it sheds its leaves annually. Its stark spiky twigs make it appear quite dead until new life bursts forth when the rising sap returns.

According to Jeremias, our Lord uses this image to direct our attention, not towards the dreadful portents of the end time, but towards the new life that will be manifested when he comes in glory.

When will this end time of life's definitive triumph over death come? No one knows. But in the meantime, we can anticipate this final triumph by intermediate ones, as Sid Caesar's victory shows.

We may still have tough times to go through—like death striking our family, accidents happening, losing our job or being let down by friends. But because Christ has already won the victory for us, we will not let these tough times defeat us.

Instead, we will turn them around into triumphs of some kind—like entering new relationships, taking on new tasks or developing new outlooks.

Television preacher Robert Schuller likes to say: "Tough times don't last. Tough people do."

We must not lose hope, then, if tough times come upon us or even if we make twenty-year mistakes the way Sid Caesar did. For the Lord promises to stay with our fig tree during the tough times of winter and draw new life from its branches.

May today's Psalm 16 be our prayer during the tough times:

> Lord, it is you who hold fast our destiny.
> With you at our right hand, we shall never be disturbed.
> Show us the path to life.
> Lead us to the fullness of joys in your presence.

Christ the King                                        Dn 7:13-14   Jn 18:33-37

# KINGSHIP DRAMA

In 1956 actor Yul Brynner won an Academy Award for his role as the bald autocratic King of Siam in the movie *The King and I*. The film was based on the musical written by Rodgers and Hammerstein for Broadway, where Brynner also played the part for a record number of times.

In this musical, the King of Siam imports a British governess to his exotic kingdom to educate his children. At the start they have frequent cultural clashes, but in the end the king and the governess form a true friendship.

Today we recall another king. He is not the king of some country like Siam, but the King of the whole universe—he is the Lord Jesus Christ, the Son of God.

In the first reading from the prophet Daniel, our Lord is envisioned as the Son of Man coming on the clouds of heaven to receive dominion, glory and kingship. In the gospel from John, Jesus stands trial and is questioned about his kingship by Pilate.

Fr. George MacRae points out in his commentary, *Invitation to John*, how the evangelist uses theater techniques to present the drama of Christ's passion. The stage is set by John as Pilate's praetorium. The principal actors are Jesus and Pilate.

As John's Passion Play unfolds, the theme of Christ's kingship emerges as the central plot. It is the focal point of Pilate's questions, the cause of our Lord's mock coronation by the soldiers and the substance of the inscription placed on his cross—Jesus of Nazareth, King of the Jews.

As a playwright, John uses irony to great effect. For example, although Jesus is brought to trial before Pilate, it is really Pilate who is being judged. Moreover, although Pilate hands him over to be *lifted up* on the cross in ignominy, he sets the stage for Jesus to be *lifted up* in later glory.

We can't watch good drama without getting involved. This is all the more true of John's Passion Play since it is also divinely inspired. Today we stand on the stage in place of Pilate to ask Jesus: "Are you really a king?" And Jesus answers us the same way he did Pilate: "Yes, I am a king. But my kingdom is not of this world."

In other words, his kingdom does not depend on military might, economic strength or political power. It is a spiritual kingdom that depends on faith, prayer and good works. It is not a kingdom that seeks to increase its wealth, expand its borders or inflate its image. It is a kingdom that promotes peace where there is violence, justice where there is exploitation and freedom where there is oppression.

Will we miss our chance as Pilate did and not take Christ's kingship seriously? Or will we acknowledge him as king and join in his causes to protect human rights, relieve poverty and care for the unwanted?

# C Cycle

1st Sunday of Advent                    Jr 33:14-16   Lk 21:25-28, 34-36

## ON GUARD

In the Royal Air Force Museum in Hendon, England there is an exhibition of the memorabilia of Lord Dowding. He was appointed Commander in Chief of the RAF in 1936 to take on the challenge of expanding the RAF's fighting force to meet the Nazi threat.

Dowding had less than four years to prepare the RAF for the epic Battle of Britain, while at the same time helping France as much as possible. Lord Dowding's accomplishments in getting the RAF ready are summed up on a plaque: "It has been given to few men so to employ so short a time that by their efforts they saved civilization."

Lord Dowding's vigilance and preparation while waiting for the Nazi attempt to invade Great Britain played a key role in England's victory in the early 1940's. Vigilance and preparation while waiting are part of the theme of today's Advent gospel.

Jesus says: "Watch yourselves, or your hearts will be coarsened with debauchery and drunkenness, and the cares of life, and that day will spring on you suddenly, like a trap . . . stay awake, praying at all times . . ."

Of course Jesus is not speaking about a military invasion or an impending war. He is speaking about his second coming in human history at the end of time. Yet the means of preparation are the same: we have to exercise vigilance, discipline ourselves and share with one another.

These same means are an excellent Advent preparation for Christmas, that celebration of Christ's first coming in human history.

First, we must exercise *vigilance*. It is easy for us to become absorbed in our livelihood and to forget life, or to become preoccupied with our own private projects and to miss God's great plan. That is why we must be vigilant, watch and pray.

Prayer opens our eyes to the presence of God. Prayer puts all things in proper perspective. Prayer implants peace in our hearts even in the midst of problems or poverty.

Second, we must exercise *self-discipline*. Without discipline we waste things: we waste our time; we waste our talents; we waste our natural resources. Self-discipline creates conditions for maximum effectiveness in the way we use our gifts.

By disciplining our minds, we grow in wisdom and knowledge. By disciplining our bodies, we develop strength and agility. By disciplining our appetites, we increase our capacity to enjoy and appreciate.

Only a person who is in possession of himself can give himself in love to another person. Only a person who is self-disciplined is truly free to seek and find Christ.

Third, we must have a spirit of *sharing*. When we experience shortages, sharing makes it tolerable and even joyful. When wealthy nations begin to share more with the Third World, peace on earth will become more of a reality.

Sharing does not diminish our wealth; it extends its usefulness. Sharing does not impoverish us; it enriches us with a deep sense of satisfaction. Sharing does not leave us empty-handed; it fills our lives with friendship and good feelings.

Let us not wait for another war to come before vigilance, discipline and sharing become important to us. Advent is an ideal time to develop these habits—not just in getting ready for Christ's coming at Christmas—but also for his coming in our daily lives, at the time of our death and at the end of time.

When Lord Dowding was preparing the RAF for the war, he didn't know how much time he had. We too don't know how much time we have left to live—four years or forty years; four months or four hours. That doesn't matter. May we be on guard and watching whenever the Lord comes.


2nd Sunday of Advent                                              Ba 5:1-9   Lk 3:1-6

# ROCK STARS

When rock stars like Michael Jackson and Bruce Springsteen make a tour, elaborate preparations are made for their coming. If they come to the Silverdome in Pontiac, Michigan, for example, their entourage comes ahead of time to get things ready for their concert.

Their publicity staff hypes up the local media, their travel agents arrange for luxurious accommodations and their technicians set up spectacular light and sound systems.

By the time a rock star arrives, most of the rough edges have been smoothed out and most of the kinks straightened out. Such elaborate preparations almost guarantee a successful stay and a very profitable show.

It is not surprising, then, that rock stars like Michael Jackson and Bruce Springsteen are almost worshipped like gods, and that their entourages resemble the prophets of old heralding the coming of the Lord. In fact, one wonders if today's gospel about John the Baptist proclaiming the coming of Jesus applies more to modern rock stars than it does to the true Messiah.

That shouldn't be, but unfortunately it is. Where have we failed if 70,000 screaming teenagers will pay $30 a ticket to see a rock star, and yet will not come to Sunday Mass and give even 30 cents to support the Church?

It is useless to blame society or the media, or point the finger of guilt at parents or pastors. It would be better if we were to look at ourselves to see where we have failed personally.

Advent is still a penitential season, even though it has joyous strains throughout. Today's readings are an example.

On the one hand, in the first reading from the prophet Baruch, the Lord's word is one of celebration and joy because his people are about to return home from exile.

On the other hand, in the gospel, the word of the Lord comes to us through John the Baptist, and it is a word of repentance and forgiveness of sins: "Prepare a way for the Lord, make his paths straight."

So the hard questions we have to ask ourselves during Advent are: How have I failed to herald the Lord's coming? How have I failed to witness personally to his good news of salvation?

If we really believe that Jesus is Lord, then we will make sure that everything is ready for his coming—whether he comes at special times like Christmas or at ordinary times in our daily lives. We will honestly face up to those spiritual valleys in ourselves that need to be filled up—those valleys we create by our bitterness and resentment, fears and worries, or anger and hostility.

If we sincerely believe that Jesus is Savior, then we will openly admit that there are some spiritual hills that need to be leveled off—those hills we build with our greed and materialism, self-indulgence and lust, or pride and self-righteousness.

If we truly believe that Jesus is indeed God's Son and the Messiah, then we will do all we can to straighten out our lives—our crooked attitudes toward people and our distorted views of them; our roundabout ways and detours to avoid meeting the Lord.

Only when we put the same energy and enthusiasm into making ourselves spiritually ready for the Lord's coming, as promoters put into the material preparations for the coming of a rock star, will Christianity begin again to make a significant difference in the world and attract youth.

Only when we put the same care and commitment into our spiritual Christmas preparations, as rock stars put into their musical performances, will "all mankind begin to see the salvation of God."

3rd Sunday of Advent                                           Zp 3:14-18   Lk 3:10-18

# ANTICIPATION

Carly Simon once wrote and sang a song called "Anticipation" that became very popular. In it she describes how she waits for her beloved to come, imagines what their being together will be like and rehearses what she will say to him.

Anticipation is looking forward to some future event. The anticipated event is almost certain to happen and it arouses in us considerable thought and feeling. We eagerly anticipate important moments in our lives like graduations and weddings; we get all excited about things like the new Ford Aerostar or a new Rocky movie; we waited 75 years in anticipation of the return of Halley's comet.

Anticipation is one of the moods of today's readings.

In the first reading, the prophet Zephaniah moves our emotions in expectation of the Lord's coming: "Shout for joy, daughter of Zion . . . Rejoice, exult with all your heart . . . Zion, have no fear . . . Yahweh your God is in your midst . . . He will renew you by his love."

In the gospel, the prophet John the Baptist has been preaching about the coming Messiah. The crowd, tax collectors and even soldiers are full of anticipation and ask John what they can do to get ready for the Messiah's coming.

We are not unlike these people in the gospel. We too are full of anticipation, especially for Christmas Day. The delight of children going to see Santa Claus, the buying and wrapping of Christmas presents, the decorating of Christmas trees, the preparing of Christmas dinner—all of these Advent activities express our great expectation and anticipation of something wonderful about to happen.

If our anticipation focuses only on the *holiday* dimensions of Christmas—decorations, parties, presents and vacations—our anticipation will end up as a great big illusion and leave us disappointed.

But if our anticipation also includes the *holyday* dimensions of Christmas—God's grace, new birth, peace on earth and good will to all—our anticipation will culminate in a true celebration and leave us with a sense of fulfillment.

The Church's Advent liturgy tries to prepare us spiritually for this kind of celebration.

Our *Advent prayers*, for example, address our desires to the Father with such phrases as: "Increase our longing for Christ our Savior"; "The day draws near for a waiting world to see the glory of your Son"; "We look forward to the birthday of our Savior."

Our *Advent readings* typify this theme of anticipation. Besides today's readings which we have already mentioned, recall the opening sentence from the First Sunday of Advent: "See, the days are coming—it is Yahweh, who speaks—when I am going to fulfill the promise I made to the house of Israel" (Jr 33:14).

Our *Advent songs* express anticipation—songs like the traditional "O Come, O Come, Emmanuel," or Charles Wesley's beautiful hymn "Come, Thou Long-Expected Jesus."

As our Advent days dwindle down, may we focus, not so much on the secular aspects of Christmas, as on its sacred dimensions. May we look forward with eager anticipation to the coming of Jesus in a new and deeper way—into our hearts and homes, into our thoughts and feelings, and into our dreams and desires.

4th Sunday of Advent                                     Mi 5:1-4   Lk 1:39-45

## JOY

In the prologue to his book *Joy*, William Schutz tells how the birth of his son Ethan inspired him to write the book. Ethan begins his life by giving joy to his parents. The joy continues as Ethan sees, touches, tastes and hears things for the first time.

But something happens to Ethan as it does to all of us. Somehow his joy diminishes with growth, never to return fully. Schutz wrote his book to help readers recapture some of this joy.

Like Ethan, Jesus too begins his life by giving joy. Even before he is born his very presence brings joy to people. When Mary greets her kinswoman, Elizabeth is filled with the Holy Spirit and cries out: "Why should I be honored with a visit from the mother of my Lord? For the moment your greeting reached my ears, the child in my womb leapt for joy."

Now it is our turn to leap for joy as we approach the celebration of Christmas. But how authentic will our joy be? Will it be a forced joy that can only be achieved by drinking alcohol? Will it be a joy of escapism from responsibility through the frantic pursuit of pleasure? Or will it be the superficial joy of prosperity suggested by slick television commercials?

To be authentic, our Christmas joy must be something deeper than these false substitutes. Psychologist William Schutz offers in his book *Joy* some sound suggestions as to how we might attain this kind of real joy.

His approach is based on the conviction that joy is a feeling that comes from the fulfillment of one's potential. Schutz explores the different areas where we can develop our full human potential.

First, *the body*. Health, energy level, muscle tone and breathing all play a role in how much we enjoy our body. Adequate exercise, sufficient sleep and proper diet are important for the well-being of our body.

Second, *personal functions*. Developing skills, increasing sensory awareness, improving our mind and getting in touch with our feelings all contribute to a fuller enjoyment of life.

Third, *interpersonal relations*. We experience joy when we achieve a balance in being with people and being alone, in being independent and in receiving support, and in being affectionate without getting engulfed.

Fourth, *organizational relations*. To realize our potential we need the support of society—we need a warm family, a congenial place to work and a government concerned about our welfare.

All of Schutz's suggestions to attain authentic joy are excellent, as far as human psychology can take us. But they still leave us short of that ultimate joy that can only come through Jesus.

His very presence in our midst is the source of this kind of joy. His presence in creation, in the sacraments and in his people should make us jump for joy the way John the Baptist did.

Even when we cannot achieve our full human potential in some of those areas Schutz outlines, we can still experience a profound interior joy because Jesus is in our midst. The power of his presence enables us to endure any difficulty, transcend any trial or overcome any obstacle.

His presence can bring peace where there is anxiety, sharing where there is selfishness and dreams where there is despair.

Isaac Watts was right when he composed a Christmas carol entitled "Joy to the World!" Indeed, there is real joy in the world at Christmas time because the Lord is come. He is *Emmanuel*, God with us!


Christmas — Mass During the Day (A, B, C)    Is 52:7-10    Jn 1:1-18

# HE DWELT AMONG US

The play *Seventh Heaven* is a story of love and regeneration. The hero is Chico, a sewer worker—manly, honest and honorable. The heroine is Diane, a street woman—abused, hostile and forlorn.

Chico rescues Diane from the streets and takes her to his sky parlor on the 7th floor of a slum tenement in Paris. Their relationship is honorable. Chico refuses to believe he loves her until he is called to serve in the French army during World War I.

For the next four years Diane starves and suffers in that dingy Paris attic, but never falters in her faith that her beloved Chico would return from the war. Chico does return—but he is blind. Nonetheless, in spite of her poverty and his handicap, their love for each other transforms their tenement attic into a *Seventh Heaven*.

This play gives us some insight into the meaning of Christmas when the Word was made flesh and dwelt among us: "And we saw his glory, the glory that is his as the only Son of the Father, full of grace and truth."

By being born as a baby from Mary's womb, Jesus took on our human condition. Except for sin he could now share in our sufferings, hurts and frailties. Jesus was truly human.

And yet he remained divine. Jesus was still the eternal Word, God's only Son, and the fullness of grace and truth. He is truly, according to John Marsh, "a human embodiment of a heavenly reality." Consequently, Jesus is *Emmanuel*, a name which means "God is with us."

The clause "dwelt among us" contains Old Testament allusions to God's presence among his people. We recall, for example, how God literally "pitched his tent" among the Israelites by dwelling in the tabernacle during their Exodus.

Moreover, the glory or the presence of God was made visible by the cloud that was seen above the tabernacle during the day and by the fire that was seen in the cloud during the night. God's presence in the tabernacle accompanied the Israelites at every stage of their journey through the wilderness.

Christmas means that God's presence among his people is now being brought to fulfillment in the very flesh of Jesus. His human body is the new tabernacle, the new and supreme sign of God's dwelling among us.

The consequences of this new mode of divine presence—now available to us in the Eucharist—are staggering. Because Jesus dwells among us, he is able to do for us what Chico and Diane did for each other—transform any situation into a *Seventh Heaven*.

All through history this meaning of Christmas has inspired Christians to see the glory and the presence of God, not only in the marvels of nature, the grandeur of art and the beauty of people, but even in the poverty of a slum, the mud of a battlefield and the refuse of a hospital ward.

It's easy to see God's glory in times of success, good fortune or fame. But it takes faith to say that God dwells among us when we're out of work, handicapped or unwanted. Yet people like Chico and Diane have been doing it for centuries.

If Christmas signifies anything, it should be that God truly dwells among us to transform any situation into a place where his glory is seen: kitchens become cathedrals, factories become temples, classrooms become shrines and slum attics become *Seventh Heavens!*

Holy Family (A, B, C)  Si 3:2-6, 12-14   Lk 2:41-52

# THE COSBY SHOW

One of TV's highest-rated programs of all time is *The Cosby Show*. It is a weekly sitcom about an upper-middle-class black family, which, for all practical purposes, has become America's First Family.

In a feature article about Bill Cosby, *Newsweek* magazine said that his show about the Huxtables is endearing but not cutesy, its parents are hassled but never hapless and there is clowning but no guff.

*The Cosby Show* is popular because the family situations it portrays have an air of universality and reality about them. Any family can identify with both the irritations and misunderstandings that arise on the show, and with the truly humorous and heartwarming things that happen.

While Dr. Cliff Huxtable, his lawyer-wife Clair and their four children may not be the perfect counterpart of the Holy Family, they do picture for us in modern terms what some of the qualities of family life should be.

Today's readings suggest some of these qualities.

The first reading from the book of Sirach emphasizes the authority and dignity that parents possess, and the honor, respect and care that children owe them.

In the second reading, St. Paul sums up how members of a family are to interact: with mercy, kindness, patience and forgiveness; by bearing with and loving one another; by playing and praying together (Col 3:12-21).

The gospel story about Jesus getting lost reminds us that celebrations like the Passover or Christmas are an important part of family life. But it also illustrates how sorrow, pain and worry are part of every family's experience, too.

Apparently Bill Cosby's television family is a facsimile of his real family. In real life Bill Cosby and his wife Camille have four daughters and one son. Bill Cosby says this about his wife Camille:

> It's hard to describe a relationship with so much growth in it. It goes past just missing her when she's not here. I'm just very, very fortunate that the person I trust the most trusts me, and the person I love the most loves me. I love her so much.

Another real-life family is that of Dr. Paul Kelley, his wife Mary Margaret, and their three sons and three daughters. Dr. Kelley is an orthopedic surgeon in Ann Arbor, Michigan and has given talks on marriage and family under the title of "The Seven C's."

First, *commitment*—a complete, lifelong caring for the other, no matter what may happen.

Second, *communication*—a willingness to take time to listen, dialogue and share one's feelings.

Third, *compatibility*—the ability to get along, adjust and be flexible.

Fourth, *compassion*—the capacity to understand weakness and sympathize with failure.

Fifth, *confession*—the readiness to say "I'm sorry," be reconciled and forgiven.

Sixth, *conviviality*—a sense of humor to laugh at oneself and make others smile.

Seventh, *children*—one's own, adopted, godchildren or nephews and nieces with whom we can share life and love.

"The Seven C's" suggested by Dr. Kelley are seen in Dr. Huxtable's family on *The Cosby Show*. They also sum up today's readings about how to become a holy family instead of a broken family. May these "Seven C's" serve as our guide to grow together in wisdom and age and grace before God and each other.

January 1 — Mary, Mother of God (A, B, C)  Nb 6:22-27  Lk 2:16-21

# MEMORIES

Rose Kennedy will go down in history as one of America's and the Church's most memorable mothers. During her 94 years she has seen in her children moments of triumph and moments of tragedy.

No other mother in U.S. history has had three sons elected to the U.S. Senate and one to the White House as President. Few mothers have lost three sons as Rose Kennedy did: Joe Jr. in an air crash, and John and Bobby by assassination.

Yet through it all, she has kept her faith: "I have always believed that God never gives a cross to bear larger than we can carry. I believe in heaven and expect to see my husband Joe there, my three sons, and my daughter Kathleen."

Looking back over her life she says: "I would rather have been the mother of a great son than to have written a great book or painted a great masterpiece." Maybe someday Rose Kennedy will be canonized; but even if she isn't, her faith in her role as a mother mirrors to us the faith of another mother we honor today—Mary, the Mother of Jesus.

In the gospel from Luke we are told that Mary, too, treasured all the things that were happening to her as a mother and reflected on them in her heart. She too would know supreme moments of triumph through her son as well as sorrowful moments of tragedy.

Motherhood and memories seem to go together. Mothers like Mary and Rose Kennedy seem to be bearers of family memories. By reflecting on important family events they not only store them in their memory, but also draw from them meaning and significance.

Mothers thus keep alive the family heritage and traditions, and pass them on to their children and grandchildren. By remembering and retelling the stories about our ancestors, mothers anchor our roots in the past and call on us to contribute our own part to this collective family history.

In his book *The Living Reminder*, Fr. Henri Nouwen says that among the best things we can give each other are good memories, such as "kind words, signs of affection, gestures of sympathy, peaceful silences, and joyful celebrations."

We owe so much to our mothers for these kinds of memories—not only in the sense of the family's history which they pass on to us, but also in the sense of their own good deeds and kind words which we remember.

Fr. Nouwen says that these memories—whether conscious or unconscious—enter so deeply into our being that, indeed, we become our memories. They take on flesh and blood in us.

As a result, whether we are aware of it or not, these memories serve as sources of strength in times of trial, as guides in times of confusion and as motivators to leave our own good memories to others.

If this is true of our own physical mothers and the memories they leave us, how much more true is it of our spiritual mother Mary.

Through St. Paul today, Mary points to Jesus to remind us of our glorious heritage—we are indeed children of God who can cry out "Abba!" that is, "Father!" (Gal 4:6).

Through the liturgy's memorial acclamation she urges us to: "Keep in mind that Jesus Christ has died for us and is risen from the dead. He is our saving Lord, he is joy for all ages."

Through the Christmas season Mary helps us to remember its true meaning as expressed in the Christmas Preface: "In the wonder of the Incarnation we see our God made visible and so are caught up in love of the God we cannot see."

In other words, Mary our mother helps us recall that great vision of the angels and shepherds at Bethlehem, and she inspires us to make that vision become visible again in our own lives, especially during this new year.


2nd Sunday of Christmas (A, B, C)                    Si 24:1-4, 8-12   Jn 1:1-18

## FULLNESS OF LIFE

In his autobiography *Man in Black*, country music star Johnny Cash describes the year 1967 as a turning point in his life. From the time he wrote and sang his first hit in 1955, "Folsom Prison Blues," Johnny Cash gradually got addicted to drugs.

But in 1967, after being thrown in jail and then almost killing himself when released, Johnny Cash got help from his wife June Carter and Dr. Nat Winston, and kicked the habit. He tells how during his forty days of withdrawal in the wilderness of his room, his every breath was a fighting prayer asking God for help.

Since then Johnny Cash has regained his faith in Jesus, attends church regularly, reads his Bible, helps Billy Graham with some of his Crusades and has written a novel about St. Paul entitled *Man in White*.

Today another John proclaims Jesus as Savior—John the evangelist. And to what John the evangelist says about Jesus in his gospel, Johnny Cash would probably add, "Amen."

"Through him all things came to be," John writes, "not one thing had its being but through him . . . Indeed, from his fullness we have, all of us, received—yes, grace in return for grace."

It took Johnny Cash a while to learn that apart from Jesus nothing comes to be. You can have success, fame and money, but without Jesus they mean nothing. In fact, such things prove to be destructive apart from God because they deceive us with empty promises of happiness.

We can wear fancy clothes, drive luxury cars and dine at the best restaurants, but without Jesus all these things leave us unfulfilled. In fact, they prove to be detrimental apart from God because they drive us to want more and more.

The Word of God became flesh in Jesus to share his fullness with us, to fill up our emptiness with his presence and our hearts with his love. Jesus came among us so that we could find life in him—real, deep down life and not just something superficial, abundant life and not just something minimal.

If there's a lot of loneliness in our lives, it's because we have not yet found the fullness of Jesus. If there's anxiety in our hearts, it's because the peace of Jesus has not yet penetrated them.

Imagine a world without music or songs from people like Johnny Cash, or a world without art and color, or a world without any depth or perspective. In such a world our existence would be dull, unimaginative and flat. That's the way it is without Jesus.

But with Jesus we find the fullness of life—we can hear sounds of music even amidst cries of pain; we can see rainbows of color even in pockets of poverty; and we can discover new dimensions even in death.

Imagine a world without rivers and lakes, landscapes without flowers and trees, tables without food and drink. Such a world would make life dry, barren and empty. That's what a life without Jesus is like.

But with Jesus we experience the fullness of life—his living waters spring up within us; his vine makes our branches fruitful; his bread of life satisfies our deepest hungers.

That's the meaning of Christmas—"From his fullness we have all received a share." At least country-singer Johnny Cash and the evangelist John think so. Do we?


Epiphany (A, B, C)                                      Is 60:1-6   Mt 2:1-12

# THE STAR

In Arthur C. Clarke's short story "The Star," we read about a Jesuit astrophysicist who makes a space trip with other scientists to a distant galaxy called the Phoenix Nebula. There they chance upon a solitary planet still orbiting the remnant of a central sun which had exploded thousands of years ago.

The explorers land their spacecraft on this planet and examine the scorched surface caused by that cosmic detonation. They discover a melted-down monolithic marker at the entrance of a great vault in which they find the carefully stored treasures and records of an advanced civilization.

On their return trip to Earth in our own galaxy, the Jesuit astrophysicist calculates the exact time when the light from this cosmic explosion in the Phoenix Nebula reached Earth. It was the date of Christ's birth when the light from that fire was seen as a bright new star appearing in the East.

But now that he had solved an ancient mystery, he had a greater mystery to grapple with. How could a loving God allow a whole planet of intelligent beings to be given to a galactic conflagration, so that the symbol of their passing might shine above Bethlehem at his Son's birth?

This science-fiction story about the star of Bethlehem has its source in today's gospel. Matthew's narration of the Magi uses the star as its central symbol. From its rising in the East to its coming to a standstill over Bethlehem, the star leads and guides the astrologers.

Arthur Clarke's science-fiction story about the Jesuit astrophysicist and Matthew's colorful story about the Magi are both stories of faith, but in different ways.

On the one hand, Clarke's story culminates in a *crisis of faith*. His priest-scientist reaches a point where he is overwhelmed by the mystery of how the cosmic destruction of a whole civilization can be reconciled with a loving God. His faith in God is on the verge of faltering.

Do we recognize ourselves in this kind of crisis of faith? Although we aren't threatened by some colossal explosion of the sun in our own solar system, we are threatened every day by nuclear explosions which could destroy the Earth.

Moreover, individuals die every day because of accidents, cancer and crime. Though their number is not as staggering as the count of the victims of a nuclear war would be, nonetheless their loss to us is equally painful and perplexing.

We should not be surprised, then, if our faith falters sometimes. Faith is not truly faith until it is tested. Only when all our reasons for believing are removed will we find out what faith really means.

On the other hand, Matthew's story ends in the *simplicity of faith*. The

Magi step out in faith when they risk leaving their homeland for a foreign country. They put their trust in the guidance of a star. Upon finding a little child and his mother, they worship him as a newborn king. Finally, their decision about how to return is determined by a dream.

"What naive, foolish men," we might say, "to let stars and dreams determine their destiny!" And yet in their simplicity of faith they found a peace which surpassed all expectations and a joy beyond all telling.

Their story is told to affirm our own faith as we make our own journey through life, and to give us some assurance in our own search for God.

Baptism of the Lord (A, B, C)  Is 42:1-4, 6-7  Lk 3:15-16, 21-22

## SOLIDARITY

The movie *Gandhi* is a three-hour epic depicting the life of Mahatma Gandhi: a man of faith and a writer, a politician and a pacifist. To lead the oppressed people of India to freedom from British rule, Gandhi adopted a pacifist approach.

By means of fasting from food, long vigils of prayer, marches, protests and civil disobedience, Gandhi persuaded the British to grant independence to India in 1947.

Even though a civil war between the Muslims and Hindus of India followed, and even though Gandhi himself was assassinated in 1948, he nevertheless began an immense movement toward freedom, peace and justice.

One of the reasons why Gandhi put on a loincloth and fasted from food almost to the point of death was to show solidarity with his Indian people and to identify with them in their suffering.

This is one of the reasons why Jesus was baptized in today's gospel—to show solidarity with us and to identify more deeply with us.

In his Pelican commentary on Luke's gospel, George Caird asks the question: "Why was Jesus baptized?" After all, to be baptized was to ask God's forgiveness, and it is the consistent witness of the New Testament that Jesus had no sins of his own to confess.

Moreover, Jesus uttered scathing criticisms of empty formalism. So it would seem that Jesus would not have undergone baptism unless the ritual had profound significance for himself and for us. Caird writes:

> Jesus went to be baptized, then, not for private reasons, but as a man with a public calling. John the Baptist had summoned all Israel to repentance, and with Israel Jesus too must go. Jesus dwelt in the midst of a sinful people, and could not separate himself from them. Rather he must be fully identified with them in their movement towards God.

In other words, Jesus did not have to be baptized. He was always God's beloved Son on whom his favor rested. Yet he freely chose to be baptized to identify himself with our need for forgiveness and with our longing for redemption. To lead us into the kingdom, he himself would enter by the only door open to us, the door of baptism.

Perhaps the life and death of both Gandhi and Jesus give us a hint about what we must do to live a meaningful life in a senseless world and to leave it better than we found it. We must identify ourselves with the poor and the oppressed and do what we can to relieve their burdens—whether by passive means of prayer and fasting, or by active means of nonviolent protest and the sharing of our material goods.

Like Gandhi and Jesus, we too have to hear today's words from Isaiah as addressed to ourselves: we have to see ourselves as God's chosen servants upon whom he has put his Spirit when we were baptized; we have to be the ones who will not break the bruised reeds of people who are jobless, nor quench the smoldering wicks of people who are at the point of despair.

If the Lord isn't calling us for the victory of justice, then whom is he calling? If the Lord isn't sending us to bring light where there is darkness and ignorance, sight where there is blindness and racism, or freedom where there is oppression and ill-treatment, then whom is he sending?

Gandhi and Jesus both had a strong sense of solidarity with their suffering people. By our baptism we become members of God's chosen people. But to what extent do we identify with their needs? To what degree do we want to express our solidarity with them? To what lengths are we willing to go to do good works among them?

*C Cycle* 217

1st Sunday of Lent                        Dt 26:4-10   Lk 4:1-13

# WRONG REASONS

In his play *Murder in the Cathedral*, playwright T.S. Eliot describes how St. Thomas Becket struggles with the threat of martyrdom. He is not afraid to die because of the sufferings of martyrdom, but because he may not be properly motivated.

As he defends the Church of England against King Henry II, Thomas wonders whether or not he is doing this out of pride. "Nothing would be more tragic," he says, "than to do the right thing for the wrong reason; to do what is noble for reasons of vanity."

The temptations that faced Thomas Becket are similar to those that confronted Jesus in today's gospel. In his Pelican commentary on Luke, G.B. Caird sums up the three temptations this way:

> It is unlikely that Jesus ever felt any temptation to do things which are commonly regarded as immoral . . . But that does not mean that his temptations were the less real . . . All temptation is to do what is attractive, and the subtlest and strongest temptation is to do what appears to be good.

Caird goes on to show that since Jesus was a man of fervent and dedicated spirit, his temptations were of three types. First, to allow the good to usurp the place of the best. Second, to seek His Father's ends by means alien to God's character. Third, to force the hand of the Father by taking short cuts to success.

In the first temptation, Jesus is hungry from fasting for forty days. The devil invites him to turn stones into loaves of bread. To eat when one is hungry is a good thing. But when eating dulls our senses to supreme values in life, we allow the good to usurp the place of the best.

If we care only about the instant gratification of our immediate physical needs, then we fail to notice the needs of our neighbor or the poor. By giving priority to the physical, we give up the special place of the spiritual in our lives. We deny what Jesus himself quotes from Scripture: "Man does not live on bread alone."

In the second temptation, Jesus is offered power over all the kingdoms of the world. Although the purpose of his messianic mission was to establish his rule, the way he would do this is his Father's way—the way of defeat on the cross and not the way of conquest; the way of weakness and obedience and not the way of power and independence.

Many are the times we seek God's ends, but by means alien to his will: we want prosperity, but at the expense of the unemployed; pleasure, but by exploiting other people; status, but by snubbing undesirables.

In the third temptation, the faith of Christ is tested. If he were to cast himself down from the pinnacle of the Temple, could he not trust that his Father would keep him safe? Would not this spectacular proof of the power of faith compel our assent?

This is the temptation to force God's hand by taking short cuts to success: we want world peace, but by nuclear arms; women's rights, but by allowing abortion; prayers answered, but by buying God's favor.

Thomas Becket prayed that he might not do a good thing—become a martyr—for the wrong reason—out of vanity.

We too would do well to pray during Lent for the following: first, that we seek always what is best, and not substitute what is only good; second, that we seek God's ends by using God's means; third, that we put our faith in God and not force his hand.


2nd Sunday of Lent                    Gn 15:5-12, 17-18    Lk 9:28-36

# TOPAZ

Precious stones have a magical quality about them, as anyone who has visited the Tower of London to see the Crown Jewels can testify. One such precious stone is the exquisite and priceless blue topaz.

Blue topaz is chemically a silicate of aluminum, which of itself has no beauty or brilliance. But under great pressure and heat exerted over millions of years, this dull opaque silicate is transformed into a transparent crystal with a remarkable blue color and clarity.

Today's readings tell us about other striking transformations.

In the first reading from Genesis, not only is Abram's name changed by God to Abraham, but his whole destiny is changed as he now becomes the father of many nations.

In the second reading, Paul says that our homeland is in heaven. It is from there that our Savior will come "to transfigure those wretched bodies of ours into copies of his glorious body" (Ph 3:21).

Finally, in the gospel Luke describes the transfiguration of our Lord in the presence of his disciples: "As he prayed, the aspect of his face was changed and his clothing became brilliant as lightning."

The gospel is a goldmine rich with symbolism. In the publication *Share the Word*, Fr. Laurence Brett explores this mine at some length. What follows is a summary of his findings.

Moses and Elijah represent the Age of the Law and the Age of the Prophets. With the appearance of Jesus, the *central age* of history has now dawned.

Last week we heard how the title *Son of God* was used by the devil during the temptations. This week we hear the same title given to Jesus by his own Father to establish his identity: "This is my Son, my chosen one."

As for *time*, Luke places the transfiguration about eight days after Peter's confession of faith. Perhaps he is hinting at the resurrection to come when Jesus will rise on the eighth day, Easter Sunday, the first day of the new creation.

As for *place*, the mountain is not named. It is a theological mountain, a place where God reveals himself to Jesus as he did to Moses and Elijah earlier.

The purpose of going to the mountain is to *pray*. It was while Jesus was praying that he was transfigured. Prayer marked every significant stage in his life and we will find him praying again on Mount Calvary.

The theme of *glory* recalls the birth of Jesus at Bethlehem and the Old Testament revelations that took place on Sinai.

The word *passage* is the same one used for the Exodus from Egypt and it anticipates the Passover which Jesus will make from death to life.

The change in Christ's *face* reminds us of the radiance on the face of Moses when he came down from Mount Sinai, except here Jesus is resplendent with his own glory.

The three *booths* or tents take us back to the wanderings of the Jews for forty years in the desert.

The *cloud* is a sign of God's presence just as it was during the Exodus when it covered the Tent of Meeting.

As we come down with Jesus from the mountain to follow him on his way to Jerusalem—where he will be put to death—we have this transfiguration scene to remind us that the journey will not end in death, but in life; not in ignominy, but in glory.

So too with us. Our sufferings during Lent will be transformed into the joy of Easter. Our penances will be transfigured into the glory of the Paschal feast.

If minerals like silicate of aluminum can be changed by immense pressure and heat into the brilliance of blue topaz, how much more can the ordinary elements of our own life—with all the pressures and forces that bear upon us—be transformed by God's grace into something radiant and beautiful.

But for this to happen, we have to be like Abraham and put our faith in God.


3rd Sunday of Lent                                    Ex 3:1-8, 13-15   Lk 13:1-9

# ONE MORE CHANCE

Just before Christmas in 1985, our country was shocked by an air crash in Newfoundland, Canada. That crash killed more than 200 American soldiers on their way home for the Christmas holidays.

A few months later in 1986, we were stunned again by another national tragedy when the space shuttle Challenger exploded only 74 seconds after liftoff. Seven astronauts were killed in that catastrophe.

Today's gospel gives us two other examples of disasters that occurred in Christ's lifetime. One of the incidents was the ruthless murder of some Galileans while they were in the middle of their Temple sacrifices. The victims were probably political agitators and this was Pilate's way of silencing them.

The other incident was a construction accident which happened near the Temple during the building of a water aqueduct. Apparently it was a project hated by the Jews because Temple funds were stolen by Pilate to finance it.

These two incidents are brought up because the Jews presumed that those who were killed were being punished by God for their sins. But Jesus denies this. Instead, he asserts that what really destroys life is our unwillingness to repent and change our lives.

Jesus says, not once, but twice by way of emphasis: "Unless you repent, you will all perish as they did." The repetition of this teaching is followed by a parable about a fig tree.

Usually it takes a fig tree three years to mature and bear fruit. If it is not producing fruit by that time, it likely never will and so it can be cut down. But this fig tree had already been given twice the allotted number of years it takes to produce fruit, for the owner of the vineyard had allowed three more years to pass in fruitless expectation.

And yet, the owner will give the fig tree still *one more chance*. His vinedressers will do even more than is necessary to help by hoeing and manuring it. All this on the grounds of a *perhaps* or a *maybe*.

This parable is a perennial one for us. Every Lent God gives us *one more chance* to produce more fruit in our lives. God is more than generous with the opportunities he gives us to reform our lives.

All of us have some areas that need changing: maybe we watch too much television, smoke too often or eat the wrong kind of food; perhaps we criticize too much, are too impatient or too demanding; maybe we waste too much time, neglect our work or avoid unpleasant tasks.

But if year after year our lives are fruitless in personal growth, sterile in prayer and empty of good works, then we are a barren fig tree. We can't blame accidents or sickness or other people for our condition. We have to take responsibility for our own lives.

Even terminal cancer patients can cultivate the will to live productively with the time they have left. For example, before she died, Jory Graham wrote a newspaper column to encourage other victims of cancer. Even amputees can take on new challenges. For example, Ted Kennedy, Jr. relearned how to ski.

What destroys life in us then are not accidents or tragedies, but our unwillingness to accept difficulties and overcome them; to accept suffering and transform it. What makes our lives fruitless are not their circumstances or limitations, but our refusal to give it one more try and hoe our ground for one more year.

This Lent is a season of grace. It may be our last one as it was for the people who died since last Easter. Now is the time for us to reform our lives so that they will be more productive. Now is the time to make whatever changes are necessary so that our fig tree in the Lord's vineyard will bear more fruit in personal growth, prayer and community service.

4th Sunday of Lent  Jos 5:1, 10-12   Lk 15:1-3, 11-32

# PRODIGAL SON

*Matt Houston* is a television program about a wealthy Texan now turned private investigator. In its premiere showing it gave some background to Matt Houston's life. His mother died giving birth to him. His father was so depressed that he gave up Matt for adoption to his closest friend.

The father then drifted away, eventually becoming an alcoholic and a criminal. Many years later he finds out that Matt's life is being threatened because of a case he is working on. So the father returns to warn him. As the story unfolds, their true relationship is revealed.

At first Matt refuses to accept his real father. But when the father steps in front of a bullet aimed for his son, Matt's eyes are opened and he realizes how much his father loves him. The story ends with the father dying in his son's arms—forgiven by his son Matt and embraced in love.

This television story is really an adaptation of today's gospel parable, except that the roles are reversed. In the gospel story told by Jesus it was a son who went away and wasted his life, only to return and be forgiven by his father. In the *Matt Houston* story it was the father who went away and wasted his life, only to return and be reconciled with his son.

Both versions show us what a magnificent love there is between parents and children, and, consequently, how boundless God's love is for us. In his book *Rediscovering the Parables*, Joachim Jeremias says that the Prodigal Son story tells us with impressive simplicity what God is like—a God of incredible goodness, grace and mercy.

Almost every detail of the story emphasizes the immense, reckless love God has for us: the way the father looked every day for his son, ran with abandon to meet him and refused to listen to his son's well-rehearsed speech; the manner in which the father dressed him with the finest robe, ring and sandals; and how he threw an extravagant feast to celebrate his son's return and tried to persuade his older son to share in the joyous occasion.

Every detail of this carefully crafted story is charged with symbolism to reveal the incredible, unconditional love God has for us. If only we could realize this, we wouldn't be like the younger prodigal son in the sense that we would be afraid to approach our heavenly Father or hesitate to come to him.

The Father doesn't wait for us. He goes out—he runs out—to meet us. The Father doesn't want to listen to our litany of sins when we pray. He interrupts to tell us how precious we are to him, how glad he is to have us back and how much he is going to do for us.

If only we could appreciate God's boundless love for us, we wouldn't pout like the older son and approach our Father as if we were a hired hand. We are not slaves, but sons of God. We don't have to calculate our wages, but simply trust in his generosity.

The Father doesn't want us to make snide remarks about our brothers and sisters, or to think that we are superior to them. Instead he wants us to forgive one another as family, share in one another's sorrows and joys, and celebrate the way he brings us back to life when we are dead and finds us when we are lost.

Matt Houston realized too late the tender love his father had for him. While we know that the prodigal son came to this kind of awareness before his father died, we never really know if the elder son ever did. Before time runs out on us, pray that we may come to know, experience and respond to the tremendous love God our Father has for us.


5th Sunday of Lent                                     Is 43:16-21   Jn 8:1-11

# THE SCARLET LETTER

In 1850 Nathaniel Hawthorne published *The Scarlet Letter*. Its setting was a Puritan community in Boston in early New England. Hawthorne's novel tells the story of Hester Prynne who was forced to wear the scarlet letter "A" for "adultery" because she had given birth to an illegitimate child.

The child's secret father was none other than the community's minister, Arthur Dimmesdale. Hester had to bear public scorn and humiliation, while the minister had merely to bear the pangs of conscience.

After many years the minister finally confessed his secret sin to the people and later died in peace. Hester meanwhile went on to live like a saint, bringing happiness to her disturbed illegitimate daughter and helping others in their troubles.

*The Scarlet Letter* has several similarities with today's gospel story about the woman caught in adultery.

First, the women. Both women were implicated in acts of adultery and were consequently subject to the penalties imposed by the law.

Second, the punishment. By today's standards Hester was dealt with harshly by always having to wear her scarlet letter "A" on her dress. But harsh as that punishment may have been, it was still not as severe as the stoning-to-death penalty that threatened the woman in the gospel episode.

Third, the men. In *The Scarlet Letter* the guilty minister enjoyed the respect of the people, while Hester was held in contempt. For many years he lived a hypocritical life, until his conscience finally compelled him to confess. In the gospel, the hypocritical scribes and Pharisees boldly accuse the woman of her sins but lack the courage to confess their own sins.

Fourth, there is conversion. Hester suffers much for her sin but becomes a saintly person in the end. The woman in the gospel is forgiven by our Lord and is given a chance to make a new life for herself.

What are we to learn from comparing these two stories? Perhaps two lessons.

First, the lesson that *sin is real*. The tendency in modern society is to deny that some things are sinful, such as stealing from stores, using addictive drugs or having abortions.

Another tendency is to excuse sin by invoking sociology or psychology. For example, some justify premarital sex as a necessary experience for growth in maturity.

But in the gospel there is no indication that Christ is denying the existence of sin. He forgives the woman not because what she did was harmless, but because he loved her in spite of her adulterous act.

Moreover, Jesus is quite clear in his directions to the woman. She is to go in peace, but from now on she is to avoid this sin.

The second lesson we can learn is *the generosity of God's forgiveness*. The woman's adultery, which others would have condemned and killed her for, is dramatically forgiven by our Lord.

Where others might dole out forgiveness piecemeal or in installments, Jesus blots out the whole debt of guilt all at once. We can't help but recall here St. Augustine's observation on this gospel that in the end only two persons remained representing *misery* and *mercy*, and *mercy* won the day.

Christ's generosity might upset some of us. Surely he should have first denounced her indulgence of the flesh. Surely he should have waited at least until she said that she was sorry.

It's too bad that Jesus did not consult us first. We would have warned him how easy it is to abuse such generosity.

Christ's generosity is almost too good to be true. He trusts in her honor to respond the right way. He believes in her sincerity. Did he ever do less for us?

Palm Sunday                                          Lk 19:28-40   Lk 22:14-23:56

## FEARLESS RESOLVE

Hollywood heroes often capture our imagination because they symbolize something that we admire. For example, when we watch Charles Bronson in *Death Wish*, Clint Eastwood in *Dirty Harry* or Sylvester Stallone in *Rambo*, it is not their violent actions that attract us, but their cool courage in confronting danger.

We're inspired whenever we see these film heroes walk fearlessly into what they know are high-risk situations, because they have resolved to do what they have to do to right some wrong.

Spontaneously we almost want to stand up and cheer for them as they defy death and demonstrate daring, because we wish that we too could face our own challenges with the same kind of courage.

On this Palm Sunday we see another hero enter a high-risk situation determined to do what he has to do. The hero is Jesus, who knew that his enemies were plotting his death, yet, in the opening verses of today's gospel, "went on ahead, going up to Jerusalem."

In these few words Luke captures the courage and resolve which marked Christ's journey to Jerusalem. It's one of the reasons why we stand up with palm branches and cheer for Jesus: "Hosanna! Blessed is he who comes as king!"

These same qualities of courage and resolve were in the mind of the prophet Isaiah when he had the Suffering Servant say: "So, too, I set my face like flint; I know I shall not be shamed" (Is 50:7).

When we read Luke's account of the passion, there, too, we saw Christ advance unflinchingly to his crucifixion and death. At the Last Supper he instituted the Eucharist to signify his body that would be broken and his blood that would be shed for us.

During his agony in the garden, Jesus balked momentarily over the cup of suffering he had to drink. But an angel from heaven came to strengthen him in his set purpose to do his Father's will.

When Jesus was struck and taunted by the armed guards, he kept his composure and remained silent. During his interrogation by the Sanhedrin he spoke out confidently: "From now on the Son of Man will be seated at the right hand of the Power of God."

On the way to Calvary, Jesus was helped by Simon of Cyrene to carry the cross, but only to make sure that he would reach his destination. On the cross Jesus refused to come down and save himself. Instead he commended his spirit into his Father's hands and died for us.

Unlike our mythical film heroes, Jesus did die. He was not invincible, but vulnerable to death. Nevertheless, Jesus conquered death in a way that supersedes the greatest exploits of our film heroes: he rose from the dead on the third day.

There is, then, a twofold purpose to Palm Sunday. On the one hand, it introduces Holy Week by presenting the passion and death of Jesus. On the other hand, it anticipates next Easter Sunday by presenting Christ's triumphal entry into Jerusalem, a sort of sneak preview of his climactic triumph over death through his resurrection.

May our Lord's courage and resolve in going to Jerusalem to die inspire us to meet our own challenges the same way and to set our faces like flint when we would rather quit.

May our Lord's ultimate victory over death also encourage us, when all seems lost, to commend ourselves with faith into the Father's hands.

In this way, the palms blessed today will signify both our pledge to journey with Jesus to Jerusalem for his passion, as well as his promise that one day we will be with him in paradise.

Easter (A, B, C)   Ac 10:34, 37-43   Lk 24:1-12

## A NEW CREATION

Andrew Lloyd Weber's musical, *Cats*, is a delightful, whimsical production based on a poetical work by T.S. Eliot. Although this imaginative musical is sheer fantasy, the cat characters it sketches personify enough human qualities to make Eliot's point: "You have now learned enough to see / That cats are much like you and me."

This is especially true in the climactic Jellicle Moon scene when one cat is selected to go to cat heaven and be reborn to a new cat life. The sentimental choice is the bedraggled fallen feline, Grizabella, the cat counterpart of Mary Magdalene in the gospels.

In her torn attire, Grizabella symbolizes the scum of society, the so-called street people like prostitutes, drunks and drug addicts. So when she is chosen to be reborn to a new life, we almost want to stand up and cheer "Alleluia!"

In its own theatrical way, *Cats* is a resurrection story corresponding to the Easter story in today's gospel. On the first day of the week, at dawn, Mary Magdalene and some other women come to the tomb to anoint the dead body of Jesus. Two angels tell them: "Why look among the dead for someone who is alive? He is not here; he has risen."

We're no longer on a stage of fantasy, but in a setting of salvation history. While Grizabella's rebirth was pure imagination, our Lord's resurrection is divine revelation. Where *Cats* could only awaken our deepest hopes for another and better life, Christ's resurrection confirms these expectations as true.

Moreover, there are scriptural overtones to some of the lyrics of the hit song from *Cats*, a song entitled "Memories." When Grizabella sings about the day dawning at sunrise and a new life beginning, we can parallel her with Mary Magdalene's coming at dawn on the first day of the week to the empty tomb where she will hear about our Lord's new risen life.

According to Fr. Eugene LaVerdiere, the "first day" means much more than Sunday, the first day of the week. For the early Christians "first day" was heavily charged with symbolism, because it put them in the context of the creation story of Genesis where the term was introduced.

We recall how in the beginning darkness covered the earth. Then God said, "Let there be light," and light was made. God called the light "day," and the darkness he called "night." "Thus evening came, and morning followed—the first day."

In other words, the phrase "first day" was canonized as a creation expression signifying the beginning of everything. So it was only natural for the evangelists to use the same words, "first day," together with the word "dawn," to communicate to us the meaning of Christ's resurrection as God's new creation, his new beginning for everything.

This is a very exciting insight, for it tells us that however dark our surroundings may be at times—because of failures, tragedy and even death—Jesus has conquered that darkness by his resurrection from the dead.

No matter how down-and-out we may become like the outcast cat Grizabella, there is always hope for us that a new life can begin even here and that we can find the meaning of what happiness is.

2nd Sunday of Easter                                           Ac 5:12-16   Jn 20:19-31

## BREAKTHROUGH

The story of Helen Keller and Ann Sullivan is told in the movie *The Miracle Worker* and it serves as a counterpoint to the story of Thomas the apostle today. For Helen Keller the senses of hearing and seeing were barriers instead of bridges to the world. Unable to see or hear or communicate, she spent her childhood in a dark and silent world.

Nonetheless, under the patient guidance of Ann Sullivan, Helen Keller learned how to speak and write. Eventually she became a distinguished lecturer, the author of many books and a world traveler proficient in several languages.

As she herself put it, she was able to "break through the barrier of the senses." Today's gospel represents another such breakthrough, but in a different way. Thomas the apostle can see and hear but is unable to believe in the risen Lord until Jesus himself appears, speaks and commands Thomas to touch his hands and his side.

It seems that it was now unnecessary for Thomas to actually touch our Lord. Seeing and hearing Jesus were enough for Thomas to make the breakthrough of his senses to reach the point of faith. Jesus said to Thomas: "You believe because you can see me. Happy are those who have not seen and yet believe."

This episode in John's gospel is especially significant for us. When this gospel was being written, the disciples who had actually seen the risen Lord had died. Now many were coming to believe in Jesus even though they had never seen him.

Thomas thus becomes a key link between the age of the apostles who saw the Lord with their own eyes and all future ages of disciples who will never see Jesus in this life and yet will believe in him.

We are part of this final age of time and we can thank Thomas for occasioning our Lord's last beatitude, as it were: "Happy are those who have not seen and yet believe."

The key to making a breakthrough of the barrier of our senses is faith. Certainly much can be demonstrated with the help of our senses. Our scientific labs and law courts depend on what we see, hear and touch to prove things. But there is a realm of experience and knowledge that transcends our senses, a realm where the senses actually become a barrier.

We sometimes call this realm the inner world of our memory and imagination, of intuition and creativity, of religion and mysticism. To penetrate this inner world we have to let go of our external senses, which will only distract us or cause interference, and trust in our inner powers.

We call this faith, a belief in some reality for which there are no external signs to prove it exists, yet which somehow we know does exist.

Many are the times we have to make our own personal breakthrough of the senses by an act of faith. When people get married they stake their whole future together on an act of faith. When students choose a college to attend they place immense trust in their teachers. When priests get ordained or religious take vows, they commit themselves to Jesus—someone they cannot see, yet in whom they believe.

We need faith to persevere when we cannot see our goal or to be patient when we cannot see any results; we need faith to make decisions when we have little evidence to go on or to pray when we're not sure if anyone is listening, let alone speaking to us.

When St. Thomas Aquinas composed his hymns to the unseen Christ present in the visible Eucharist, faith played a key part. Many are the times we have sung: "What our senses fail to fathom, let us grasp through faith's consent."

May we renew that faith today and make another break through the barrier of our senses.

3rd Sunday of Easter                                    Ac 5:27-32, 40-41   Jn 21:1-19

# WELCOME TABLE

Before he died in 1975 at age 82, the Rev. Eugene Huffman "did whatever his black hands could find to do." At various times, he had worked as a chauffeur and butler for movie stars like John Hall and Bette Davis, held jobs as a short-order cook and a Pullman porter, was a newspaper columnist and radio commentator, and had written novels and plays.

Then Eugene Huffman became a minister and in 1961 founded a church in San Francisco. In his storefront church where he held his Sunday services he had a Welcome Table. Following their worship, poor people of all races and creeds were invited to sit down to share a meal at this Welcome Table.

When his church was thriving during the 1960's, Rev. Huffman's Welcome Table fed as many as fifty people a day and his seven-room apartment above the church provided shelter for 14 homeless men.

If asked why he had a Welcome Table, Rev. Huffman would quote today's gospel from John, in which our Lord asks Peter three times if he loves him and then tells him three times to "feed my lambs."

A footnote in *The New American Bible* on this text stresses its juridical aspect. The First Vatican Council cited this text in defining the supreme authority and power which Jesus gave to Peter as head of his Church. But Rev. Huffman interpreted the text differently. When Jesus says to Peter, "Feed my lambs," Rev. Huffman took the words as addressed to us literally.

In other words, Rev. Huffman said that Christ is not only telling us to feed his people sacramentally with the word of Scripture and the bread of the Eucharist, but also physically with real food and drink.

Rev. Huffman felt that food and fellowship should go together. If we are one in fellowship because of our common faith in Jesus, then we should also be one in the food we share because of our love for one another.

Rev. Huffman's interpretation of this text from John is supported by other sections of the gospel. John's gospel is the only one that does not give an account of the institution of the Eucharist at the Last Supper. Instead it gives a description of Jesus washing the feet of his disciples and then telling them about fraternal charity.

It seems then that the significance of the Eucharist for John is not just eating and drinking. It means serving and ministering. The Lord's supper is not just liturgy and ceremony. It means loving and sharing.

If we take Christ's words to Peter seriously, as Rev. Huffman did, then we literally have to feed his sheep in some way by our generosity. For example, we have to sustain the life of the unborn by the protection we provide for them, or feed the mentally deficient by fulfilling their hunger for acceptance as human beings.

Feeding sheep might take on the form of nourishing our youth by our openness and readiness to communicate with them, or supporting our aged by holding them in high esteeem and showing them appreciation.

The Jews in the desert complained because they did not get enough food and drink. People like Rev. Huffman complain because they don't have enough food and drink to give away.

Peter complained because Jesus wanted to wash his feet. Later he complained because our Lord asked him three times if he loved him. But Peter was a stubborn man, and it was our Lord's only way to show him the meaning of the Eucharist, namely, unselfish service to others and a ministry of giving.

Jesus asks us: "Do you love me? If you do, then after you finish your Eucharistic meal, go and feed my people—the unborn child, the frustrated teenager, the mentally handicapped and the lonely elderly."

4th Sunday of Easter                              Ac 13:14, 43-52   Jn 10:27-30

## ABANDONED? NEVER!

In his book *Alive: The Story of the Andes Survivors*, Piers Paul Read tells how 16 people escaped safely from an airplane crash in the Andes Mountains in 1972. For 71 days they endured the hostile environment of that remote, rugged mountain terrain before they were rescued.

There in the snow with no food and only light clothing, they saw planes fly over the area from time to time, but the planes never spotted them. Then on a transistor radio they heard the awful news that the official search for the crashed airplane had been abandoned as futile.

To keep alive they decided to eat parts of the bodies of the dead.

Eventually, two of the survivors left the crash site to find a way out, and after struggling for 10 terrible days they came upon some cowboys. Rescue of the other 14 survivors followed.

This story of the Andes survivors tells us something about today's gospel. Jesus says: "I know my sheep and they follow me. I give them eternal life; they will never be lost and no one will ever steal them from me."

In other words, other people may sometimes give up on us, but the Lord Jesus never will. Because of the circumstances, the official search for the Andes survivors had to be abandoned. But the Lord never abandoned them.

In fact, neither the paralyzing cold nor the avalanches of snow, neither their injuries nor their illnesses could snatch them out of the hand of the Lord. In spite of the perils that threatened them, Christ protected his sheep so that they did not perish during the ordeal.

Now we might ask: "What about the 11 people who died in the crash? Didn't they perish? Or what about the 16 who lived through the crash but died shortly after because of their injuries? Didn't they perish too?"

In a sense, yes, they did perish—but only in this life. Through our faith in Jesus we believe that they received from him in exchange a better life—one that is eternal. Their death did not snatch them out of the hand of the Lord. On the contrary, it secured their place in his presence in a permanent way.

Their situation is described in today's second reading from the book of Revelation: "They will never hunger or thirst again . . . because the Lamb who is at the throne will be their shepherd and will lead them to springs of living water" (Rv 7:16-17).

So it doesn't matter how great is the peril that threatens us. Whether we live or whether we die, according to St. Paul, we belong to the Lord, and no one or anything can snatch us out of his hand.

People may sometimes give up on us—and with good reasons—but never our Good Shepherd. Our spouse may have to give up on us because we drink or gamble too much, but never the Lord. He always goes on searching for a lost sheep.

Our employer may have to give up on us and fire us from our job because of our dishonesty, but never the Lord. He always offers us reconciliation as he did the good thief on the cross.

Our political colleagues may have to give up on us and try to remove us from office, but never the Lord. As we sang in Psalm 100, "His kindness endures forever," regardless of how many mistakes we may make.

So even though we are not saved from sorrow or suffering or death, we can still be like the disciples in the first reading from Acts and "be filled with joy and the Holy Spirit," because we know that no one will ever snatch us out of the hands of Christ.

5th Sunday of Easter　　　　　　　　　　　　　　　Ac 14:21-27　Jn 13:31-33, 34-35

# GREATNESS

In Shakespeare's play, *Twelfth Night*, there is a famous line that reads: "Some are born great, some achieve greatness, and some have greatness thrust upon them."

As we look around we see how true this is.

Some are born great, at least financially, because their parents are very rich. We think of Henry Clay Ford or Nelson Rockefeller, for example.

Some achieve greatness because of what they accomplished with a lot of effort. Luciano Pavarotti and Beverly Sills come to mind here.

And some have greatness thrust upon them because they reacted heroically or nobly in certain situations. St. Maximilian Kolbe and Anne Frank are examples.

If we look into today's readings we see again how true Shakespeare's words are.

In the first reading from Acts, the apostles Paul and Barnabas establish a principle for achieving Christian greatness: "We have to experience many hardships before we enter the kingdom of God."

In the gospel, greatness is translated into the word *glory*: "Now has the Son of Man been glorified, and in him God has been glorified." The meaning of this hour of glory or greatness is unmistakable. The scene is the Last Supper. The betrayer Judas has just left the upper room. Our Lord's passion and death are about to begin.

How can Jesus call the hour of his death the hour of his glory? In the same way we designate any hour of crisis or challenge as an hour of glory.

In sports we recognize certain athletes as superstars because they perform their best when the pressure is the greatest. We think of Kirk Gibson hitting a home run to win the 1984 World Series for the Tigers, or of Jack Nicklaus charging from behind to win the Masters' Golf Tournament in 1986.

In the field of skilled professions, the surgeons and lawyers who have great reputations are the ones who take on the greatest challenges in the operating room or in the courtroom and who excel in the process.

In times of war, we honor as heroes and heroines the men and women who make the supreme sacrifice for their country by dying for it.

So it is not surprising to see Jesus approaching his hour of death as the supreme hour that will give the greatest glory to his Father and that will glorify the Son forever.

Too often we look on our trials and challenges as something to avoid and run away from at all costs. How mistaken we are, because these are opportunities to achieve greatness. This is not to say that we should go running around looking for troubles and crises. But when they do come to us, we should view them as potential hours of glory.

Psychologists tell us that crises and challenges are times either for *breakdowns* or *breakthroughs* with respect to growth in maturity—and, we might add, with respect to growth in spirituality.

In other words, when a crisis occurs in our marriage or work, or in our studies or health, we can, on the one hand, *break down* under the pressure by damaging a relationship, copping out on the job, giving up in our studies or indulging in self-pity.

Or we can, on the other hand, *break through* the challenge by deepening a relationship, conquering the task, persevering in our studies or coping with our health problems.

True greatness is not measured by how much fame we attain, but by how we react to crises and challenges the way Jesus did—by seeing them as hours of glory and as opportunities for growth.

6th Sunday of Easter　　　　　　　　　　Ac 15:1-2, 22-29　Jn 14:23-29

# PATHFINDERS

In a best-selling book entitled *Pathfinders*, author Gail Sheehy follows the lives of 200 persons who took the risk of blazing new, less obvious trails.

For example, Al Oerter was a four-time Olympic gold medal winner as a discus thrower. As a young man, Al nurtured the classic male fantasy of virility: perfection of physical strength.

At age 32 he departed from that male stereotype to develop the other aspects of his personality, such as gentleness, in order to be a better family man. Al Oerter is a *pathfinder* who was willing to seek a new horizon of intimacy and love to balance his earlier cultivation of athletic brawn and prowess.

*Pathfinders* like Al Oerter are willing to re-evaluate their lives, are ready to risk change and dare to make new decisions. We see this spirit illustrated in today's readings.

In the first reading, the early Church was confronted with a controversy about retaining some Mosaic practices such as circumcision. It was a situation that had never arisen before. The early Christians had to make decisions they never dreamed of. But under the direction of the Holy Spirit, they pioneered the Church to move along uncharted paths.

This pattern has been repeated down through the ages to our own day as we have to confront new questions like test-tube babies, environmental pollution and nuclear energy. Jesus never told us in his Sermon on the Mount how we should use television and computers. But he did give us the Holy Spirit to guide us in our roles as *pathfinders* in the new age of technology and electronics.

We have his promise to do this in the gospel for today: "I have said these things to you while still with you; but the Advocate, the Holy Spirit, whom the Father will send in my name, will teach you everything and remind you of all I have said to you."

In his book *Preaching the New Lectionary*, Reginald Fuller remarks that it is not the function of the Spirit to convey ever new revelations; rather, it is "to unfold in ever new understanding, ever new interpretations and applications the once-for-all revelation of Jesus Christ." The work of the Holy Spirit is more than a reminiscence of all that Jesus said and did; it is also "a living representation, a creative exploitation of the gospel."

If Christianity is going to be relevant in the face of contemporary issues, then we have to be *pathfinders* in government and law, entertainment and education, and in health care and business.

We may not know exactly what to do, but we should not hesitate because the Holy Spirit will enlighten us. We may not know what kind of opposition we may encounter, but we should not be intimidated because the Holy Spirit will strengthen us. We may not know what far-reaching consequences our decisions may have, but we should not be fainthearted because the Holy Spirit dwells within us.

When society marks out certain routes for us to follow regarding abortion, pornography and materialism, we have to take risks of being counter-cultural and blaze our own trails with such movements as Pro-Life, The Christian Culture Series and Bread for the World.

Christians who are *pathfinders* are not content with a cozy, card-carrying kind of commitment. They search for new ways to apply their Christianity to current events. Christians who are *pathfinders* are not satisfied with a routine practice of their faith. They explore creative modes and contemporary forms to express their faith.


Ascension                                              Ac 1:1-11  Lk 24:46-53

## SOARING HIGHER

At the conclusion of Part One of Richard Bach's book *Jonathan Livingston Seagull*, two radiant birds come as Jonathan's brothers to take him higher, to take him home. Jonathan balks, but the birds insist: "But you can, Jonathan, for you have learned. One school is finished, and the time has come for another to begin."

It was a moment of enlightenment for Jonathan. He realized that he "*could* fly higher, and it *was* time to go home." Taking one last long glance across the sky and land where he had learned so much, Jonathan Livingston Seagull "rose with the two star-bright gulls to disappear into a perfect dark sky."

There are striking similarities between this episode in Bach's book and Luke's account of our Lord's Ascension in today's readings.

First, the "school" and "learning" mentioned in *Jonathan* recall how Jesus "taught" his apostles until the day he was taken up to heaven.

Second, the "time for another school to begin" for Jonathan reflects Christ's promise to send the Holy Spirit upon his apostles so that they could begin their new mission of being his "witnesses to the ends of the world."

Third, the two "star-bright gulls" suggest the presence of the "two men dressed in white" who spoke to the apostles after Jesus ascended.

Fourth, when Jonathan "rose to disappear into the sky," it was reminiscent of Jesus being "lifted up in a cloud which took him from their sight."

The *Jonathan Livingston Seagull* story can be taken, then, as a modern myth to help us understand the significance of Christ's Ascension. Our Lord's leaving was not the termination of his redemptive activity. Rather, his glorification is an extension of it among his people.

The time of Christ's saving work on earth in its visible and incarnational dimension was finished, but the time for his saving work in heaven in its invisible and sacramental dimension was beginning. The time for his own personal preaching was at an end, whereas the time for the power of the Holy Spirit to become operative in the Church was at hand.

The time for preparing his apostles for their mission of establishing his Church was over, while the time for their participation in the expansion of that Church was starting. The time for his physical presence in our midst was completed, but the time for his presence in our midst through prayer, Eucharist and service was commencing.

Indeed, as Bach writes, "one school is finished, and the time has come for another to begin." The pattern is the same for us. Whether we graduate, or get married, or get ordained, or retire, we are merely finishing one phase of our life in order to begin the next one.

In this life our tasks are never completed, our challenges never end, our schooling is never concluded. There is always one more project to begin, one more person to visit, one more book to read, one more cause to support, and so on.

All of us are Jonathans capable of flying higher to discover new dimensions of self-growth and interpersonal relationships. All of us are called to transcend our self-concern to experience the excitement of completing Christ's work on earth by serving others in ever newer ways.

In a sense, liturgy is like life. We come to church to praise God, hear his word and eat his bread. But we don't stand here all day looking up to heaven. We leave to witness to him in the world, proclaim his good news and show by our love that he is indeed always with us.

For Jonathans like ourselves, life is not dull, but dynamic; not static, but energetic; not a settling down, but a never-ending search. Our story is yet to be finished. Our best chapters may not yet have been written.

7th Sunday of Easter                      Ac 7:55-60    Jn 17:20-26

# STREAM OF CONSCIOUSNESS

In 1922 author James Joyce completed his book entitled *Ulysses*. It was an experimental work that turned out to be a masterpiece of the stream-of-consciousness school.

The setting for Joyce's novel is Dublin. The time is June 16, 1904. The whole story covers approximately 16 hours. It is a modern allegory in which Joyce's hero, Stephen Dedalus, goes in search of his father. His search follows closely the framework of the wanderings of Ulysses in Homer's ancient Greek classic, the *Odyssey*.

Throughout the book Joyce uses various literary techniques such as dreams, musings, interior monologues and free association to reveal the innermost thoughts and feelings of Stephen Dedalus and the other characters.

While John's gospel is much more edifying to read than James Joyce's controversial *Ulysses*, the literary form of today's reading is somewhat like Joyce's stream-of-consciousness style.

The setting for today's gospel is the Last Supper before Jesus died. The reading is from our Lord's last discourse to his disciples. It is the part where Jesus prays aloud to his Father in the presence of his disciples: "Father, may they be one in us, as you are in me and I am in you . . . I have made your name known to them . . . so that the love with which you loved me may be in them, so that I may be in them."

Since it is part of our Lord's farewell address, the prayer seems to race over a lot of his last-minute concerns. With so little time left, only the urgent issues surface to his human consciousness.

Jesus is worried about our unity with one another. He is anxious about how we will love each other. He is wondering about whether we will end up sharing his glory.

This stream-of-consciousness type of prayer is significant to us not only because of the ultimate issues it raises, but also because it is a model of how we should pray sometimes.

Too often we restrict our praying to a recitation of set prayers and formulas, like the rosary or a litany or the invocations of some novena ritual. Such prayers in themselves are excellent. But they are not the only way we can pray.

Sometimes we can use our stream of consciousness to pray, the way Jesus did in John's gospel.

As our worries surface, we can speak about them to God our Father, for he cares about us more than many sparrows or the lilies of the field.

As our fears make themselves felt, we can share them with the Lord Jesus, for he too knows what it felt like to be afraid.

As our dreams and hopes reveal themselves, we can set them before the Holy Spirit, for he may be the inspiration behind them and he is the one who can bring them to completion.

One of the nice things about this stream-of-consciousness form of praying is that we can easily slip into it anywhere and anytime. We can be walking, jogging or driving and pray this way. We can be washing the dishes or mowing the lawn and pray this way. We can be waiting in a doctor's office or in a supermarket checkout line and pray this way.

Stream-of-consciousness praying is different from ordinary daydreaming in that it is not aimless reverie. No, it is daydreaming that is gently directed to God. It is being lost in one's thoughts and feelings, but in the presence of God.

Moreover, it is not a selfish kind of prayer. Stream-of-consciousness praying makes us more aware of the needs of other people—especially those closest to us.

Like Jesus, we end up praying for unity and love in our family and parish; for food and work for the poor; for freedom and justice throughout the world.

Pentecost (A, B, C)   Gn 11:1-9   Ac 2:1-11   Jn 20:19-23

# LANGUAGE

Almost 100 years ago Dr. Zamenhof, a Polish linguist, constructed a new language that could be shared by people throughout the world. The artificial language Dr. Zamenhof created is called Esperanto, "the language of hope."

The name signifies the hope of humankind that a common language might heal the divisions that exist among the different peoples of the earth. We even use the slang expression, "speaking the same language," to indicate harmony or unity of purpose on a certain issue.

The Feast of Pentecost is the Church's celebration of her unity and universality in the Holy Spirit, and so some of the readings used express this in terms of language.

One of the optional readings for Pentecost is the Genesis story about the Tower of Babel. It presupposes that before the building of the tower, people were united and spoke the same language. But in punishment for humankind's pride and arrogance, God confused their speech. Divisions resulted and different languages were developed.

Whether or not the events at Babel actually took place that way is not important. What is important is that sin somehow makes it difficult for us to communicate with each other and to understand each other.

Today's reading from Acts describes the descent of the Holy Spirit on the disciples at Pentecost. With the Tower of Babel story in the background, the reading underlines one of the key outcomes of the Holy Spirit's coming—the disciples spoke in a foreign tongue, yet each nationality present heard and understood them in their own language.

In other words, the confusion of tongues attributed to sin in the story of the Tower of Babel is now removed. Instead the Holy Spirit restores, at least momentarily, a common understanding and a sense of unity.

Ever since, we've been trying to recover that Pentecostal experience of unity and understanding. Dr. Zamenhof's invention of a universal language like Esperanto has been followed by: establishing the United Nations Assembly, holding summit meetings, having cultural exchanges and reviving the Olympic Games.

Occasionally people from different countries make a breakthrough in communicating with and understanding one another—not so much in the arena of politics or economics, as on the level of art, music and dance.

For example, pianist Vladimir Horowitz recently returned to his homeland, Russia, for a concert after more than 60 years of absence. He became an instant good-will ambassador because he moved the hearts of the Russian people—not by what he said, but by the music he played.

We don't need a translator to appreciate such things as the Bolshoi Ballet, or a Picasso painting, or a Calder sculpture. Great works of art seem to transcend spoken languages and touch our spirits to unite us at the deepest levels of our being.

But Pentecost is more than a work of art or music. Pentecost is a new outpouring of God's Holy Spirit into our hearts to kindle in us the fire of his love. The new language that will unite us is not Esperanto so much as the language of love. Even before a child learns how to speak, it already knows that it is loved by its mother.

Even though a word was never exchanged, the Jew who was beaten by robbers knew that he was loved by the Good Samaritan. Even though victims of earthquakes or floods may live in foreign countries, they welcome the message of love we send in relief aid.

Acts of kindness and mercy destroy divisions and build bridges between people. Gestures of peace and forgiveness reduce hostility and forge bonds of unity.

Tongues of fire may not come down on us today as they did on the first disciples at Pentecost. But may the Holy Spirit fill our hearts anew so that we can speak his language of love to each other and to all the world.


Holy Trinity                                          Pr 8:22-31   Jn 16:12-15

# TRINITARIAN COMPARISONS

In her book *The Mind of the Maker*, Dorothy Sayers explores the mystery of the Trinity. She uses different comparisons to help us understand a little how it is possible for there to be one God, but three Persons.

Sayers quotes, for example, two comparisons suggested by St. Augustine. First, whenever we use our sight there is an inseparable trinity present: the form that is seen, the act of vision and the mental attention which correlates the two. Second, every thought is an inseparable trinity of memory, understanding and will.

Dorothy Sayers then goes on to analyze the creative experiences of writers, painters and other artists, "for every work (or act) of creation is threefold, an earthly trinity to match the heavenly."

Thus a play by Shakespeare is first in the mind of the author as an intuitive idea or insight. This is the image of the Father. Second, there is the incarnation of the idea in written words. This corresponds to the Son. Third, there is the meaning of the work and its response in the reader. This represents the Holy Spirit. These three elements are distinct, yet form a single creative act.

So even though the mystery of the Trinity is indeed beyond our comprehension, comparisons do make it more meaningful to some extent. In addition, each of the three readings from Scripture gives us some insight about God to inspire us.

The first reading from Proverbs extols the *creative* power of God in the wonders of the universe. As we contemplate God's handiwork ranging from sea to sky, we can't help but reaffirm our faith in God's creative power at work in us.

Our lives may be surrounded sometimes by disorder and chaos, yet somehow God remains a craftsman who can still create something good and beautiful in and through and around us.

In the second reading from Romans the message is one of *hope*. Every life has moments of suffering. Sickness, losing someone dear through death, hurt feelings and anxieties seem to afflict all of us from time to time.

Nonetheless we are able to endure these sufferings because "the love of God has been poured into our hearts through the Holy Spirit" (Rm 5:5). Our hope in God's abiding presence is not deceptive nor will it leave us disappointed.

Finally, in the gospel from John we hear Jesus promise to send the *Spirit of truth* to guide us to all truth. We are surrounded by conflicting claims to the truth about the meaning of life and the way to live.

The movie and television industries of Hollywood and New York have their gospel; the gambling strips of Las Vegas have theirs; the Playboy Penthouses of Chicago have their version; the Madison Avenue promoters in New York have theirs.

We need the Holy Spirit to lead us through this maze of messages to hear what God has to say. God spoke to us in a significant way through his

Son Jesus Christ. God continues to speak to us through his Holy Spirit. The Holy Spirit is the ultimate revelation about how much God loves us and wants to be with us. The Holy Spirit is our supreme guide to discover the truth about life and the way we should live it.

John F. Kennedy once wrote: "There are three things which are real: God, human folly and laughter. The first two are beyond comprehension, so we must do what we can with the third." Although there is not much we can do with the Trinity, at least we can dispose ourselves to receive their creative influence, gift of love and guidance to all truth.

Corpus Christi                                                  Gn 14:18-20   Lk 9:11-17

# SHARING

*Coming Out of the Ice* is a book written by Victor Herman that was later made into a television drama. It tells the story of how Victor spent 45 years of his life in Russia.

As a 16-year-old boy he left his hometown of Detroit in 1931 to go to Russia where his father was to help set up an auto plant. In 1934 Victor became a celebrity in Russia by breaking the world parachute jumping record. In 1938, at age 23, he was arrested as a spy.

For the next 18 years he miraculously survived the Russian prisons and labor camps until he was pardoned after Stalin's death. But it took another 20 years before Victor was allowed to return to Detroit in 1976.

In one labor camp incident, Victor was left to die on the ground after he had been confined to isolation for a year. His prisoner friend, Red Loon, took him into his hut, scrounged for food to feed him and nursed him back to health. Because Red shared what he had with Victor, he saved Victor's life.

In a sense, this heroic act of sharing is a type of the sharing that should take place with the Eucharist. In the gospel, Jesus looks out at a tired and hungry crowd in an out-of-the-way place. The five loaves and two fish which his disciples had were obviously inadequate to feed the multitude.

Nonetheless, Jesus instructs his disciples to get the people seated, prays to his Father, pronounces a blessing over the five loaves and two fish, and gives them to the Twelve to distribute to the crowd. They all ate until they were satisfied, and there were twelve baskets of food left over.

This scenario of taking bread, giving thanks, breaking and giving will occur again at the Last Supper. In other words, the miracle of feeding the multitude is Eucharistic in significance, especially under the aspect of sharing.

It seemed that the disciples wouldn't have enough to go around, let alone take care of themselves. Still Jesus told them to give away what they had. The bread and fish were not first multiplied, stockpiled and counted to make sure there was plenty available. Instead, the miracle took place as the five loaves and two fish were being distributed.

What a lesson of *trust* and *sharing*! We don't have to wait until we make sure we've got enough to take care of all our needs, real and imagined, before we share with others. The Lord invites us to share what we have precisely at those times when we don't seem to have enough.

We don't have to wait until we get all our debts paid, a certain amount of savings in the bank and our freezers stuffed with food before we share with others. Sharing should be going on all the time, especially when we have only a little—whether it is five loaves and two fish, or limited time and energy.

This is a hard teaching to accept. To try it we have to have *faith* in the Lord's power to multiply our resources. We have to *love* our brothers and sisters who are hurting more than we. We have to *hope* that all of us will be satisfied with enough leftovers to fill twelve baskets.

This is the miracle of the Eucharist—by sharing what we have with one another, God's love is multiplied many times over through us. This is what happened when Red Loon shared his food and bunk with Victor Herman in that Siberian labor camp. Red's sharing even the little he had and in the worst of circumstances saved Victor's life.

Moreover, the inspiration of Red's heroic generosity continues to multiply as the story of *Coming Out of the Ice* is retold. That is the meaning of Eucharist.

Eucharist is not just the bread of the Lord Jesus whose presence we honor in the *liturgy*. Eucharist is also the bread of ourselves that we have to share with others in *life*.

2nd Sunday of the Year  Is 62:1-5  Jn 2:1-12

# THE BEST IS YET TO BE

In a drama written for television entitled *Love Among the Ruins*, Laurence Olivier and Katharine Hepburn star as two old friends who were childhood sweethearts forty years ago. Still a single man, Laurence Olivier is now a prominent lawyer near the age of retirement. Katharine Hepburn is now a widow who comes by chance to Olivier's office for some legal help.

Their old romance flares up again, and this time Olivier gets up enough courage to ask Hepburn to marry him. To convince her to say "Yes," he quotes these verses from Robert Browning's poetry:

> Grow old along with me!
> The best is yet to be,
> The last of life,
> For which the first was made.
> Our times are in his hands.

This television drama about love and marriage, and about "the best is yet to be," throws some light on today's gospel story about the wedding at Cana. In his book *John: The Different Gospel*, Fr. Michael Taylor points out that unlike the other evangelists, John calls Jesus' works of wonder *signs* instead of miracles. John does this because they reveal in a visible way the inner and spiritual identity of Jesus.

This is the reason why Christ's first sign at Cana is used to complete the Epiphany cycle of manifestations about him. The *star* of the Epiphany Feast itself revealed to the wise men the newborn Savior. Our Lord's *baptism* last week revealed to John the Baptist that Jesus was God's beloved Son. The *wedding* at Cana today reveals some of the meaning of Christ's role as Messiah.

The first symbol which strikes us in the story is the *marriage* itself. The first reading from the prophet Isaiah is but one of many Old Testament examples which use the intimate and ultimate love between a husband and wife as an image to describe the deep personal love God has for his people. This love is now being revealed through his Son Jesus.

The second symbol is the set of *six water jars* which were used for Jewish ceremonial washings. John chose the number six to indicate the imperfection of the Old Testament purification of the Mosaic Law compared to the perfect New Testament purifications from sin that would be accomplished by Jesus.

A third symbol in the Cana story is the *wine*, another Old Testament image associated with the messianic age. When Jesus took the water and changed it into an abundant quantity of wine (some 150 gallons) of choicest quality, this symbolized that the Messiah was now here and that the new age had begun.

The Old Testament, signified by the water, is *not* being cast aside; it is being transformed by Jesus into something better—the new wine of the New Testament. Indeed, this *hour* that has finally come is the best that is to be in human history because it is characterized by the abundance and excellence of God's glory being revealed in Jesus.

So much for the symbolism of the wedding at Cana. How do we fit into the story? The story begins and ends on a note of *faith*—Mary's faith at the beginning when she informs her Son about the shortage of wine, and the disciples' faith at the end when they believed in him.

Whether we see ourselves as the wedding couple or the waiter or the guests isn't important. What is important is that we see God's glory being revealed in our midst here and now through Jesus, and that we respond to him in faith.

What matters is that we see how Jesus continually takes whatever stands for imperfect water in our lives—our mistakes, our emptiness, our disappointments, our hurts, our sins—and transforms them into the best of wine: new hope, new dreams, new courage, new efforts, new life.

What Laurence Olivier said to Katharine Hepburn in their television love story, Jesus says to us:

> Come along with me.
> The best is yet to be,
> The last of life,
> For which the first was made.
> Your times are in my hands.

C Cycle 247

3rd Sunday of the Year    Ne 8:2-4, 5-6, 8-10    Lk 1:1-4; 4:14-21

## INAUGURAL ADDRESSES

When U.S. presidents are sworn into office it is customary for them to deliver inaugural speeches. These addresses usually outline the challenges which face them and the ideals by which they will try to govern.

Such inaugural speeches are more often remembered, however, for their inspirational sayings.

We recall, for example, Woodrow Wilson's statement in 1913: "This is the high enterprise of the new day . . . we shall restore, not destroy."

Famous too are Franklin Delano Roosevelt's words in 1933: "This great nation will endure as it has endured . . . The only thing we have to fear is fear itself."

John F. Kennedy's exhortation in 1961 is equally memorable: "And so, my fellow Americans, ask not what your country can do for you. Ask what you can do for your country."

More recently we call to mind Ronald Reagan's American Song theme in 1985: "Hopeful, big-hearted, idealistic—daring, decent and fair. That's our heritage, that's our song . . . We raise our voices to the God who is the author of this most tender music."

Today's gospel reads somewhat like one of these presidential inaugural addresses. Jesus had already been appointed officially by his Father to his office as Messiah when he was baptized. Although he has yet to select his cabinet—the twelve apostles—he now begins his teaching ministry by standing up in public in a synagogue and making his inaugural address.

In his speech he quotes the prophet Isaiah to outline the challenges facing him as the Messiah and to give us a glimpse of the ideals by which he will try to live. Empowered by the Spirit, he will bring glad tidings to the poor and proclaim liberty to captives; he will restore sight to the blind and free the imprisoned.

Then he makes the dramatic and daring declaration that all this is happening right then and right there: "This text is being fulfilled today even as you listen."

Many presidents have made more eloquent inaugural speeches, but none has ever had the power to implement his promises in a perfect way. Only Jesus could do that, because he is the Son of God and anointed by the Holy Spirit.

No president can accomplish his goals for the good of his people unless they actively support him with their labor, military service and taxes. In the same way, Jesus cannot continue to accomplish his messianic work in our time and place unless we put our faith in him, follow his way and fight for his causes.

Just as no country can survive, let alone prosper, when it has too many freeloaders for citizens, so too the kingdom of God cannot thrive when it has too many do-nothing Christians.

If the world is in such a sorry state today, we can't put the blame on Christ and Christianity. We have to blame ourselves in part, especially if we are merely card-carrying Christians—that is, Christians who claim to believe in Christ, but are uncommitted to his causes.

G.K. Chesterton was right when he said: "Christianity has not been tried and found wanting; it has been found difficult and not tried."

So it is not enough to be moved emotionally by Christ's inaugural speech today; we have to do something about it. We have to seek out the oppressed and outcasts and support their quest for justice. We have to reach out to the unwanted and unloved and reaffirm their dignity. We have to listen to the cries of the wounded and poor and lift them up with compassion.

If we don't believe in Christ's causes, then we shouldn't stand up and recite the Creed. But if we do believe in Jesus Christ as Lord, and if we believe in committing ourselves to him, then we should stand up with conviction and courage and proclaim the Creed!

4th Sunday of the Year        Jr 1:4-5, 17-19   Lk 4:21-30

## UNPOPULAR PROPHETS

The movie *Black Like Me* is based on a book by the same title written by John Howard Griffin. It documents his experiences when he had his skin darkened to pose as a Negro and traveled for a month through the Deep South in the late 1950's.

John Howard Griffin was born in Dallas of a mother who was a concert pianist. As a youth he studied psychiatry in France. During World War II he was wounded while serving in the army and went blind as a result. In 1947 Griffin returned to Texas to study Braille and become a novelist.

After ten years of blindness, he recovered his eyesight in a dramatic way and was able to see his wife and two children for the first time. Griffin then got a job with a Negro magazine. It was during this time that he undertook his *Black Like Me* adventure.

Griffin went on to become a leader in the Civil Rights Movement, thus incurring a backlash of hatred from white racists, ranging from threatening mail and phone calls to being hung in effigy by his own townspeople. Griffin died in 1980.

The opposition John Howard Griffin encountered in his prophetic work for civil rights finds a parallel in today's readings.

In the first reading, God calls Jeremiah to be a prophet and predicts the resistance he will meet: "They will fight against you, but shall not overcome you, for I am with you to deliver you."

In the gospel, Jesus proclaims himself as a prophet to his own townspeople. He is promptly expelled from the synagogue and almost killed at the outskirts of Nazareth, causing him to remark: "No prophet is ever accepted in his own country."

Although none of us will ever likely be interviewed by Mike Wallace on *60 Minutes* for making some protest, we are still called by the Lord to be prophets in some manner and to proclaim his message according to our position in life.

Whether we are factory worker or housewife, salesman or secretary, we are sent by the Lord to be his witness in the world. Whether we are married, widowed or single, we are designated by Christ to denounce injustice and to decry violence; to defend the weak and to demand human rights.

For example, to stand up for the protection of the unborn child is to take a prophetic stance against abortion. This will not make us popular with a lot of people. In fact, it may invite accusations and opposition.

To stand up for nuclear disarmament is to take a prophetic stance against militarism. This too may mean going against the crowd. In fact, we may be denounced as unpatriotic or labeled as a Communist sympathizer.

To stand up for decency in literature, movies and television is to take a prophetic stance against sexual permissiveness. As a result, we may end up being ridiculed and mocked as old-fashioned.

It is never easy to be a prophet—whether in the time of Jeremiah and

Jesus or in the time of John Howard Griffin and John Paul II. But prophets we must be if we claim to be Christian.

Although we will encounter resistance, we should not be afraid because we have the Lord's promise to be with us. Like Jesus in the gospel, we should move with daring through the crowd, confident that God will strengthen us in the face of the challenges we meet.

5th Sunday of the Year                                         Is 6:1-8   Lk 5:1-11

## LAUNCH OUT

In Arthur Miller's play *Death of a Salesman* the main character, Willie Loman, is a tragic symbol of futility. As a salesman, Willie drives around in his car dutifully to make his calls on prospective customers. However, except for a few minor successes, his efforts repeatedly end in failure.

Since Willie seems to be only "spinning his wheels," his life becomes an intolerable drudgery. He becomes so preoccupied with his setbacks that he loses all perspective and kills himself.

If only Willie had been able to really see and not just look at what he had—a loving wife, two sons, his health, his religion—he might not have let his defeats drown him in despair. Instead, he might have been able to discover his true value in the sight of God the way Isaiah and Peter did in today's readings.

Both the prophet and the apostle were overcome by a profound sense of sin and unworthiness before God. "Woe is me . . . for I am a man of unclean lips," cried Isaiah. "Leave me, Lord, I am a sinful man," said Peter.

But they didn't stay there. They stepped out in faith to answer the Lord's call to holiness and ministry. "Here I am. Send me," offered Isaiah. "I will follow you, Lord," said Peter.

Like Willie Loman, Peter too knew the frustration one feels when our best efforts end in failure. He and the other disciples had been fishing hard all night but caught nothing.

Haven't we been there too? We toil hard in the kitchen, and our meals still turn out disappointments. We work hard on the job, yet we seem to be getting nowhere. We study hard in school, but our test results don't show it. We try hard to mix socially, yet no one seems to care.

At such times it's easy to get discouraged and want to quit. That's why we need to hear today's gospel. For it is precisely at such moments of futility that the Lord stands by to help us. When Peter's boat was empty, it was then that Jesus stepped into it.

We also need to be reminded that it takes faith to find a way out of a sense of failure and futility. It was only after Peter followed Christ's directions to "launch into deep water and lower your nets for a catch," that they hauled in a huge number of fish.

To overcome feelings of futility, then, it takes faith—faith in our Lord's presence and faith in following his directions. We may have to give it that one more try or launch out into deeper waters, but if we have faith in Jesus, then fish we didn't see before will appear.

Unfortunately, Willie Loman didn't have this kind of faith. But Anne Sexton did. Dying of cancer and searching for meaning, she expressed her feelings in a poem.

At first Anne Sexton describes her futility in trying to row towards God:

> I am rowing, I am rowing
> though the oarlocks stick and are rusty
> and the sea blinks and rolls
> . . . but I am rowing, I am rowing
> though the wind pushes me back.

Nonetheless, her poem ends on a note of hope that God will somehow be reached through all the absurdities of her sickness and embrace her in love. Anne's poem ends with her still rowing.

6th Sunday of the Year                    Jr 17:5-8   Lk 6:17, 20-26

## HAPPINESS MYTHS

Dr. Harold Treffert is the director of the Winnebago Mental Health Institute in Wisconsin. In an article entitled "The American Fairy Tale," he discusses five dangerous ideas we have about the meaning of happiness.

First, happiness is *things*. The more you accumulate and have, the happier you will be.

Second, happiness is *what you do*. The more you produce and earn, the happier you will be.

Third, happiness is being the *same as others*. The more you are fashionable and conform with the times, the happier you will be.

Fourth, happiness is *mental health*. The fewer problems you have and the more carefree you are, the happier you will be.

Fifth, happiness is *communicating with electronic gadgets*. The more you can communicate with a television set, a satellite or a computer, the happier you will be.

According to Dr. Treffert, these five myths about happiness are the cause of many mental health problems today. If happiness cannot be found through these five myths of "The American Fairy Tale," then where do we find it?

Jesus gave us an answer when he outlined the beatitudes in today's reading from Luke. Unlike Matthew's version which contains the more familiar listing of eight beatitudes, Luke's gospel mentions only four beatitudes, which are then followed by four corresponding woes.

Whether there are precisely eight or four beatitudes is not crucial. What is crucial is their revolutionary character as an agenda for finding happiness. They represent a complete reversal of the world's values.

Dr. Treffert summarized the world's values of today in terms of five American myths. In his day our Lord summarized them under four headings: prosperity, comfort, fun and popularity. And Jesus not only rejected these four things, he also attached woes to them: "Woe to you who are rich . . . who have your fill now . . . who laugh now . . . who have others praise you."

It is not that Jesus is against wealth as such, or pleasure, or good times, or popularity. He is against them when they are attained by exploiting people or when they are made into objects of happiness instead of being the means to happiness.

By contrast he proclaims that people can be happy even when they don't have these things: "Blessed are you" who are poor or hungry, or weep or are hated.

"How is this possible?" we might ask. It is possible because the kingdom of God has already come in the person of Jesus, though not yet in its fullness. To belong to this kingdom one doesn't have to have what the world considers important or essential.

C Cycle 253

The good news Jesus brought about God's forgiveness, compassion, and desire to share his divine life with us is something that can be received by the poor as well as the rich. In fact, the poor might be in a better position than the rich to welcome this good news precisely because they stand so empty before God and realize their needs.

The beatitudes declare that happiness does not come from what we *have* but from what we *are*—God's chosen people who are precious in his sight. Happiness does not derive from what we *achieve* but from what we *receive*—God's gift of himself.

The beatitudes are not, then, some pipe dream or fairy tale. They are God's own word revealing to us the secret for finding happiness regardless of our state in life.


7th Sunday of the Year    1 S 26:2, 7-9, 12-13, 22-23    Lk 6:27-38

## FORGIVENESS AND FEELINGS

The Rev. Richard Wurmbrand was born a Jew in Rumania, became a Christian convert, switched to atheistic Communism and finally was ordained a Lutheran minister. When Stalin's forces took over Rumania, Richard Wurmbrand was arrested for publicly defending the Christian faith and put in prison for fourteen years.

Because he continued to talk about Christ to the prisoners, the Communists tortured him with spiked closets, ice treatments, starving rats and hot irons. Yet, Wurmbrand would always emerge and say, "Before I was interrupted, I was telling you about Christ." His full story is told in a book entitled *Tortured for Christ*.

Before the Stalin takeover, the Nazis had their Jewish holocaust in Rumania. In talking with a Nazi soldier, Richard Wurmbrand learned that this was the very man who had killed his Jewish wife Sabrina's entire family. Sabrina was now a Christian.

This Nazi did not believe in either guilt or forgiveness. So Richard brought his wife Sabrina to this man and told her what he had done to her family. Sabrina embraced the Nazi, kissed him and said: "As God forgives you, I forgive you."

Sabrina Wurmbrand could do what seems impossible to us, because she believed in Christ's words in today's gospel: "Love your enemies and do good to those who hate you. Be compassionate as your Father is compassionate. Forgive, and you will be forgiven."

*The Interpreter's Bible* acknowledges the difficulty of feeling any kind of love toward someone who has hurt us deeply. But it insists that even though "to *love* is not necessarily to *like*," we should still *want* for someone "the best in life that God can help us make available for him or her."

In other words, Jesus is not asking for nice feelings, which we cannot control. He is asking us to want nothing but the highest good for someone. Sabrina Wurmbrand understood this. Her husband was unfaithful to her at one time. Although she condemned his infidelity, she would not condemn him.

The Nazi soldier had killed her parents, three brothers and two sisters. To his utter amazement, Sabrina did not demand revenge. Instead she disarmed him with forgiveness.

Sabrina wanted nothing but the best for her husband Richard and for the soldier—their reconciliation and healing, a new vision and direction, and a place in God's kingdom.

We see David doing the same thing for Saul in the first reading. Saul had tried several times to kill David. Yet, when David had a chance to kill Saul in his sleep, he spared his life.

By contrast, how many times have we figuratively put the sword to someone who injured us, either by making a snide remark or by leaving them in the lurch or by giving them the cold shoulder?

Obviously, Christ isn't saying that we should give away our second family car to some thief who has just made off with the first car. But he is saying that we should love those who hurt us in some way, at least by *willing* their *highest good*; that we should take some initiative to reach out in forgiveness, instead of seeking revenge.

We don't have to *feel* like doing it, but we do have to have *faith* in it. The paradox is that by doing good to others, it will come back to us in surprising ways. By giving only what will help someone, God's graces will be given to us in good measure.

C Cycle 255

8th Sunday of the Year  Si 27:4-7  Lk 6:39-45

# TRUE EXCELLENCE

*Iacocca, An Autobiography* became an instant best seller when it was published in 1984. It marked another achievement for a man whose name has become synonymous with success.

In 1964 Lee Iacocca was hailed as the mastermind behind the introduction of the ever-popular Ford Mustang. In 1970 he became president of the Ford Motor Company. In 1983 he was touted as an industrial folk hero for saving and rebuilding the Chrysler Corporation.

Lee Iacocca is a paradox because he is a corporate capitalist with populist appeal. He's loved by executives and workers alike. According to Joseph Califano, "He's real, and he cares—I think that comes through."

People such as Lee Iacocca are recognized for their excellence because their exterior successes seem to flow from their interior qualities. This is why we acclaim coach Bear Bryant, the winningest coach in the history of college football, or actress Helen Hayes, the First Lady of the Theater.

What is true in the world of industry, sports and entertainment is also true in the world of spirituality. At least Jesus seems to think so in today's gospel when he uses the example of good and bad trees: "For every tree can be told by its own fruit . . . A good man draws what is good from the state of goodness in his heart . . . For a man's words flow out of what fills his heart."

Remarking on this passage in his Pelican commentary on Luke, G.B. Caird underlines the relation that exists between character and influence:

> The leader can only guide if he first sees the way. The teacher can impart only what he himself has learned . . . Sound influence is the fruit growing on the tree of sound character, the overflow of an inner abundance.

In other words, we can't move, inspire or influence people unless there is something genuine and attractive within us. That's why people such as Lee Iacocca, Bear Bryant and Helen Hayes capture our imagination. We intuitively sense their inner spark and become excited when we see them in action. They enliven and energize us with their presence.

So if we want to make any impact on people's lives as disciples of the

Lord, we have to strive to become good persons with a goodness that is real and authentic.

It means that we have to put on the *mind* of Christ: denouncing hypocrisy in the name of truth; crying out for justice in the face of oppression; challenging indifference in the midst of complacency.

It means that we have to feel with the Lord's *heart*: reaching out to the downtrodden; forgiving the wayward; sharing with the poor.

It means that we have to *pray* the way Jesus did: praising God for his goodness; thanking him for his gifts; trusting in him for his help.

As we become good people in the image of Christ, our lives will become more and more transparent. People will see goodness in us and be inspired by it. They will recognize our genuineness and respond to it.

Then what we say will have force, because it will flow from our inner convictions. Then what we do will make a difference for others, because it will come from the depth of our being.

9th Sunday of the Year                    1 K 8:41-43   Lk 7:1-10

# CHARIOTS OF FIRE

The film *Chariots of Fire* won an Oscar in 1982 for Best Picture. It tells the story of two British sprinters and their pursuit of gold medals in the 1924 Olympics. One of the runners is a Jew named Harold Abrahams who uses his running to combat anti-Semitism and to fulfill his own compulsive need to win.

The other runner is a Scottish missionary named Eric Liddell. He looked at his quickness as a gift from God and his development of that talent as a religious act. He said: "God made me for a purpose, but he also made me fast. When I run, I can feel his pleasure."

When Eric Liddell found out that his heat in the 100 meter race was scheduled for a Sunday, he refused to run on the Sabbath in spite of great pressure and ridicule. On Monday, Liddell entered another race—the 400 meter event—for which he had not trained. Before the race, a stranger gave him a piece of paper on which was written a line from 1 Samuel 2:30: "I will honor those who honor me."

Liddell had put his faith in God to enter this race and the note only served to confirm it. He won the gold medal in that race and set a new world's record in doing so.

Today's gospel tells another story of extraordinary faith. When Jesus comes to save a centurion's servant who was dying, the centurion sends some friends to say to Jesus: "Lord, I am not worthy to have you under my roof. But give the word and let my servant be cured."

Jesus is amazed at the centurion's faith, praises him in front of the crowd, and cures his servant instantly from a distance.

This was a significant story for the early Church because it signaled that non-Jews were worthy to enter the kingdom of God, and because it showed that Jesus could exercise his power without being physically present. In a sense, that is the essence of Christian faith—to believe in Jesus without seeing him, to affirm his power without feeling his physical presence.

No one knew this better than Helen Keller when she wrote that she thanked God every day for setting in her darkness the lamp of faith as a source of strength and as a guide. Eric Liddell knew this too when he seemed to stand alone on the track because of his religious convictions, yet believed in his heart that the Lord's power would be with him.

We have our own opportunities to practice this kind of faith.

Maybe we've been coasting along for years in good health and suddenly find ourselves facing open heart surgery or cancer tests. The nearness of God is not so real anymore.

Perhaps our family life, which had been a happy one up until now, is being torn apart by an alcohol or drug problem. "Where is God now?" we question.

Possibly we've enjoyed a work situation that had been stable and secure, and now unexpectedly find ourselves laid off or even unemployed. The apparent absence of God becomes disturbing.

Death sometimes takes away a loved one whose presence meant very much to us. With that person's departure, God too seems to have disappeared.

These are times when we can say with the centurion that we are not worthy of Christ's presence, yet ask him in faith to say but a word to bless us in some way: a word of encouragement to rally us, a word of hope to reassure us, a word of promise to inspire us.

With faith we can face any future, however bleak, and exclaim with the poet William Blake:

Bring me my Bow of burning gold:
Bring me my Arrows of desire:
Bring me my Spear: O clouds unfold!
Bring me my Chariot of Fire.

10th Sunday of the Year          1 K 17:17-24  Lk 7:11-17

## WIDOWS AND ONLY SONS

The movie entitled *Witness* tells the story of an Amish widow and her 5-year-old son. The little boy witnesses a murder committed by a police officer and becomes a murder target himself in a police cover-up.

Throughout this fast-paced movie of intrigue, suspense and narrow escapes, we share in the worries and fears of the Amish widow trying to protect her only son. We find our hearts reaching out with compassion toward her: "Good Lord," we pray, "she's already lost her husband. Don't let any harm come to her little boy now."

These feelings aroused in our hearts by the movie *Witness* are the same as those felt by Elijah and Jesus in today's readings. In parallel stories, both Elijah and Jesus encounter widows who have just lost their only sons. The hearts of Elijah and Jesus are moved with pity, and they bring the sons back to life.

To appreciate the impact of these miracles, we must recall that in the Bible the widow was a frequent symbol of the poor and the helpless. In biblical times there was no job market for women, nor was there any welfare system as we know today.

So when Elijah and Jesus come across a widow who has lost not only her husband (which is bad enough), but also (to make matters worse) her only son, they meet someone who is indeed the poorest of the poor in their time. So they are moved with compassion to restore the women's sons.

Commentator William Barclay remarks that, on the one hand, these stories are unparalleled for their pathos and poignancy in presenting human misery. But, on the other hand, they are overpowering for their revelations of divine mercy.

If we focus on just the gospel story, we find that it is highly symbolic.

First, the two crowds which converge. One crowd is a funeral procession following a dead man. The other crowd is a group of disciples following Jesus, the Lord of life.

For a moment, life triumphs over death, a foreshadowing of the more definitive triumph that will take place later when Jesus himself will be raised from the dead once and for all.

Second, in the opening episode of this chapter, Jesus healed a centurion's servant who was sick *to* the point of death. In today's episode, Jesus restores a young man who had passed *beyond* the point of death.

By putting these two stories together consecutively, Luke is making a significant statement: no suffering is beyond God's power to relieve; no death is beyond God's power to conquer.

Third, there is the element of faith. In previous miracle stories, like that of the centurion's servant, faith was at work in the recipients beforehand. But here, in the widow of Naim story, faith is neither demanded nor sought beforehand. Instead, it is given as a gift afterwards. The whole incident is charged with God's gracious and unconditional love.

Is this not the way God intervenes sometimes in our lives, too, when we've done nothing to earn or merit his amazing grace? Even when he's uninvited, he sometimes invades the ground of our being and brings unexpected blessings for us.

Inspiring as the widow of Naim story is, it still leaves some of us asking: "If God is so good, why didn't he bring back to life my husband or wife when they passed away? Why didn't he restore my son or daughter when they died?"

Perhaps the only answer is: The Lord did not raise them from the dead when we wanted—but one day, in his own time, he will.

What is needed from us are not more questions, but silence in the presence of God; not more demands or ultimatums, but trust as we place our destiny in his hands.

11th Sunday of the Year                    2 S 12:7-10, 13   Lk 7:36-50

## FORGIVENESS STORIES

In the movie *Under the Volcano*, Albert Finney plays a British diplomat in South America. His personal life and career have been on a steady downgrade. He is an alcoholic, his wife has left him and he's been assigned to a remote diplomatic office.

His wife returns to help him salvage his life before he destroys himself completely. But the diplomat comes to a tragic end, not because he dies an alcoholic at the hands of violent men, but because he dies without being able to accept his wife's loving forgiveness or to forgive himself.

Forgiveness is the subject of today's readings from Scripture. But unlike the movie *Under the Volcano* where forgiveness is refused, these readings are stories of forgiveness received.

The Old Testament reading tells how Nathan confronts King David with his sins of adultery and murder. David acknowledges his guilt and is then forgiven by God.

In the gospel a woman—the town sinner, so to speak—dares to approach Jesus at a dinner. With profound and sincere gestures she acts out her contrition. After telling the host Simon a short parable about forgiveness and gratitude, Jesus tells the woman that her many sins are forgiven because of her faith and love.

These biblical texts abound with contrasts.

First, King David acts like a villain, but with God's forgiveness he recovers his lost virtue. His fall occasions a greater fidelity.

Second, in the gospel, Simon the Pharisee sees himself as a self-styled saint; but in fact he is a sinner who needs to be forgiven for pride and a sense of superiority. In the eyes of all the townsfolk, the woman is one of their worst sinners—but under the gaze of the Lord, she is also one of their greatest lovers.

Third, according to his parable, Jesus implies that both Simon and the woman are forgiven—but while the woman accepts the gift, Simon does not.

Fourth, as the host, Simon should have shown more hospitality to our Lord who was his guest. By contrast the repentant woman, who was a complete stranger to Jesus, overwhelms him with affection.

Simon seems to hold back and never gets close to Jesus, or to anyone else for that matter. The woman is not afraid to express her feelings and outdoes herself in repentance, just as she had outdone herself in sinfulness before.

Fifth, the use of oil is pivotal to the story. Simon withheld from Jesus an anointing with even a little ordinary olive oil. The sinful woman literally poured out on Jesus a whole vase of expensive perfumed oil—a symbol of both the vastness of her love and of the forgiveness she received.

How do we face our own sinfulness and accept forgiveness? Unless we honestly confess our sins we miss out on the miracle of God's mercy, the way Simon the Pharisee did. Unless we open our hearts to accept the gift of forgiveness from God, from others and ourselves, we can waste a lifetime the way the diplomat did in the movie *Under the Volcano*.

But if we are man enough like David or woman enough like the gospel sinner to confess our sins and seek forgiveness, then Christ can do great things for us. He can transform our vices into virtues, make guilt give way to gladness and change dead ends into new beginnings.

The Lord's kingdom does not consist of people who have never sinned, but of people who have sinned and been forgiven; of people who have failed, even grievously, yet found grace.

So we don't have to pretend to be perfect as Simon did. All we have to do is place ourselves at the feet of Jesus as the penitent woman did and experience the pardon and peace of his unconditional love.


12th Sunday of the Year                           Zc 12:10-11   Lk 9:18-24

# SUFFERING AND SUCCESS

In recent years several movies have reflected the connection that exists between suffering and success. The *Rocky* series about boxing, *Chariots of Fire* about track, and *Vision Quest* about wrestling illustrate how pain is the price an athlete has to pay for victory.

We get the same message from television, too. *Paper Chase* about lawyers, *St. Elsewhere* about doctors, and *Fame* about theater performers emphasize how long hours of study and training are necessary to become a true professional.

In other words, the common athletic locker room slogan of "No pain, no gain" fits equally well in libraries, labs and dressing rooms. The message is the same—without self-discipline there can be no development; without self-denial, no dedication; without some suffering, no success.

A similar message appears in today's readings.

By way of prophecy, the Old Testament reading from Zechariah pictures God pouring out on the house of David a spirit of grace but in a situation of suffering: "They will look on the one whom they have pierced; they will mourn for him as for an only son."

In the gospel Jesus proclaims that he will fulfill this messianic prophecy by enduring suffering, rejection and death before he is raised up in triumph. Jesus then goes on to spell out for us a definition of discipleship. If we want to be his disciples, then we must deny ourselves, take up our cross each day and follow in his steps.

There are two kinds of suffering in discipleship.

The first kind is shown in the movies and television programs mentioned earlier—suffering we take on ourselves in the form of self-denial, discipline and training. The purpose of this type of suffering is not to experience pain or discomfort, but to prepare ourselves for some kind of worthwhile performance or achievement.

We do the same in our spiritual life. Whenever we voluntarily fast, pray or give alms, we deny ourselves some pleasure or material thing in order to explore our own inner powers and to experience the presence of God.

The second kind of suffering in discipleship is the kind that happens to us beyond our control, in spite of our best efforts. Catching the flu, getting hit by a reckless driver or being laid off from our job are just a few examples of this kind of suffering.

Such suffering seems useless and senseless to us. Its happening seems to contradict our idea of a God who is all good and just. It was the kind of suffering that Jesus went through during his passion and death.

And yet, somehow, even this kind of suffering can serve a higher purpose. We have within us the capacity to draw good out of evil, to convert losses into gains and to find meaning amidst pain.

God our Father did this when he raised Jesus from the dead to new life. He continues to do this in and through us every time we refuse to indulge in self-pity when we're hurting and reach out to help others; or deny ourselves the luxury of quitting and take up our cross with courage; or weather the darkness of doubt and despair and renew our faith and hope.

Once we decide to follow Jesus as disciples, we are destined to share in his sufferings, but only that we might save ourselves in the process and also share in his glory.

13th Sunday of the Year  1 K 19:16, 19-21   Lk 9:51-62

# WORLD CLASS

In a recent issue of *Sports Illustrated*, there was an article on Bela Karolyi, a Rumanian gymnastic coach. He was once the coach of the national Rumanian team that produced the world and Olympic champion Nadia Comaneci.

In 1981 Bela Karolyi defected to the U.S. with a suitcase, leaving everything else behind including his Mercedes. Today he trains more than 300 youth at his Sundance Athletic Club in Houston.

To attain world class status in gymnastics the way Nadia Comaneci did, an athlete must become a disciple of a master like Bela Karolyi. First, she must sacrifice her own personal comfort and follow a strenuous training program. Second, she must reorder her priorities, attach supreme importance to gymnastics and subordinate everything else to it. Third, she must make a single-minded commitment to persevere in spite of difficulties and disappointments.

These same three elements of discipleship are required of our Lord's followers in today's gospel. In responding to three individuals who offer to become his disciples, Jesus talks about three conditions:

First, not having a place to lay one's head. In other words, a willingness to make sacrifices with little concern for personal comfort.

Second, leaving the dead to bury the dead, even in one's own family. In other words, giving the kingdom of God absolute priority, especially when conflicts of interest arise.

Third, putting one's hand to the plow without looking back. In other words, a disciple must make an unswerving commitment to his mission.

If such is the case, who of us is fit to be a follower of Christ? Who of us would dare to be one of his disciples? The answer is, "All of us." If we understand these three conditions correctly, every one of us is destined to this kind of discipleship.

In his commentary on this gospel, Scripture scholar Carroll Stuhlmueller claims that the sayings of Jesus must be understood in the Semitic background of contrast and exaggeration. Jesus was deliberately trying to startle us, to stir up thought, to compel us to count the cost of committing ourselves to his cause—the kingdom of God.

Or, to put it another way, Jesus is warning us against cheap grace. Our call to discipleship demands that we make difficult choices—not always between good and evil, but between the good and the best; not always without ambiguity, but with the risk of faith.

First, there are times when we have to sacrifice our own personal comfort in order to minister to the sick, visit the elderly, share with the poor or listen to the lonely.

Second, there are times when we have to reorder our priorities and duties in order to allot time for meditation as well as for our recreation, spend time with our family as well as with our work, or give time to parish programs as well as to our own personal projects.

Third, there are times when we need single-minded dedication to persevere in the face of obstacles in order to keep our hand to the plow of chastity when the public promotes pornography, remain faithful to our marriage promises when divorce would be an easy way out, and not look back in pushing ahead for a Constitutional Amendment to protect the unborn.

None of us will probably ever become a world-class gymnast—even under a master like Bela Karolyi. But all of us can become world-class Christians by firmly resolving to follow Jesus—not only when we have plenty, but even in poverty; not only when we feel like it, but even when all we have is faith to go on; not only to Jerusalem, but even as far as Calvary.

14th Sunday of the Year                    Is 66:10-14    Lk 10:1-12, 17-20

## SUPERSTARS

What is it that makes an athlete a superstar? What is it that puts an athlete in a class by himself or herself? Perhaps what makes a superstar shine more brightly than others is his or her confidence and capacity to perform consistently with excellence, especially in pressure situations.

One thinks, for example, of the great quarterbacks in pro football, of men like Joe Montana, who with two minutes left in a game can lead his team downfield to snatch a victory out of the clutches of defeat.

When the going gets tough you want superstars like Wade Boggs in the batter's box in the bottom of the ninth inning, or Larry Bird with the basketball in the final seconds of overtime.

When the pressure is the greatest, you can almost sense that a superstar like Jack Nicklaus will sink that long putt on the 18th green, or that Wayne Gretzky will put the puck in the net in the last minute of play.

Now what is true of superstars in sports is also true of saints in the Christian life. They have the confidence and the capacity to come through when the pressure is the greatest. Today's readings from Scripture show why.

In the first reading from Isaiah, the Chosen People are in exile and yet the prophet tells them to exult: "Rejoice, Jerusalem, be glad for her . . . all you who mourned her . . . Now towards her I send flowing peace, like a river . . . To his servants Yahweh will reveal his hand."

In the gospel Jesus sends 72 of his disciples on a mission to proclaim his peace, to heal in his name and to announce the here and now presence of the kingdom of God. When the 72 come back rejoicing, Jesus says to them, "Yes, I have given you power to tread underfoot serpents and scorpions and the whole strength of the enemy."

In explaining this gospel passage, Fr. Laurence Brett writes in *Share the Word*:

> Ultimately, despite rejection, the disciples' mission will be victorious. Why? Because their master has empowered them. Jesus watched Satan fall; they watch demons fall.

In other words, the ultimate triumph of the kingdom is assured. The decisive victory has already been accomplished through the death and resurrection of Christ. It only remains to be revealed and worked out in our own human history.

That is why we can be confident! We have been empowered by the Lord to perform with poise under pressure.

Jesus sends us with the command: "Be on your way. Go into your homes and parish churches, your studios and theaters, and there proclaim my peace, heal in my name and make my presence felt."

"I have given you power," Jesus says, "to tread on the forces of the enemy. There is no loss from which you cannot recover; no setback from which you may not start again; no hurt you've experienced that cannot be healed."

What confidence we should have then in Isaiah's vision of how the Lord can transform our sorrow into joy, our slavery into freedom and our barrenness into fruitfulness!

What strength we should feel from our Lord's promises in the gospel! With his power we can be steadfast in suffering, keep calm in crises and remain undaunted by disappointment.

Like superstars in sports we can come through under pressure because the Lord is with us. Because of his presence, no failure need ever be final and no sin need ever be the last word to our story. Even death cannot destroy us completely, because our names are written in the kingdom of heaven.


15th Sunday of the Year                                    Dt 30:10-14   Lk 10:25-37

## THE GOOD SAMARITAN

In the movie *Limelight*, Charlie Chaplin is Calvero, an aging vaudeville performer, and Claire Bloom is Thereza, a suicide-prone ballerina. In his prime, Calvero was a famous comedian—but now in his decline, coupled with his drinking problem, he bores the audience.

As Calvero staggers home one night, he comes upon Thereza trying to commit suicide. He rescues her and allows her to share his apartment to recuperate. They begin a platonic relationship.

Calvero encourages Thereza to try ballet again. When she loses confidence on her opening night, Calvero forces her to go onstage. The strain is too much for the aging Calvero. He dies from a heart attack while Thereza pirouettes on the stage with renewed hope.

This touching story about a caring man is almost like a film version of our Lord's Good Samaritan parable. Both Calvero and the Good Samaritan were moved with compassion at the sight of someone half-dead, intervened to save them and then cared for them at their own expense.

To appreciate more our Lord's parable, we should recall how much the Jews and Samaritans hated each other for reasons of race, politics and religion. Today it would be like an Irish Catholic helping an Ulster Protestant or a black person assisting a member of the Ku Klux Klan.

In contrast to the Good Samaritan, the priest and the Levite both saw the beaten man, but passed by. If the man were dead and they touched him, then they would become ritually impure for temple worship. So it seems that they were more concerned about ritual than in taking a risk to help someone in dire need.

In what category do we fall? As we travel from our own Jerichos to Jerusalem how do we react to people in need? We are not talking about picking up hitchhikers or derelicts. No, we are talking about people in our own parish or place of work or neighborhood. We are talking especially about people in our own family or home, for Jericho to Jerusalem can be as far as from our bedroom to the kitchen.

Whenever we find people hurting in some way from illness or loneliness, poverty or senility, depression or rejection, we are forced to make a decision. We either look without compassion and pass by, or we are moved by love and offer to help.

In her reflections on this parable, Sr. Nadine Koza points out that too often we pass people by because we dislike, mistrust or feel prejudiced against them. But if we can search inside to touch our own woundedness, then we can see in the other's brokenness a reflection of our own and reach out to help them.

The clown Calvero and the Good Samaritan did this. They rejected all the reasons why they shouldn't get involved and risked responding for the only reason that really mattered: someone near was hurting like themselves and needed them.

Let us not line up with the lawyer in the gospel and ask the wrong question: "*Who* is my neighbor?" Instead, let us take our stance with Jesus and Calvero and ask "*How* can I be a neighbor?"

Let us not ask the wrong question as the priest and Levite did: "What will happen to *me* if I stop?" Instead, let us ask the question of the Good Samaritan: "What will happen to *him* if I don't stop?"

16th Sunday of the Year                Gn 18:1-10   Lk 10:38-42

# TENDER MERCIES

In the movie *Tender Mercies*, Robert Duvall is Mac Sledge, a washed-up country singer who is an alcoholic. Abandoned by a companion at a run-down motel along a desolate Texas highway, Mac pays for the room by going to work for Rosa Lee, a young widow who runs the motel.

Mac Sledge needs a steady job, and so Rosa Lee hires him to stay on as a handyman. Her only ultimatum is that he not drink while on the job.

Out there on the prairie, pumping gas or puttering around the grounds, with no one but the widow and her little boy for company, the broken-down Mac Sledge becomes whole again.

Nurtured by the *tender mercies* of Rosa Lee, Mac Sledge gradually quits drinking altogether, finds peace and falls in love with her. Rosa Lee's hospitality transforms his life in such a powerful way that he is literally reborn like the legendary Phoenix.

The virtue of hospitality is a central theme of today's readings.

In the first reading from Genesis, Abraham and Sarah welcome three strangers to their tent and afford them the customary desert amenities of shelter, water and food.

In the gospel, the sisters Martha and Mary welcome our Lord to their home. Martha busies herself with all the details of hospitality, while Mary entertains Jesus by sitting at his feet and listening to his words.

We are inclined to contrast the two sisters and characterize them as symbols of action as opposed to contemplation. However, we would be closer to the spirit of the gospel if we view their roles as completing one another—that is, as two different but complementary forms of hospitality.

Martha is the female counterpart of the Good Samaritan of last week's gospel. Her actions on behalf of Jesus her guest recall all the details of the Good Samaritan's care for the victim he found. Martha is indeed one who has gone and done the same. She is unselfishly and generously showing compassion to Jesus through her hospitality.

Mary anticipates next week's gospel. She is the female counterpart of the disciples who ask Jesus to teach them how to pray and then listen to his words of instruction. Mary, too, listens to our Lord's words. She understands that we do not live on bread alone, but on the word of God. Jesus approves her insight that the bread of his word is better nourishment than ordinary food.

So Martha and Mary are not in conflict in the way they welcome Jesus. Rather, they accompany each other by expressing their hospitality in different ways: Mary by being a listener; Martha by being a doer.

St. Basil the Great preached and practiced hospitality. In one of his sermons he said: "The Christian should offer his brethren simple and unpretentious hospitality." He founded an impressive village near Caesarea to provide lodging for pilgrims, orphans, aged people and the sick.

In the Eucharist, Christ welcomes us as guests and extends to us his hospitality. Like Mary he sits by us and listens—he shares with us the feelings of our hearts and the thoughts of our minds.

Like Martha and Abraham, Jesus does everything he can for his guests—he uplifts us with forgiveness, inspires us through Scripture and feeds us with the food of the Eucharist.

Through his hospitality Jesus shows *tender mercy* to us as weary travelers. Can we do the same for one another? Can we show *tender mercy* to fellow pilgrims on the road of life and invite people like Mac Sledge to heal their wounds, discover their best selves and experience God's blessings?

17th Sunday of the Year                                              Gn 18:20-32   Lk 11:1-13

## ASK, SEEK AND KNOCK

In Ingmar Bergman's film *The Seventh Seal*, a Knight returns from the Crusades and passes through a country plagued with the Black Death. The Knight is trying to catch up with God before Death catches up with him.

To stall for more time in his search for God, the Knight challenges Death to a game of chess. The Knight says to Death: "I want knowledge, not faith . . . I want God to stretch out his hand towards me, reveal himself and speak to me . . . Why should he hide himself in a mist of half-spoken promises and unseen parables? I call out to him in the dark but no one seems to be there.

Death responds, "Perhaps no one is there."

But the Knight remains undaunted in his search for God and meaning. He finds it in the simple and beautiful love between a young married couple and their child whose company he enjoys for a while. Before Death finally takes him, the Knight finds fulfillment for himself by delaying Death one more time to allow the family to escape safely.

*The Seventh Seal* gives us some insight about today's readings.

In the first reading we see Abraham bargaining as the Knight did, but this time it is with God.

Although the city of Sodom is doomed by God for its grave sins,

Abraham petitions him to spare the city if there are as few as ten just people there. He is persistent in prayer—although in the end, Sodom was found not to have even ten righteous people, and was destroyed.

In the gospel, Jesus teaches a parable about persistence in prayer and then adds these words of emphasis: "Ask and it will be given to you; seek, and you will find; knock, and the door will be opened to you."

If Jesus were to appear before us today, he might say further: "Ask, seek and knock the way the Knight did in Bergman's film or the way Abraham did in the Genesis story."

Christ's story and statements about persistence in prayer sound nice, but they don't square off with real life. All prayers are not answered. All kinds of good people ask for cures and don't receive them, seek justice and don't find it or knock for jobs and don't get them.

It might help us to understand that our Lord is trying to make only one point with his parable—namely, that we should be persistent in prayer. He even gives us reasons why: we have a loving Father who cares for us, listens to us and rejoices to give us what we truly need.

But Jesus also leaves a lot unsaid. He doesn't say that all our ills will be healed, or that all our problems will be solved, or that death will disappear. After all, we are still in our human condition and not in heaven.

But Jesus does say that we cannot ask, seek or knock in vain. In our troubles, pains and sorrows we will be given the Holy Spirit to support us, strengthen us and inspire us.

In his book *Our Prayer*, Louis Evely suggests how we can find meaning in every circumstance of our lives, even in tragedies. God does not cause them, but he shows us how to overcome them. Evely writes:

> God does not prevent disasters or death; he is with us in them. He offers us the grace to be happier poor than we would have been rich; to be happier in misfortune than when everything is going well.

So we should be persistent in prayer—not so much to persuade God about what we want—but to prepare ourselves to receive what we really need. We might want prosperity, success or health. But what we might really need is patience, wisdom and peace.

Ask for these things, and we will receive them. Seek after these higher gifts, and we will find them. Knock in faith for things that are of real value, and in fact they will be given to us.

18th Sunday of the Year    Ec 1:2; 2:21-23    Lk 12:13-21

# STOCKPILING

As a young man Bill Glass was an all-pro football player for the Detroit Lions and the Cleveland Browns. Today he is an evangelist who is an all-pro preacher of God's word.

In one of his talks, Bill Glass tells the story of a multi-millionaire Texas oil man. He wanted to be buried when he died in a solid gold, custom-made Cadillac surrounded by all his wealth.

At his funeral, a vast crowd assembled to pay their last respects. The dead man was dressed in his finest glittering apparel—the kind Liberace wore when he performed—and was propped up in the front seat of his golden Cadillac. As the car was lowered into the grave a young boy in the crowd said: "Man, that's really livin'!"

Bill Glass goes on to emphasize the point of his parable. What we often think of as "really livin' " is actually "really dyin'." What we often pursue under the illusion of a "full life" leads only to an "empty grave."

Today's readings say much the same thing.

In the first reading from the book of Ecclesiastes, the wise man ponders the vanity and futility of life: "For so it is that a man who has labored . . . must leave what is his own to someone who has not toiled for it at all . . . what does he gain for all the toil and strain that he has undergone?"

In the gospel, Jesus tells the parable of the rich man who built bigger barns to stock up his goods. Just when he figured that he was super-secure for the future, he died. Everything he stockpiled had to be left behind.

In his commentary on this parable, Fr. Carroll Stuhlmueller makes an interesting remark. He says that the man's sudden death is not really essential to the story. Even if the rich man had continued to live, he was already dead. The moment he became greedy, he died to the only kind of life worth living—a life of trust in God and sharing with others.

That is exactly the point Bill Glass was making. When we make possessions or pleasure or power our top priority instead of spiritual riches, we die to the joy of giving, the satisfaction of self-discipline and the happiness of sharing. When we devote all our time and energy to selfish pursuits, death merely discloses the opportunities we've wasted and our poverty of good works.

If we want to really live, now is the time to use our resources wisely and not save them foolishly. Now is the time to exercise our stewardship over God's gifts and not set them aside as if we owned the gifts.

Certainly we are not talking about *necessary savings* we need to educate our children or to provide for the security of our retirement. We are talking about *excessive savings* that reflect a lack of trust in God, a basic greed in our attitude and a callous heart to the poor.

It seems that when we have too much today, we hold a garage or yard sale. St. Leo the Great said:

> Extend to the poor a more open-handed generosity . . . In these acts of giving do not fear a lack of means. A generous spirit is itself great wealth . . . The giver should be free from anxiety and full of joy. His gain will be greatest when he keeps back least for himself.

In the Eucharist we have an example of giving and sharing. Christ did not institute the Eucharist to be stored up and left in our tabernacles. He gave us the Eucharist as food to be distributed and shared as a community.

Jesus challenges us to re-examine our priorities and the way we use our possessions. Instead of growing rich for ourselves, he invites us to grow rich in the sight of God.


19th Sunday of the Year                    Ws 18:6-9   Lk 12:35-40

## SUDDEN DEATH

The movie *West Side Story* is a modern version of Shakespeare's play *Romeo and Juliet*. The setting is New York City and the hero and heroine are Tony and Maria, two youths who belong to different ethnic groups at war with each other.

Nonetheless, Tony and Maria fall in love with each other. As the story reaches its climax, they are about to escape together from the hatred of the West Side when their dreams are destroyed by Tony's tragic death in a senseless fight.

Tony never expected that night to be his last. He was anticipating his marriage to Maria and the new life they would enjoy together. He had even borrowed money to get them started. Tony was making plans to live, not die.

But, as today's gospel points out, death often comes in sudden and unexpected ways. Jesus said to his disciples: "You too must stand ready, because the Son of Man is coming at an hour you do not expect."

According to William Barclay, Jesus' words have two senses. In the narrower sense they refer to his Second Coming at the end of the world. In the wider sense they refer to the time of our death when Jesus will summon us from life.

If we take Christ's words with respect to our own death, then they assume a note of urgency. Christ is warning us to be always prepared—to have our belts fastened and our lamps burning ready—like servants awaiting their master's return.

The note is one of urgency because we don't know how much time we have left. It might be very little, or it might be a lengthy period. We might die soon and suddenly as Tony did in *West Side Story* at a youthful age, or we might die much later and very slowly, as actor and dancer Fred Astaire did at age 88.

In either case, we have to be ready. Perhaps the best way to be always prepared is to live by the *as if* principle: to live *as if* the Lord were going to meet us today in death; *as if* this were the last day of our life; *as if* there were no tomorrow.

If we apply the *as if* principle, we are more likely to live with greater awareness and intensity, with greater urgency and vigor. For example, we will be more sensitive to the needs of people dearest to us and respond to fulfill those needs while there is still time. We will be more attuned to the opportunities that surround us and arouse ourselves to use them before they disappear forever.

After his wife's death, Thomas Carlyle wrote: "Oh, if I could see her once more to let her know that I always loved her. She never did know it."

Perhaps it was this experience of a lost opportunity that prompted Carlyle to write: "Our main business is not to see what lies dimly at a distance, but to do what lies clearly at hand."

We don't know the day or hour when the Lord will come for us or for our loved ones. So we have to live *as if* we were never to get another chance to do some good for someone; *as if* this were the last time they would hear us call them over the phone, visit them at home or write them a letter; *as if* this were our last chance to let them know that we truly care for them and are concerned about them.

The Son of Man will come when we least expect him. So we have to celebrate this Mass—to use the words of a plaque—"*as if* it were our first Mass; *as if* it were our last Mass; *as if* it were our only Mass."

If we pray every day with this sense of urgency, we will be ready for the Lord when he does come to welcome us to his heavenly banquet.


20th Sunday of the Year                                     Jr 38:4-6, 8-10   Lk 12:49-53

## A FIRE TO KINDLE

In June of 1968 Senator Robert F. Kennedy was assassinated in Los Angeles. According to his brother, Senator Edward M. Kennedy, what Bobby Kennedy stood for, lived for and died for was best summed up in a speech he made to the young people of South Africa in 1966.

In that speech, Robert Kennedy reflected on the evils of the world: discrimination and slavery, starvation and slaughter, poverty and repression. He asked, "What can one man or one woman do against such an enormous array of world ills?" He answered:

> Few of us will have the greatness to bend history itself, but each one of us can work to change a small portion of events, and in the sum total of all those acts will be written the history of this generation.

That is the way Robert Kennedy lived and died. In the words of his brother Edward Kennedy: "Bobby was simply a good and decent man, who saw wrong and tried to right it, saw suffering and tried to heal it, saw war and tried to stop it."

The life and death of Robert Kennedy bear some similarity to that of both Jeremiah and Jesus in today's readings. They too lived and died trying to change the course of human history by denouncing evil and doing good.

In the first reading, the prophet Jeremiah had appealed to his people to return to God to avoid a national disaster. For his efforts he is convicted as a traitor and thrown into a muddy cistern to die. This time he is saved from death through the intervention of an Ethiopian, but later he will be murdered by his own countrymen when his prophecies come true.

In the gospel, Jesus talks about his mission by using the metaphor of lighting a fire, and he refers to his passion by using the image of a baptism to be received. History repeats itself—like Jeremiah before him, Jesus dies a prophet's death in Jerusalem.

Jeremiah, Jesus and Robert Kennedy—all three were dedicated to doing good for their people; all three occasioned controversy and division; all three were martyred for their cause.

Can our call to Christian discipleship be any different? Can we look at the world's evils of brutality and violence, injustice and oppression, sensuality and greed, and not be inflamed by them?

Jeremiah, Jesus and Robert Kennedy were never content with the *status quo*. They were men of vision who saw how things should be. They were men of energy who acted to make them happen.

How then can we close our eyes and pretend that today's evils are invisible? How can we cling to our illusions of security and not reach out to touch someone who is hurting because of these evils?

We might say, "What difference will it make if I help one poor family when whole nations are starving? Or if I prevent one abortion when millions are performed every year? Or if I protest excessive government spending on nuclear arms when billions are spent anyway?"

Robert Kennedy answered this way:

> Each time a man stands up for an ideal, or acts to improve the lot of others, or strikes out against injustice, he sends forth a tiny ripple of hope. And crossing each other from a million different centers of energy and daring, those ripples build a current that can sweep down the mightiest walls of oppression and resistance.

All of us have been created by the divine spark to light a fire on the earth. Pray that we may have our Lord's desire to ignite that blaze by the way we live; that we may have Jeremiah's courage to fan that flame by the way we speak; that we may have Robert Kennedy's faith to spread that fire by the way we dream.

Robert Kennedy often said: "Some men see things as they are and say 'Why?' I dream of things that never were and say, 'Why not?' "

21st Sunday of the Year                                                      Is 66:18-21    Lk 13:22-30

# THE LAST WILL BE FIRST

Barbara Hutton, the Woolworth heiress, was known as the "poor little rich girl." Since her mother died when she was five, Barbara Hutton described her childhood as an unhappy one. She said, "Though I had millions of dollars, I had no mother and no home."

Nor was her adult life a very happy one. She was married seven times and was a princess three of those times. A virtual recluse, she died in 1979 at age 66. A newspaper article summed up her life with the words: "Barbara Hutton died unmarried and alone, a symbol of the cliché that money doesn't buy happiness."

By way of contrast, consider the life of Dorothy Day. She was known as "the mother of the faceless poor and of the city's offscouring." She always felt that she existed for a special purpose. She discovered that purpose when she became a Catholic at age 30 and dedicated her life to help the poor.

Dorothy Day founded and edited the *Catholic Worker* newspaper, went to prison as a suffragist and pacifist, and established farm communes and hospices for the dispossessed. When she died in 1980 at age 83, *Time* magazine called her a "secular saint."

Barbara Hutton and Dorothy Day illustrate somewhat the proverb cited by our Lord today: "There are those now last who will be first, and those now first who will be last."

On the one hand, during her lifetime Barbara Hutton had the first pick of almost anything she wanted because of her wealth—husbands, mansions, dresses, etc. But in the end, none of these things brought her happiness, fulfillment or peace.

On the other hand, Dorothy Day would probably come up last in those surveys that list the most beautiful women, the most famous women, the best dressed women, etc. But in the end, she was first in the hearts of the countless poor people whom she helped and, consequently, will take a first place in the kingdom of God.

But what about us who are neither first nor last when it comes to wealth, status or virtue? How do Christ's words apply to us who are in-between people? *The Interpreter's Bible* emphasizes four points in response to these questions.

First, the kingdom door is narrow. The door is open, but it is narrow. This means that we have to struggle strenuously to enter through it: we have to discipline ourselves, carry our crosses and develop our talents.

Second, the time is short. The door is open, but it will soon be closed for some of us. None of us will live here forever. Already the door is being closed on today's opportunities. We can't afford to waste the time we have left.

Third, there is no favoritism in the kingdom. People will enter from the East and West, from the North and South. People will come from the black and the white, the Democrats and the Republicans, the rich and the poor. All of us will sit down together at the feast in God's kingdom where there are no favorites.

Fourth, some reversals and surprises will occur. The first may be last, and the last may be first. Many of our expectations and calculations will be upended and overthrown. The poor may step ahead of the rich, the simple surpass the clever and the sinner outshine the pious.

We must not ask, then, irrelevant questions like *who* will get in or *how many* will enter. Christ challenges us to try our best to come in through the narrow door and to use wisely the little time we have left.

We should not preoccupy ourselves with foolish comparisons about who seems to be luckier or has it easier than ourselves. Such speculations are useless, for God has no favorites. He is an equal-opportunity God.

What does it take to convince us that, like Dorothy Day, we are destined for greatness? We might be surprised to discover one day that our cross was really our crown, that our agony was really our glory and that our last place was really a first place.


22nd Sunday of the Year                          Si 3:17-18, 20, 28-29   Lk 14:1, 7-14

# HUMILITY

Dr. Richard Evans is a psychologist at the University of Houston who has developed an interesting series of films. They consist of interviews Evans did with some of the great leaders in the fields of psychology and psychiatry—people like Carl Jung, Eric Fromm, Erik Erikson, Carl Rogers, B.F. Skinner and Jean Piaget.

Surprisingly, the major thing Evans learned from these great figures was the need for humility:

> What these great thinkers profess to know and their assessment of it is usually rather humble. Some people tend to oversell what psychology and psychiatry can do to help people solve their problems. Not so with the really great personages in these fields. The really important people have a more modest view of what they have contributed, much less what the field has contributed in general.

Humility is a mark of all truly great people. The first reading from Sirach states: "Humble yourself the more, the greater you are, and you will find favor with God."

Humility is a quality Jesus himself has. In Matthew's gospel he says: "Learn of me, for I am gentle and humble of heart" (Mt 11:29). In today's gospel from Luke he says: "Everyone who exalts himself will be humbled, and he who humbles himself will be exalted."

The virtue of humility has fallen on hard times in our day. Books abound promoting aggressive behavior, assertive training and affirmative action. In today's marketplace humility is not what we would call the "in-thing" that turns people on.

And yet humility remains at the root of the Christian life. It ranks right up there with the great gospel reversals: to lose one's life is to find it; the last shall be first; the humble shall be exalted.

The reason for this dilemma is that humility is misunderstood. The humility which the world despises and rightly rejects is a pseudo-humility. A pseudo-humility is pretentious self-effacement and a phony denial of our gifts. It is easily seen in the award winner who mouths, "I really don't deserve this award, but . . ." or in the habitual drunk who says, "I'm no good," because it gives him an excuse for not changing his ways.

By way of contrast, authentic Christian humility is an honest recognition of our true status before God.

On the one hand, humility is a joyful acceptance of our gifts, talents and abilities as coming from God. It inspires us to use these blessings for our own enrichment and for God's glory.

On the other hand, genuine humility does not deny our human limitations and weaknesses. It enables us to make a candid admission that we are sinners, but sinners who have been forgiven and will continue to need forgiveness.

In other words, humble people can look at both the heights and the depths of their personalities without becoming proud over the one, or discouraged by the other. This is the secret of truly great people.

Their humility empowers them to take on difficult challenges, explore the unknown and attempt what seems impossible because they are aware of their own inner resources and strengths. Their humility also allows them to accept their mistakes, admit their limitations and even laugh at their failures.

A healthy sense of humor is closer to humility than serious self-depreciation. Pope John XXIII once remarked: "Anybody can be pope; the proof of this is that I have become pope."

If we seek to be truly great, then we have to become humble. St. Augustine says:

> Do you wish to raise yourself? Begin by humbling yourself. Are you dreaming of building an edifice that will tower to the skies? Begin by laying the foundation of humility.

23rd Sunday of the Year          Ws 9:13-18   Lk 14:25-33

## BRIDGE-BUILDING

In the early 1980's, two famous bridges had anniversaries. In November of 1982, festivities marked the 25th anniversary of the opening of the Mackinac Bridge in northern Michigan. In May of 1983, there was a celebration to mark the 100th anniversary of the Brooklyn Bridge.

Both bridges are regarded as remarkable accomplishments for the particular eras in which they were constructed. The Mackinac Bridge and the Brooklyn Bridge stand as monuments to excellence in design, architecture and engineering.

By contrast, the Zilwaukee Bridge near Saginaw, Michigan is becoming infamous for faulty design, engineering blunders and excessive cost. If the historical Jesus were with us today, he would probably use the Zilwaukee Bridge to illustrate the first of his twin parables in today's gospel.

We can imagine Jesus saying: "If one of you decides to build a

Zilwaukee Bridge, would you not first sit down to examine the blueprints, calculate your costs and hire the best engineers? Wouldn't you do that for fear of laying the foundation and then not being able to complete the work; at which all who saw it would jeer at you, saying, 'That man began to build what he could not finish.' "

Of course, Jesus would not be giving a lecture on bridge-building to us. Instead he would be telling us something about discipleship. The point of the parables in today's gospel is to make us realize that becoming a disciple of Jesus is not something we do because of a sudden whim or flight of fancy.

Discipleship is a serious commitment that requires much thought and careful deliberation. Becoming a follower of Christ is the most important enterprise we will ever undertake. Consequently, it requires at least as much consideration as we would give to any important business or political decision.

Discipleship is a venture that demands total dedication. Everything else must become secondary if Jesus is to be the Lord of our life. When Jesus says that we must *hate* our families, he is using a Semitic expression meaning that we must *prefer* him above anyone else in our life. If a conflict of interest arises, a disciple will prefer to follow Jesus and not let family ties or work or leisure activities interfere.

We have to count the cost before we commit ourselves to accompany Jesus on his journey to Jerusalem, where he will die and rise. If we're unwilling to give up some sinful situation, or change a lifestyle that contradicts the gospel, or sacrifice our own convenience to love our neighbor, then we can't call ourselves serious disciples.

We might be superficial disciples who hang around Jesus hoping to catch some of his glory, but we're not serious disciples who are devoted and loyal enough to carry the cross after him.

Serious disciples are ready to renounce all their possessions should that be required by the Lord. They are willing to surrender their home, health, freedom, yes, even their loved ones, should that be the price they have to pay to follow Jesus.

Thank the Lord for again giving us an invitation to become true disciples. Praise him for giving us not only the inspiration to start our own journey to Jerusalem with him, but also the resolution to finish that journey regardless of what it may cost.

We may never be bridge-builders. But we can all be builders of the kingdom of God through our discipleship.

Moreover, we can be confident that whatever it costs us is nothing compared to the glory that will be ours in the resurrection. We can expect that whatever good work the Lord begins through us will be brought to completion by him.

24th Sunday of the Year                     Ex 32:7-11, 13-14   Lk 15:1-10

## LOST SHEEP AND COINS

In her novel *Five for Sorrow, Ten for Joy*, author Rumer Godden tells an intriguing tale. The heroine of the story is Lise, an English army girl who falls upon hard times and becomes a prostitute after the liberation of Paris in World War II.

Within a short time, she becomes the leading madame in one of Paris' smartest brothels owned by a man named Patrice. But Patrice soon tires of Madame Lise as his mistress, and so she is humiliated.

In trying to help a younger prostitute escape from the same fate she suffered, Lise shoots and kills Patrice. So she is sent to prison where she meets the French Dominican Sisters of Béthanie.

This is a community dedicated to serving whores, drug addicts and vagrants; some of the sisters were once themselves such unfortunates. Lise becomes one of the Sisters of Béthanie.

Sister Lise is a prototype of the lost sheep and lost coin in today's twin parables. She was wayward and lost, but through the Dominican Sisters of Béthanie our Lord went searching for her. And when he found her he embraced her, took her in his arms and invited her to become his spouse, a nun.

Who of us would deny that there was more joy in heaven and on earth when Jesus found Lise, than over ninety-nine of us who have never been lost that way? Does this mean God loves the ninety-nine less? No, just as parents do not love their other children less when a particular child is sick and needs to be lavished with more love for the time being.

Our Lord's two stories are so simple that it is easy to miss how sublime they are, too. In his book *Rediscovering the Parables*, Joachim Jeremias calls our attention to some of their significant details.

First, *the chief actors* in each story. A shepherd was reckoned among the "sinners" because he was suspected of driving his flocks into foreign fields and embezzling the profits. A woman was considered a second-class citizen, the mere property of man.

What a revolutionary move on Jesus' part to use them to play the role of God in his parables! It's as if he said, "Do you want to know what God is like? Then look at the shepherd or the woman in my story."

Second, *the value of what was lost*. One sheep did not cost much, but it was helpless to find its own way back and would eventually starve or be killed by a predator. The lost coin in the other story may have been part of the woman's dowry, representing her most precious possession and future security.

For us the sheep and the coin denote our unique worth as individuals in the sight of God. Society may dehumanize us, count us like a digit and reduce us to anonymity, but never God. We are always special, precious and of supreme value in his eyes.

Third, *the intensity of the search*. With unwearying persistence the shepherd pursues the wandering sheep through cliffs and crags until he finds it. The woman lights a candle and relentlessly sweeps her house until she recovers her precious coin.

No matter how far we fall or how far we wander, God never gives up on us. He searches for us with steadfast tenacity until he finds us.

Finally, *the joy of finding what was lost*. The expressions, "there is joy in heaven" and "there is joy among the angels," are both paraphrases for the unutterable divine name. In other words, *God* is the one who rejoices when the lost are found and sinners repent.

Our God is a God who celebrates when sinners are saved, delights when we do the right thing and finds joy in being generous with his mercy. Lise learned this late in life. When will we learn this and live by it?

25th Sunday of the Year                    Am 8:4-7   Lk 16:1-13

# MONEY-MAKERS

When her husband Ray Kroc died in 1984, Joan Kroc was left with an estimated $700 million. Her wealth included an 8.7-percent share of the common stock of the McDonald's food empire and full ownership of the San Diego Padres baseball franchise.

Since that time this fast-food empress has become a woman of many causes. Besides giving sizable donations to nuclear-disarmament groups, the San Diego zoo, St. Jude Children's Hospital in Memphis and the American Red Cross for African famine relief, Joan Kroc has also been a steady supporter of the arts, alcohol and drug rehabilitation, medical research, wildlife preservation and programs to combat child abuse.

Some skeptics dismiss her as a jet-set do-gooder, but close friends say that she becomes personally involved in many of the causes she supports.

Today's readings from Scripture seem to be a blueprint for Joan Kroc's use of money. She is the antithesis of the rich decried by the prophet Amos for trampling on the needy and taking unfair advantage of the poor.

The gospel reading is a collection of three separate statements Jesus made about money and material things, which Joan Kroc seems to have taken to heart.

The first statement Jesus made was: "Use money, tainted as it is, to win you friends, and thus make sure that when it fails you, they will welcome you into the tents of eternity."

On the one hand, Jesus is warning us about the temporary nature of wealth, either because we can lose it while we are still living, or because we have to leave it for others when we die.

On the other hand, Jesus is suggesting how to use our wealth wisely. If we give to the poor, then they will become our friends, both here on earth now and in heaven later. Jesus is not recommending a calculated charity, but a life of compassion and sharing with a view to eternity.

His second statement is about material things: "The man who can be trusted in little things can be trusted in great." While earthly objects have their own intrinsic value, they are not as great as the rewards of heaven. Yet it is how we use the little things of earth now that will determine our greater rewards in heaven later.

One immediate application of this point of view is our problem of environmental pollution. If we cannot learn to respect and take care of things like water, air and soil, how can we expect to be entrusted with the greater things of the kingdom where there will be a new heaven and a new earth?

Our Lord's third statement is: "No man can serve two masters. You cannot serve both God and money." Jesus is insisting on total dedication.

We cannot be completely committed to the cause of Christ, and at the same time be excessively concerned about making money.

We must not interpret this to mean that we should scorn the making of money. It is a caution not to become overanxious about making money. Actually, Jesus admired the skill and ingenuity of certain money-makers. His parable about the unjust steward is an example of this. What Jesus despised in financial matters was the attitude of greed and selfishness.

Consequently, our Lord expects us to be dedicated wage earners, but in subordination to the demands of his gospel teachings about sharing with the poor, keeping an eye on eternity and making him the master of our life.

26th Sunday of the Year                                      Am 6:1, 4-7   Lk 16:19-31

## DEAR ABBY

The "Dear Abby" column once received a letter from a 15-year-old girl which read as follows:

> Dear Abby: Happiness is not having your parents scold you if you come home late, having your own bedroom, and getting the telephone call you've been hoping for. Happiness is belonging to a popular group, being dressed as well as anybody, and having a lot of spending money. Happiness is something I don't have. "15 and Unhappy."

Shortly after the letter was published, "Dear Abby" received a reply from a 13-year-old girl who wrote:

> Dear Abby: Happiness is being able to walk and talk, to see and hear. Unhappiness is reading a letter from a 15-year-old girl who can do all four things and still says she isn't happy. I can talk, I can see, I can hear. But I can't walk. "13 and Happy."

These letters reflect two different points of view on happiness. Today's gospel parable does the same.

One of the characters is a rich man who believed that happiness is wealth, expensive clothing and sumptuous meals. If the parable were told by our Lord today, he might describe the man in terms of American Express credit cards, Cadillac cars and Cutty Sark Scotch.

The other character is a poor man named Lazarus, a beggar who is sick with sores and starving. If he were here today, Jesus might describe him as a refugee from Southeast Asia, a migrant worker from Latin America or an unemployed parishioner.

The parable continues with a sudden shift in scenes. Both the rich man and Lazarus have died. Their fortunes are completely reversed. Lazarus is now the one enjoying the higher honors, symbolized by the bosom of Abraham—while the rich man is suffering in torment, symbolized by the flames.

Since his own fate is fixed, the rich man makes a passionate appeal to send someone from the dead to warn his five brothers, but to no avail. Abraham says to him: "If they will not listen either to Moses or to the prophets, they will not be convinced even if someone should rise from the dead."

In his commentary on this parable, Joachim Jeremias says some things about what the parable is *not*. Although Jesus uses images that were popular in his time, his parable is not a teaching about life after death.

In addition, even though he contrasts the final destiny of a rich man and a poor man, his story is not a condemnation of wealth in itself, nor an approval of poverty in itself. If we react to the story by cheering for the poor man Lazarus and booing the rich man, we miss the point.

The point of the parable is the outlook we have on happiness. Happiness is not guaranteed by what we *have*, however much that may be, nor is happiness beyond our reach because of what we *don't have*.

Happiness consists in experiencing God present in our own lives—in good times and in bad times; amidst plenty and amidst poverty. Happiness means listening to God's word—as spoken through the Old Testament prophets like Moses; as spoken in the New Testament through his own Son Jesus; as spoken in our own time through one another.

Happiness is found in helping the poor lying at our gate: by showing compassion to the widowed and divorced; by caring for the aged and handicapped; by welcoming the lonely and depressed.

During this liturgy, pray that we may not make ourselves unhappy by being selfish, uncaring and insensitive. Ask the Father to help us to be happy by seeing his gifts surrounding us and by sharing these gifts with the poor.

27th Sunday of the Year                    Hab 1:2-3; 2:2-4   Lk 17:5-10

## FAITH

Not since the legendary Caruso has an opera personality had such charisma as tenor Luciano Pavarotti. In his autobiography, *Pavarotti: My Own Story*, he describes how he was trained by a great master, Arrigo Pola. "Everything Pola asked me to do, I did—day after day, blindly. For six months we did nothing but vocalize and work on vowels."

Pavarotti worked hard under Pola for two and a half years, and then worked just as hard under Maestro Ettore Campogalliani for another five years. Finally, after putting so much faith and trust in his mentors, Pavarotti made a breakthrough at a concert in Salsomaggiore where he thrilled the audience and was catapulted into fame.

This story about faith and trust leads us into today's readings which focus on the same themes.

The first reading starts with a protest by the prophet Habakkuk about human violence and misery. It ends with God's promise to right these wrongs in his own time. In the meantime, we must live by faith.

The gospel gives us one of the best examples of prayer in all Scripture, when the apostles ask Jesus to increase their faith. Pleased with their request, our Lord seems to say: "I'm glad you asked for an increase of faith. Because if you had faith even the size of a tiny mustard seed, you would have power to command trees to be uprooted and transplanted into the sea."

*The Jerome Biblical Commentary* interprets our Lord's words as an acknowledgment that faith is indeed a key factor in our lives, but also as a caution that it is the *quality* rather than the *quantity* of faith that needs to be increased.

That is why Jesus compares faith to a tiny mustard seed—a living thing whose power does not depend on its size, but on its life principle hidden deep within itself.

Unless we understand this distinction, we run the risk of deluding ourselves. We can easily end up thinking that the more prayers we say, the more faith we have; or the more good works we do, the stronger our faith becomes.

Multiplying prayers and good works, as if faith were some kind of spiritual stockpile, is to miss the meaning of faith. Faith is more like life itself—something that can grow in a qualitative sense and become deeper, richer and more fruitful.

Jesus himself never defined faith in the gospels. But from all he said about it, we might define it as an unconditional acceptance of Jesus as the Son of God. We have faith, then, if we believe in the words Jesus spoke and in the power he possesses.

It does not follow that faith will give us power to literally move trees. But faith will give us power to cope with difficulties, overcome obstacles and attempt great things for the Lord.

As Luciano Pavarotti put his trust in his master teacher, we too will put all our trust in our mentor, the Lord Jesus. We may not understand why the Lord allows some things to happen to us, but we will still put our faith in him.

We may not understand why the Lord demands that we let go of certain things, but we will still trust in him and accept his discipline. We may not understand why he invites us to take on new challenges, but we will still believe in him and say "Yes" to the challenges.

May the Lord increase this kind of faith is us, so that even though it be like a tiny mustard seed, its power will penetrate our whole being and through us permeate the whole world.

28th Sunday of the Year　　　　　　　　　　　　　2 K 5:14-17　　Lk 17:11-19

# GRATITUDE

In 1976 Louise Fletcher was awarded an Oscar for best actress for her role as Nurse Ratched in the movie *One Flew Over the Cuckoo's Nest*. She had given up acting for eleven years to raise her children before she won that role after five big-name actresses had turned it down.

In accepting her Academy Award, Louise Fletcher did a very dramatic thing. With her voice breaking with emotion she faced a national television audience and said: "For my mother and my father, I want to say thank you for teaching me to have a dream. You are seeing my dream come true."

Louise Fletcher delivered the message in sign language at the same time, because both of her parents are deaf mutes and were watching from their home in Alabama.

This touching story about gratitude is reflected in today's readings from Scripture.

In the first reading from the second book of Kings, the Syrian general Naaman comes back to the prophet Elisha to thank him with a gift for curing him of his leprosy.

In the gospel from Luke, Jesus cures ten lepers, but only one of the ten returns to praise and thank him, and this man was a Samaritan. Jesus then praises the faith of this one man who came back to give thanks.

*The Interpreter's Bible* remarks that gratitude is an instinctive human response:

> Man gives thanks for the same reason that birds sing. Children are taught how to say "Thank you," but they hardly need in the first instance to be taught how to feel it.

Even nations pause to give thanks as a community. The Israelites instituted the feast of Pentecost to thank God for the blessings of a good grain harvest. Our own American holiday of Thanksgiving Day is in the same tradition.

Books on etiquette devote many pages to proper ways of expressing gratitude, such as a thank-you note for a gift given at a wedding or for a gesture of sympathy at a funeral.

It is important, then, that we say "Thanks" often to one another and to God. Taking time to do this makes us reflect on how many blessings we have, instead of brooding over the ones we don't have.

Showing gratitude provides occasions not only to recognize our gifts from others, but also to appreciate and value these gifts in a deeper sense as signs of their love for us.

If more people practiced the art of saying "Thank you" sincerely and not just superficially, think of how much pain and hurt would be eliminated from the world and how much happiness and joy there would be instead.

When we have a spirit of gratitude for the taken-for-granted blessings of life—like the sun, the water, our health—we have an added resource to help us cope with disappointments, losses and difficulties.

Martin Rinkart's great song of praise, "Now Thank We All Our God," was composed after a war, famine and pestilence. As a minister he had buried numerous victims during those trying times. Yet he never despaired because his heart was full of gratitude for God's "countless gifts of love" that he could still see surrounding him.

*C Cycle* 289

May we too open our eyes to see the "wondrous things" God does daily for us and approach him in prayer to praise him for these gifts. May we appreciate what we do for one another every day and express our thanks by word or gesture.

May our faith in times of trouble be firm enough so that we will always find reasons to celebrate God's blessings upon us.


29th Sunday of the YearEx 17:8-13   Lk 18:1-8

# PERSISTENCE IN PRAYER

The movie *Heartland* dramatizes the story of rugged prairie life in the early 1900's. A widow named Elinore Randall answers an ad to become a housekeeper for Clyde Stewart, a taciturn cattle homesteader in Burntfork, Wyoming.

After a rocky beginning, their relationship smooths out and they eventually get married, partly out of economic convenience and partly out of deep human needs. Together they heroically endure the hardships of a stubborn soil that yields little food, freezing winter winds that decimate their herd and the death of their newborn little boy.

In the climax of the story, Clyde Stewart has given up on the cattle ranch and begins to pack their belongings. But Elinore won't let him quit. She pleads and bargains with him not to abandon their dream.

Her tenacity triumphs when a calf is born, a sign of a new beginning, new life and new hope. Clyde finally agrees to stay and give the ranch one more try.

Elinore's persistence and faith are comparable to the widow's in today's parable. The widow kept coming to the judge for her rights and eventually wore him out. Jesus uses her as an example of praying always and not losing heart.

According to *The Interpreter's Bible*, the point of the parable is not to picture God as a heartless judge but to exhort us to persevere in prayer. If persistence prevails with a judge who cares only for his own convenience and comfort, how much more will it prevail with a gracious God who loves his children?

Nonetheless, some questions still remain unanswered. Why should we have to plead and wait at all when we pray? Why are some prayers never answered, regardless of how long we pray?

*The Interpreter's Bible* makes three suggestions as possible solutions to these problems.

First, God may delay to answer prayers in our way in order to purify our motives. Is what we ask for in prayer really what we *need*, or is it something we merely *want*?

What we *want* may be nice—a raise in pay or an "A" on an exam—but it might only make us more selfish and unloving. What we might really *need* to make us a better and wiser person might be poverty or failure.

Second, God may delay in order to intensify our desire. Where there is little desire on the part of the entertainer, athlete, student or worker, they seldom reach their potential. But where there is intense desire, a person is more likely to scale the heights of excellence.

Third, God may delay to make us appreciate his gifts more. Home is dearer when the journey is long. Success is more precious when the struggle is arduous. God's gifts are sometimes valued more when we have to wait for them.

Fr. William Toohey was the chaplain for the Notre Dame football team for several years. He too struggled with prayer problems. If Notre Dame won, people said, "Your prayers worked today, Father." If Notre Dame lost, they asked, "What happened? Didn't you say the right words?"

To clarify his own understanding of prayer, Fr. Toohey made some distinctions. Prayer is not working on God to manipulate him into granting a request as if he were some kind of Aladdin's lamp. Rather, it is a surrender to God in faith to experience his *presence* even without his *presents*.

So we have to persist in prayer, not to *persuade* God to give us some gift, but to *prepare* and open our hearts to receive him who is the Giver of all gifts. We need to persevere in prayer, not because God is hard to reach, but because we are.

So maybe we need to make one more novena, light one more candle or recite one more rosary because we're not ready yet to relinquish our will to his or to receive him into our hearts.

30th Sunday of the Year           Si 35:12-14, 16-18   Lk 18:9-14

# I'M OK, YOU'RE OK

A book that was a best seller for many years is Dr. Thomas Harris' *I'm OK, You're OK*. Along with its sequel *Staying OK*, it popularized the Transactional Analysis approach to help people improve their relationships with themselves and others.

Transactional Analysis (or TA) is a learning device that enables us to realize that we are responsible for what we do in the future, no matter what has happened to us in the past.

The goal of TA is to emancipate the *adult* element in us from the archaic recordings of the *parent* and *child* elements in us, so that we can create new options for ourselves and make our own free choices.

Today's gospel story illustrates a little bit of Transactional Analysis. The selection of two extremes as characters in Jesus' story tips us off that he's setting us up.

The Pharisee was the religious pro—he did all the right things demanded by the law. The tax collector was a sinner by employment—he was guilty of breaking the law by the very work he did.

Each man prays in the Temple. If Jesus had stopped to ask us, "Who do *you* think went home justified?" we probably would have answered, "The Pharisee!" But Jesus would say, "You're wrong! The other guy is the good guy. The tax collector is the one who goes home justified."

"How come?" we would protest. Then Jesus would give us the punch line: "Everyone who exalts himself will be humbled, but he who humbles himself will be exalted."

In terms of Transactional Analysis the Pharisee was relating to God like a *parent* to a *child*. He was telling God all about the good things he was doing for him—fasting, praying, tithing and so on. He was almost demanding that God admire and approve of him.

On the other hand, the tax collector related to God like a *child* to a *parent*. He humbly acknowledged that he had done wrong but trusted in his heavenly Father's love and mercy.

How do we pray? Do we approach God as if we were the Big Daddy with all kinds of gifts to *give* to him? As if we were doing him a big favor with all our achievements?

Or do we approach God like a *child* going to a *parent* to *receive* something? Like a *child* who comes in humility to be affirmed, embraced, loved and exalted?

Also in terms of TA, by comparing himself to the tax collector, the Pharisee almost so much as said to the latter, "I'm OK, but you're not OK." He assumed a position of pretended superiority. He was playing the "pecking game" that chickens play—that is, he was pecking on someone who seemed smaller and weaker in his eyes, in order to make himself look better by comparison.

Do we pray like that? Is our prayer a monologue of "I"'s like the Pharisee's to convince ourselves that "We're OK"? Is our prayer a "pecking game" pointing out the flaws of other people to make ourselves feel satisfied because "They're not OK"?

One of the aims of TA is to make us ready to change for the better regardless of our past. Prayer, too, prepares us for change, for improvement. But this will happen only if we are humble and ready for change like the tax collector, and not proud and self-satisfied like the Pharisee.

Change for the better will happen only if we approach God the way a *child* comes to a *parent*—not to give but to receive; not to brag about ourselves but to listen to the Lord. Indeed, we are OK in God's eyes. But he wants to make us more so.

31st Sunday of the Year                              Ws 11:22-12:1  Lk 19:1-10

## SHORT AND TALL

When Calvin Murphy played professional basketball for the Houston Rockets of the NBA, he was one of the smallest players in the league at 5'9". And yet he ranks 17th on the all-time scoring list, is near the top in career Free Throw shooting percentage and holds the record for consecutive successful Free Throws.

In a game dominated by 7-foot giants, the diminutive Calvin Murphy stood tall with his achievements and records. Another remarkable man of small stature is featured in today's gospel.

His story takes place in Jericho instead of Houston, he is a tax-collector instead of a basketball player and his name is Zacchaeus instead of Calvin

Murphy. Of all the stories in the Bible, his story is not only one of the most charming, but also one of the most significant.

First, Zacchaeus is classified as a tax collector, reminiscent of last Sunday's story about the two men who went to the Temple to pray. Recall who went home justified. It was the tax collector, a sinner by occupation, instead of the Pharisee, a religious man by profession.

Not only does Zacchaeus go home justified, but he is even privileged to have Jesus himself as his guest.

Second, Zacchaeus is described as a wealthy man. This reminds us of two other rich men in Luke's gospel. One is the rich man Dives who wouldn't share anything with the poor man Lazarus. The other is the rich young man who went away sad when Jesus invited him to give all he had to the poor.

Their counterpart is Zacchaeus who accepts Christ's invitation with enthusiasm and gives away half his wealth to the poor.

Third, when Jesus defends Zacchaeus in the presence of the people grumbling about him being a sinner, he says: "The Son of Man has come to search out and save what was lost."

This groups the story with other Lost-and-Found stories in Luke: the parables about the lost sheep, the lost coin and the lost prodigal son.

Fourth, Zacchaeus climbed a tree so he could see Jesus. The crowd, too, was curious to see Jesus, but they were blind because they did not see Jesus the way Zacchaeus did—as a savior of sinners.

This follows a preceding incident in which something similar happened. As Jesus drew near Jericho, a blind man had faith to see Jesus as healer and savior, whereas the crowd which could see failed to recognize who Jesus really was.

Today we play the role of Zacchaeus as we come to church to see and hear Jesus, and Jesus invites us to hurry home so he can stay at our house as guest. But for this experience to make any impact on our life, we have to respond the way Zacchaeus did.

First, we have to face our sinfulness and start changing our ways. How can Jesus justify us if we won't repent and reform?

Second, we have to be willing to let go of certain things to follow the Lord. How can Jesus find a place in our heart if it's full of love of money, pleasure or power?

Third, we have to realize that without Jesus we would be lost. How can we stand our ground except by the grace of God?

Fourth, we must have faith to see Jesus in our midst. How can we expect to recognize Jesus in the poor, the outcast and the handicapped unless we have faith?

If we respond the way Zacchaeus did, then the following lines written by Emily Dickinson will be fulfilled in us:

> We never know how high we are
> Till we are called to rise
> And then, if we are true to plan
> Our statures touch the skies.

32nd Sunday of the Year                                         2 M 7:1-2, 9-14   Lk 20:27-38

## THE DAY AFTER

When the movie *The Day After* was shown on television in 1983, it caused quite a controversy. This was because it focused on the ultimate *what if*—the event of a global nuclear war.

*What if* the population of Kansas City is instantly reduced to vaporized silhouettes; *what if* the blistered wounded are doomed to die; *what if* some survivors are surrounded by radioactive fallout that settles like a fine white dust all over the earth?

*The Day After* was intended primarily to provoke serious reflection and discussion about nuclear disarmament. But it also provoked questions about our faith. Would a good God allow such a terrifying evil to happen? Why do we have to die at all? Is there really a resurrection?

Today's readings suggest some answers to these questions, not in the sense of complete explanations, but in the sense of strengthening our faith in Jesus Christ, the risen Son of the living God.

In the Old Testament reading from Maccabees, we hear the inspiring story of a Jewish mother whose seven sons are tortured to death for their faith. It is one of the strongest Old Testament witnesses we have to a God-given hope of being restored to life in a resurrection.

In the gospel, Jesus is challenged by an ultra-conservative group of Jews, the Sadducees, who base all their beliefs on a literal interpretation of the law of Moses and who deny any life after death.

The Sadducees pose a ridiculous problem about a woman having seven husbands to prove their point that there is no resurrection. But Jesus turns the tables on them and quotes their own Scriptures to claim that the dead do rise to life.

Jesus refers to the passage where God reveals himself to Moses at the burning bush as the God of Abraham, the God of Isaac and the God of Jacob. In other words, "God is not the God of the dead, but of the living. All are alive for him."

We don't get a satisfying answer from the Scriptures to the question, "How can a good God allow such terrible evils like the slaughter of the seven sons or the death of the Marines in Lebanon to occur?" But we do get an affirmation of our faith in an afterlife.

No matter how terrifying death may be, whether at the hands of terrorists or nuclear missiles, life will be restored. No matter how much destruction a nuclear holocaust may cause, *the day after* will never be *the last day*. A new heaven and a new earth will appear.

Even if our bodies are vaporized and atomized by a nuclear explosion, they will one day rise from the dust—restored and transformed by the Lord—because our God is a God of the *living* and not of the dead.

If this is going to be true *the day after* a possible nuclear war, then it should be no less true *any day before* such an event. Christian hope does not allow us to despair. Regardless of how close death may be, whether from cancer or radioactive fallout, we can't allow ourselves to get discouraged.

As long as we are alive, our quest for peace should reflect Christian optimism, not pessimism. As long as we are alive, our efforts to build God's kingdom should demonstrate an appreciation of the temporal order, not its abandonment. As long as we are alive, *today* is the only day that matters, not *the day after*.

With Christian faith and hope we are strong enough to survive *any today*, and if need be *any day after*.

33rd Sunday of the Year　　　　　　　　　　　　Ml 3:19-20　Lk 21:5-19

## DO NOT WORRY

In 1942 Edith Stein was driven with other naked prisoners into a gas chamber at Auschwitz. She had been a professional philosopher, teacher and writer; had served in World War I in a Red Cross hospital; became a Catholic convert in 1922; and had been a contemplative Carmelite nun known as Sister Benedicta since 1933.

But because she was of Jewish descent, Edith Stein was arrested by the Nazis at a Carmelite convent in Holland and sent to Auschwitz to die with thousands of other Jews.

Since then she has become a Catholic symbol for all the victims of the Holocaust. She was beatified in 1987, and there is a movement to have her canonized as a patron saint for professional women, intellectuals, scholars and contemplatives.

Edith Stein stands out as a victor as well as a victim because of her faith in the triumphant cross of Christ. Her final book on *The Science of the Cross* was completed on the very day she was arrested. Of this book she said:

> One can only learn the *Science of the Cross* if one feels the cross in one's own person. I was convinced of this from the very first and have said with all my heart: Hail, O Cross, our only hope.

Edith Stein's martyrdom fulfilled in a real, striking way today's readings from Scripture.

From the first reading by the prophet Malachi, we can see how a judgment day arrived blazing like an oven fire. But for her, there arose the sun of righteousness "with healing in its rays."

In reading the gospel we can't help but notice the similarities between the cosmic disaster described there and the Holocaust atrocities—wars and insurrections, manhandling and persecutions, imprisonments and trials, hatred and violence.

But the key words of our Lord that strengthened Edith Stein and which should inspire us are: "Do not worry about your defense beforehand, for I will give you an eloquence and a wisdom . . . not a hair of your head will be lost. By patient endurance you will save your lives."

"But," we might object, "how can this be true? For all her faith Edith Stein died as six million other Jews did in the Holocaust. How can we say that she was not harmed or that she was saved?"

In his commentary on this section of Luke's gospel, William Barclay tries to answer us. He quotes a World War I poem by Rupert Brooke:

We have built a house which is not for Time's throwing,
We have gained a peace unshaken by pain forever.
War knows no power. Safe shall be my going,
Secretly armed against all death's endeavor:
Safe though all safety's lost; safe where men fall.
And if these poor limbs die, safest of all.

In other words, Barclay concludes, anyone who walks with Christ may lose his life, but can never lose his soul. We will all die one way or another in this life, but we will rise with our Lord in the next life.

Few of us will ever have to face what Edith Stein did at Auschwitz or what the early Christians did when Jerusalem was destroyed. But all of us have to face our own form of trials and conflicts, resistance and opposition, sufferings and ordeals.

So we need to take heart from people like Edith Stein, who seemed crushed by the gigantic forces of an evil like the Holocaust, and yet triumphed over it because of her faith in Christ's promise to be with her.

If we have confidence in Christ's words, "Do not worry," it won't matter what kind of crisis we have to confront—whether it's a serious illness or the loss of a job or the breakup of some relationship. With Christ at our side we will find the courage we need to overcome that crisis. With patient endurance we will come through the ordeal even stronger in spirit than we were before.

Christ the King                                     2 S 5:1-3   Lk 23:35-43

# CHARISMA

President John F. Kennedy was assassinated on November 22, 1963. Even though he was president for less than three years, Kennedy captured the nation's imagination with his charisma, eloquence, decisiveness and wit. The mystique surrounding his memory is summed up in a *Time* magazine essay written by Hugh Sidey in 1983. He writes:

John F. Kennedy was the greatest actor of our time, dimming those more celluloid performers like Ronald Reagan. He was on a stage as wide as the world and in a drama of the centuries. He commanded with Marlborough and debated with Churchill, he dined with Jefferson and rode with Sherman to the sea.

Sidey goes on to call Kennedy a practical romantic who sought the company of the great, both in his fantasies and in real life. Kennedy urged his fellow Americans to follow this youthful adventure of mind and body with him. In conclusion Sidey says:

> That is why John F. Kennedy lives among us today. In death he found a place in the caravan of history's great whose thoughts and words he used, whose actions he revered.

Today we honor another great leader whose bright trajectory in history ended in midpassage—Jesus Christ our King! In the Holy Year of 1983 we commemorated the 1950th anniversary of his death on the cross.

Just as Kennedy did, Jesus too captured the imagination of his nation. He did it with his Sermon on the Mount, his miracles of healing, his outspoken criticism of the Pharisees and his sense of destiny. Christ's charisma was compelling.

Also like Kennedy, Jesus too died a violent, shocking death at the peak of his career. His death on the cross in the midst of two thieves is the scene of today's gospel.

But unlike Kennedy, Christ's life did not end at the tomb. Christ the King rose from the dead to fulfill some of his own words on the cross: "I promise you: today you will be with me in paradise."

There has been much mythmaking by the media concerning the life and death of John F. Kennedy. But the life, death and resurrection of Christ is more than a myth—it is the mystery of the invisible God becoming a visible man to save us.

As St. Paul points out in the second reading, today we give thanks to the Father for rescuing us from the power of darkness through his beloved Son and bringing us into his kingdom of light. We praise the Lord Jesus for making peace through the blood of his cross (Col 1:12-20).

In a word, we are celebrating the establishing of God's kingdom through the mystery of Christ's passion and resurrection. But to participate in that kingdom we have to be like the good thief on the cross. We have to turn to Jesus, trust in his mercy and take his promise for what it says: "Today you will be with me in paradise."

Moreover, to establish Christ's kingdom here on earth we have to promote the values of that kingdom as outlined in the Preface of this Mass: truth and life; holiness and grace; justice, love and peace.

The significance of our role was understood well by John F. Kennedy when he said:

> The hopes of all mankind for freedom and the future rest upon us. The energy, the faith, the devotion we bring to this endeavor will light our country, and the glow from that fire can truly light the world.

# Supplement

Christmas - Midnight Mass (A, B, C)    Is 9:1-6   Lk 2:1-14

# TIDINGS OF JOY

Paul Newman has directed a new film version of Tennessee Williams' play *The Glass Menagerie*. One of the principal characters of this story is Laura, played in the film by Newman's wife, Joanne Woodward.

Laura has been crippled since childhood and separated from the real world like a piece of her own glass collection. She is a symbol of all of us insofar as our existence is melancholy and joyless.

The Laura syndrome of sadness that afflicts us in varying degrees is one of the main reasons why Jesus became human. This was heralded by the angel to the shepherds in the Christmas gospel: "Do not be afraid. Behold, I bring you good tidings of *great joy*, which will be for every people. Today in the town of David, a savior has been born to you."

In a sense, a person without Jesus is a lot like Laura—handicapped and fragile, gloomy and cheerless. Without Jesus it's hard to sing "Joy to the World," even at Christmas, because our world is then like a *glass menagerie*—lifeless and immobile, unreal and breakable.

But with Jesus everything changes. Sadness and melancholy give way to joy, our hurts are healed and our loneliness is transformed by love.

Without Jesus the world is joyless. Just witness the false joy that dominates such scenes as disco clubs, gay bars, gambling casinos, rock concerts, X-rated movie houses and so on. We see here a joy that is superficial, fleeting and empty.

Contrast that with the joy that Jesus brings—a joy that is deep down, lasting and fulfilling; a joy that gives depth, meaning and purpose to our lives.

In his book *Surprised by Joy*, C.S. Lewis tells how he passed from atheism to theism to Christianity. At one stage in his journey he sought human fulfillment in what he describes as desiring joy itself through a supreme aesthetic experience.

But C.S. Lewis was disappointed in his search. He found not the wave of joy itself, but only the imprint it left on the sand. He writes:

> All images and sensations, if idolatrously mistaken for joy itself, soon honestly confessed themselves inadequate. All said, in the last resort, "It is not I. I am only a reminder. Look! Look! What do I remind you of?"

Eventually C.S. Lewis found what he had sought in joy: God himself as revealed in Jesus Christ. He went looking for joy, but as the title of his book expresses it, he was *surprised by joy*—he found Jesus.

Indeed, we will find some real joy in our Christmas dinners, gatherings and caroling. But only in Jesus will we find that genuine joy that will sustain us long after our guests have departed, our gifts are forgotten and our Christmas cards are burned.

For even if we are handicapped like Laura, with Jesus we can still be happy. We may be fragile and breakable like glass pieces, but with Jesus we can survive whatever abuse comes our way. There will be times when we will be saddened because of illness or death; nonetheless, with Jesus we can still be joyful.

Christmas - Midnight Mass (A, B, C)            Is 9:1-6    Lk 2:1-14

# GIVING

In a Christmas story narrated over the radio one year, a little girl came into a store to buy a Christmas gift. The owner of the store was an angry, bitter man who had recently lost his beloved wife in a car accident.

The little girl explained that she wanted to get a necklace for her older sister, but all she had was a few cents from her broken piggy bank. It would be their first Christmas since their mother died.

The little girl's self-forgetfulness and sincere concern for her sister so moved the heart of the store owner that he gave her a very expensive necklace in exchange for the few cents that she had.

After Christmas the older sister came to the store with the exquisite necklace and wanted to know how her little sister was able to pay for it. The store owner would not reveal the real price but only said, "She gave all that she had to buy the gift."

This story illustrates the spirit of giving that is the heart of the Christmas story: "God so loved the world that he *gave* his only Son" (Jn 3:16). God's gift to us is joyously announced by the angel to the shepherds in the Christmas gospel: "Today in the town of David *a savior* has been born to you, who is Christ the Lord."

This is the essence of Christmas—giving out of love—generously and selflessly: God giving us his only Son to be our savior because he loves us; the little girl giving her all to buy a gift for her older sister because she loves her.

We usually associate the spirit of Christmas giving with the buying, wrapping and exchanging of gifts, or with the doling out of Christmas bonuses. On the one hand, such giving is good—it's good for merchants, employees, friendships and families. On the other hand, such giving of material things often replaces entirely the deeper kind of spiritual giving that is closer to the real meaning of Christmas.

Giving out of love the way God gave to us implies giving something of ourselves. This kind of personal giving might take the form of inspiring someone to be a better person or do something great. We saw this happen in the radio story when the innocence and simplicity of the little girl moved an angry and bitter store owner to do something noble and generous.

Such Christmas giving occurs every time we demonstrate appreciation for what people do for us, recognize their accomplishments and show an interest in them. It happens whenever we bring peace to the troubled, hope to the downcast and love to the lonely.

Such Christmas giving out of love—generously and selflessly—the way God gave to us, is summed up in a poem someone wrote:

> What is the best gift to give at Christmas?
> To your offenders, forgiveness
> To your opponents, tolerance
> To your children, devotion
> To your parents, reverence
> To your fellow workers, cooperation
> To your friends, generosity
> To yourself, respect
> To all, charity.

Easter (A, B, C)                                                      Jn 20:1-9

# HE IS ALIVE

In one of its 1982 issues, *Parade* magazine had a story about 62-year-old Lana Turner. It was entitled "Lana Turns Religious." After seven husbands, an affair with alcohol and numerous scandals, Lana Turner had found religion. "God has his arms wrapped around me," she exclaimed.

The former "sweater girl" is no suddenly born-again Christian. She is simply a woman who late in life has found security in a deep, abiding faith in God. Since finding God, Lana Turner has given up booze and her reclusiveness, and is reconstructing her life. She has put aside her shady past and is walking with the Lord into a bright future.

As we celebrate Easter Sunday, it is easy to compare Lana Turner with Mary Magdalene in John's gospel. Mary comes alone to the tomb while it is still dark. Finding the stone moved away, she runs off to Simon Peter and John to say: "They have taken the Lord out of the tomb, and we don't know where they have put him."

Then later in the story, Jesus appears to Mary Magdalene in the garden. She does not recognize him until he calls her by name. Immediately he sends her to the disciples to announce that she has seen the risen Lord.

In a talk about these resurrection stories, Fr. John Bertolucci makes the following observations. Mary Magdalene had three strikes against her, and yet she was the one selected by Jesus for his first appearance after he had risen, and she is the one sent to announce to the disciples the good news of his resurrection.

First, Mary Magdalene was a woman. In Jewish society at the time of Christ, a woman was a second-class citizen, was considered inferior to men and was treated like property.

Second, Mary Magdalene had been possessed previously by seven demons. Jesus had expelled them from her, but she still needed healing to rehabilitate herself. She still needed more time to get her new act together.

Third, Mary Magdalene had a bad reputation. She was known everywhere as a prostitute, as a woman of the streets. Her association with Jesus still raised a lot of suspicious eyebrows.

Nevertheless, in spite of these three strikes against her, Mary Magdalene was selected by Jesus as the first witness to his resurrection. Jesus did not choose Peter, his designated leader, nor his beloved disciple John. Instead he chose Mary Magdalene—a woman, an ex-hooker and one formerly possessed by seven devils.

We should not be surprised if Jesus selects people like Lana Turner or Mary Magdalene to witness to his resurrection. Their past scandals and sins do not disqualify them from being born-again Christians.

On the contrary, these make them apt witnesses for the risen Lord. For once they are converted, they can say to us: "Jesus is alive. He is risen. I've seen him. I've touched him."

Lana Turner and Mary Magdalene challenge us this Easter to proclaim with our lives that Jesus is indeed alive and that he is with us now. Moreover, Jesus sends us, as he sent these two women, to announce this good news.

The Lord doesn't care about our excuses, our past failures or our state of readiness. Once we've turned to him, he wants us to give witness to others how we've seen him alive, how his power is changing us and how his hand has touched us.


Easter (A, B, C)                                   Ac 10:34, 37-43   Mt 28:1-10

## DEATH LEADING TO LIFE

Benigno Aquino, Jr. has become a Filipino folk hero. At age 22 he was mayor of his hometown. Later he became a governor and then a senator. In 1972 Aquino was preparing to run for the presidency in opposition to Ferdinand Marcos when Marcos suddenly invoked martial law, canceled the election and jailed him.

Benigno Aquino stayed in prison for eight years before he was released to travel to the U.S. for by-pass surgery in 1980. He and his family spent the next three years in voluntary exile in the Boston area.

In 1983 he decided to return to Manila to rally opposition against Marcos. He was assassinated at the Manila Airport.

But Aquino's death did not end the fight against the Marcos regime. Instead it drew more than a million marchers to his funeral and fired a people's revolt under the new leadership of his widow Corazon Aquino, who became the President of the Philippine Islands.

Benigno Aquino's bloody death thus became a source of new life for his Filipino people. His tragic end marked the beginning of a new era. In this sense, his death leading to new life is a type of the death and resurrection of Jesus.

It is true that Aquino's tomb is not empty, as is the case in our Lord's Easter story today. Nor has he been raised yet with a glorified body like Christ's.

Nevertheless, his spirit lives on through his widow Corazon Aquino, his influence is felt in a very real way among his followers and his memory will mark Filipino history for a long time.

If the life and death of a man like Benigno Aquino can create such an impact, how much more of an impact should the life and death of Jesus create? The resurrection of Jesus from the dead is not something symbolic. It is the very substance of our faith. It is not a myth whose memory we try to keep alive. It is the very mystery that gives meaning to our whole life.

The resurrection of Jesus was not an event that affected a particular people at a particular time in history. It is the very power of God raising Jesus from the dead to make him Lord of every people of every time.

If all this is true, what new impact should Easter make in our lives this year? The gospel gives us some clues to answer this. The phrase, "Do not be afraid," and the command, "Go and tell the news" appear twice in the gospel of Matthew. The women hear these words spoken to them first by the angel at the tomb, and then by our Lord after they leave the tomb.

Today these words are addressed to us.

"Do not be afraid," Jesus says. While it is true that we may not be terrorized by tyranny as the Filipino people were, we still have other things that frighten us: threats of nuclear war, unemployment, violence, sickness and death.

So we need to hear Jesus reassure us that his victory over death includes our victory over all these fears. We still have battles to fight with them, but at least we can count on the final outcome being in our favor.

"Go and tell the news," Jesus commands us. This doesn't mean that we have to call a press conference. Nevertheless, we have to find our own ways to let people know that Jesus is indeed risen and that he is alive today.

The best way is to show that Jesus makes a significant difference in our lives—perhaps because he's freed us from some bad habit, or has changed our attitude toward work, or has made us more sensitive to the sufferings of the poor, or has strengthened us in coping with our own difficulties.

As Easter 1986 marked a new beginning for the Filipino people because of the life and death of Benigno Aquino, may this Easter mean new life for us in some way because of the death and resurrection of Jesus.

Vigil of Pentecost (A, B, C)   Gn 11:1-9   Jn 7:37-39

# THIRST

In his book *The Fearful Void*, explorer Geoffrey Moorhouse describes how he crossed the scorching Sahara Desert by camel and on foot. Water was such a vital element on his trip that his route was dictated by the location of wells and oases. The wells were no more than holes in the ground and water was often mixed with mud, urine and camel-dung. Even so it was precious, for it meant the difference between living and dying in the desert.

One time when Geoffrey Moorhouse was sure that he would die from thirst, a little boy brought him some water the color of diluted blood. To Geoffrey this was the most beautiful thing in the world at that moment, more beautiful than the stained glass of Chartres or a symphony by Bach.

Our bodies need water to sustain life and health. We can go for weeks without food, but only for a few days without water before our life-sustaining systems begin to break down. In the same way, our spirits need the life-giving water of the Holy Spirit.

Jesus says this in today's gospel: "If anyone thirsts, let him come to me and drink. He who believes in me, as the Scripture has said, 'Out of his heart shall flow rivers of living water.'" The evangelist adds the comment: "Now this he said about the Spirit, which those who believed in him were to receive."

The significance of Christ's claim becomes more striking when we see it in the context of the Feast of Tabernacles. It was on the last and greatest day of this festival that Jesus stood up and cried out.

The Feast of Tabernacles commemorated the forty years the Jews lived in tents in the wilderness of the desert. Because they were sustained by miraculous water from the rock, on each of the first seven days of the Feast of Tabernacles a golden vessel was filled with water from the Pool of Siloam and was carried in procession to the Temple for libations.

But on the eighth day of the Feast no water was carried. That was the day that Jesus stood up to make his claim: "If anyone thirsts, let him come to me and drink." As mentioned earlier, he was referring to the Holy Spirit that he would give to those who believed in him.

In his commentary on this gospel, John Marsh says:

Jesus is in fact beginning to tell the festival crowd in the Temple of Jerusalem what he has already told the Samaritan woman at the well by Sychar, namely, that he or the Holy Spirit is the real quenching of thirst that is more than physical, and of which physical thirst, dreadful and critical as it can be, is but a metaphor or symbol.

All of us thirst and crave for many things in life. We thirst for material things like a nice home or a new car; for financial success and economic security; for pleasures of the body associated with food, drink and sex; for things that delight the mind like a good book or an interesting movie; for acceptance, companionship and love.

There are all kinds of things we thirst for and there are all kinds of places or people we look to in order to satisfy these thirsts. Some of these are the wrong places and the wrong people, and they leave us more thirsty than before.

Only the Holy Spirit can satisfy our thirsts on all levels by teaching us how to use material things wisely and by guiding us to put money and pleasure in proper perspective. Only the Holy Spirit can fulfill our deepest needs by enlightening us to discover our best selves and by inspiring us to see those things which will be in our best interests.

May our prayer on this Vigil of Pentecost be: "Come, Holy Spirit, and fill the hearts of your faithful. Increase our thirst for the higher values of life, for things that really count. Satisfy our thirst for personal fulfillment, peace of mind and a permanent place among God's people."

Pentecost (A, B, C)                                    Ac 2:1-11   Jn 20:19-23

# JOHNNY LINGO

The movie *Johnny Lingo* is a modern parable. The story is set on some islands in the South Seas where the custom among the natives is that the husband buys his wife. For three cows a man can get a good wife; for five cows the best wife.

On the islands there is a 19-year-old girl named Mahana whom everybody considers ugly. Mahana's father would take one cow just to get her off his hands. But along comes Johnny Lingo who offers to pay eight cows for Mahana as his wife. The islanders can't believe it. Why would Johnny Lingo, the shrewdest and handsomest man on the islands, pay eight cows for the ugly Mahana?

Well, the marriage takes place and some months later Johnny Lingo and Mahana return to the island. Again the people can't believe what they see. Mahana is no longer an ugly, awkward and shy girl. Instead she is a young woman who is radiant with beauty, poise and charm.

Johnny's love for Mahana has changed her, transformed her from a nobody into the most beautiful woman on the islands—so much so that Mahana's father accuses Johnny Lingo of cheating him. Mahana is not worth just eight cows; she is worth ten cows now.

This simple story of Johnny Lingo and Mahana is a good illustration of what happens when the Holy Spirit comes into our lives.

In the first reading from Acts, we heard how the Holy Spirit came as a driving wind and as tongues of fire to fill the hearts of the disciples. As a result of the Holy Spirit's coming, the apostles are transformed. Before they were afraid, confused and timid. Now they are full of courage, men with a mission and bold preachers of the gospel.

Like the disciples, we too need the gifts of the Holy Spirit. Like Mahana, we too need the gift of love. And so Jesus Christ comes like a Johnny Lingo into our midst to offer us the gift of his love: "Receive the Holy Spirit."

If we open our hearts to accept this gift, then like Mahana in the story or the disciples on Pentecost, we too can be transformed. Suppose we look at some of these changes under three headings—*person, presence* and *power*.

First, *person*. Under the gentle guidance of the Holy Spirit we can discover who we really are as a person. We are not an ugly Mahana not worth even one cow, but a beautiful Mahana worth more than all the animals in the world. We are lovable because we are children of God who have received the Spirit of adoption.

Second, *presence*. Jesus promised to send the Holy Spirit to be with us always. Consequently, we don't ever have to feel rejected or left out as Mahana did at the beginning of the story. Instead, we should feel secure and loved because the Holy Spirit is always with us. We may feel lonely at times, but we will never be alone. People may hurt us at times, but the Holy Spirit will heal us with his presence.

Third, *power*. Jesus promised to send the Holy Spirit to give the apostles the power to preach and perform miracles. This same power of the Spirit is given to us to do whatever is necessary to change our lives for the better: to overcome our depressions and neuroses, and experience the peace and joy of the Spirit; to become less dependent on alcohol, drugs and tobacco, and be free to become our very best selves.

Pray that we may receive the Holy Spirit anew so he can show us how lovable we are as *persons*, be *present* with us in good times and bad times, and give us the *power* to change our lives for the better and renew the face of the earth.

Vigil of the Assumption (A, B, C)　　　1 Ch 15:3-4, 15, 16; 16:1-2　　Lk 11:27-28

## MY FAIR LADY

*My Fair Lady* is a musical based on George Bernard Shaw's play *Pygmalion*. It tells the story of a linguistics professor named Henry Higgins and a lowly cockney flower girl named Eliza Doolittle.

To demonstrate his genius in phonetics, the egotistical Henry Higgins takes on the crude guttersnipe Eliza and tries to transform her in three months into a woman of culture and grace. With persistence and patience, he makes good his boast to be able to do this, and Eliza indeed becomes a "Fair Lady."

In fact, Henry Higgins does his work so well that Eliza Doolittle falls in love with him and wants to live with him all the days of her life.

This romantic story reflects in a faint way the amazing transformation that happened to another woman, Mary, the mother of Jesus. On this feast of her Assumption we celebrate the marvelous way God raised her from the dead and took her with him into heaven. There God can truly call her *My Fair Lady*.

Because of the way Mary bore Christ in her womb and in her heart, she is indeed the "ark of God" mentioned in the reading from the first book of Chronicles. She has been taken—body and soul—"to the place prepared" for her in the tent of God's eternal dwelling.

Because her "corruptible frame has taken on incorruptibility and her mortal body immortality," she has already made real St. Paul's dream in the second reading. Like her son Jesus, Mary has defeated death and can now glory in her victory (1 Cor 15:54-57).

Finally, because of her faith and love, Mary deserves to be called "Blessed"—the gospel equivalent of her title, *My Fair Lady*. She not only bore, nursed and raised her son Jesus with great devotion, but also heard and kept God's word every moment of her life.

That's some of the good news from Scripture about Mary's Assumption. But what does it have to do with us? Is Mary way out there in some place we call heaven while we're still down here struggling on earth?

Not really, at least not according to the Dutch Catechism. It claims that just as Christ's resurrection effected a new and more forceful presence by him in the world, so too Mary's Assumption brought about a new and more powerful way of her being with us:

> This means that Mary is more in the world than any other woman. Cleopatra is remembered. Mary is addressed. She is the most closely present of all women.

Furthermore, the magnificent transformation Mary experienced is meant for us too. It is the sign and promise of our resurrection and assumption into glory.

In his book titled *Catholicism*, Fr. Richard McBrien writes:

> The dogma of the Assumption asserts something about human existence in asserting something about Mary: that human existence is bodily existence, and that we are destined for glory not only in the realm of the spiritual but in the realm of the material as well.

Consequently, because Mary is with us "right here" and not "out there," we can honor her with shrines, praise her with songs, and pray to and through her with our rosaries.

Moreover, because her Assumption is a preview of our own future transformation, we can find encouragement in times of suffering and sorrow when we wonder if it's all worthwhile; or find hope in experiences of destruction and death when we question our destiny.

The Polish people believe this. Even though they are oppressed by Communism, their faith in Our Lady of Czestochowa and all that the Black Madonna symbolizes enables them to sing proudly their National Anthem: *Jeszcze Polska nie Zginela*—"Poland is not yet lost."

May Mary's feast of the Assumption continue to inspire oppressed people like the Poles in their quest for freedom and strengthen us in our own struggles on our pilgrim way.

The Assumption of Mary (A, B, C)  Rv 11:19; 12:1-6, 10  Lk 1:39-56

## TAJ MAHAL

The Taj Mahal in India has been described as a "love song in marble." Completed in 1645, this magnificent marble mausoleum was built by Shah Jahan, India's Mogul emperor, in memory of his favorite wife, Princess Arjemand. Shah Jahan loved her deeply, calling her his *Taj Mahal*, meaning "The Pearl of the Palace."

But Princess Arjemand died giving birth to their fourteenth child and the emperor was inconsolable. So he summoned a great architect from Persia to build the Taj Mahal, telling him that it must be "the one perfect thing in the world."

Seventeen years were needed to build this enchanting edifice of gleaming white marble embroidered with flashing jewels. It is an enduring monument to love that still inspires tourists, artists and writers from all over the world.

This beautiful love story gives us some idea of how much God must love Mary, the mother of Jesus. Today's feast of her Assumption into heaven is proof of this. By raising her from the dead and taking her into heaven—body and soul—God demonstrated his undying love for Mary.

Like Shah Jahan, God couldn't bear the death of his beloved. However, God could do what the Indian emperor could not do—raise his beloved from the dead and restore her to life even more beautiful than before.

Moreover, God didn't have to build a Taj Mahal to memorialize Mary. Her own glorified body is itself a magnificent temple of the Holy Spirit. As the first reading from Revelation describes her, she is "adorned with the sun, standing on the moon, and with the twelve stars on her head for a crown."

No wonder the gospel has Mary again singing her *Magnificat*: "My soul proclaims the greatness of the Lord, and my spirit exults in God my

Savior . . . from this day forward all generations will call me blessed, for the Almighty has done great things for me."

The meaning of Mary's Assumption is summed up in the Preface of this Mass: "The virgin Mother of God was taken up into heaven to be the beginning and the pattern of the Church in its perfection and a sign of hope and comfort for your people on their pilgrim way."

In other words, Mary's glorification is not only a personal privilege—comparable to the resurrection and ascension of her son Jesus—but also a promise and pledge of our own glorification one day. It not only emphasizes her unique dignity as the mother of Jesus, but also underscores our own destiny.

Mary experienced the human fact of death but was preserved from its effects of decay and disintegration. Her Assumption is a reminder that on the last day we, too, shall rise from the dead, and our bodies will be clothed with incorruptibility and immortality.

Another consequence of Mary's glorification is the extension of her influence in our lives. As our mother she has not abandoned us like orphans by leaving us physically. Rather, she is more present to us than ever before in a spiritual way. Her disappearance from our sight was not a departure implying absence. Rather, it inaugurated a hidden presence that is more powerful than physical presence.

John Paul II alluded to this in 1979 when he visited the Shrine of Our Lady of Guadalupe in Mexico City:

> In a wonderful way Mary is always found in the mystery of Christ, her only Son, because she is present whenever men and women, his brothers and sisters, are present, whenever the Church is present.

What a source of encouragement to feel Mary's presence by faith when worries and anxieties mount or when confusion and uncertainty assail us! What an anchor of strength to know that she is with us when tensions and stress beset us or when sufferings and hurts overwhelm us!

We don't have to go to some distant Taj Mahal to show our love for Mary. She's as near as we let her be to the shrine of our hearts to help us in our journey to glory.

All Saints (A, B, C)                                                  Rv 7:2-4, 9-14    Mt 5:1-12

## ORDINARY PEOPLE

*Harry, My Friend* is the true story of Harry Guttenplan—a crippled Jewish beggar—whom author Stephan Grosso met on the streets of New York City. Every week for three years, Stephan would visit Harry at his welfare-paid apartment and at his hospital bedside until Harry died in 1970.

To all appearances, Harry was an ordinary man who had a lot of ailments. He had a withered right arm and leg caused by infantile paralysis as a youth; he was mentally impaired somewhat because of brain damage caused by several strokes; he had asthma that continually clogged his nose, throat and chest; and he was afflicted with Parkinson's disease.

Occasionally Harry would get angry with God, lose his temper with his sister or complain about feeling sad. But most often he prayed with immense trust, gave people more credit than they deserved for being the slightest bit kind to him, and celebrated simple pleasures like eating his favorite ham and potato salad.

Stephan Grosso wrote a book about Harry Guttenplan because he is convinced that Harry was a saint—"a holy man who had passed through incredible stages of suffering, and who had immersed himself in great life-changing experiences and had arrived at a childlike purity and simplicity."

On today's feast of All Saints we honor people like Harry—ordinary people who achieved extraordinary sanctity; ordinary people whose lives seemed to us very humdrum but in God's eyes were very holy; ordinary people who didn't always *do* saintly things, yet always strove to *be* good people.

We honor these ordinary people, who, in the words of the first reading from Revelation, "stand before the throne and the Lamb, dressed in long white robes and hold palm branches in their hands."

Today we join Jesus in the gospel and call them "Blessed," because in their own quiet way they were poor in spirit, hungered and thirsted for what was right, showed mercy to others and were peacemakers.

Where do we find all these saints, these ordinary people? On the streets, where Stephan Grosso found Harry Guttenplan; in the places where we work; in our neighborhood community; and, especially, in our own family.

These saints are seldom cited for awards or given medals. But if you look hard, you will see them overcoming their adversities, forgiving those who hurt them, offering to help others and sharing whatever they have.

According to psychiatrist Abraham Maslow, one of the traits self-actualizing people have is "the wonderful capacity to appreciate again and again, freshly and naively, the basic good of life with awe, pleasure, wonder, and even ecstasy, however stale these experiences may have become to others."

The same could be said of ordinary people like Harry who have become saints. They have a capacity to experience God's presence in what seems monotonous and dull, to see his blessings in the routine and commonplace.

Praise God for ordinary people like Harry who show us how to see God where others do not. Thank God for all the saints who inspire us to struggle on when others would quit. Glorify God for giving common folk like us the call and the capacity to become saints ourselves.

All Saints (A, B, C)     Rv 7:2-4, 9-14    Mt 5:1-12

# DREAMERS AND DOERS

On December 2, 1980 Maryknoll Sister Ita Ford was martyred in El Salvador. Four months before her death she wrote a letter to her niece, Jennifer Sullivan of Brooklyn, on the occasion of Jennifer's 16th birthday. In that letter Sr. Ita described what a terrible time it was for youth in El Salvador. A lot of idealism and life was being snuffed out.

Nonetheless, she felt that the youths who had died for their freedom had fulfilled a purpose with their lives. Sr. Ita then urged Jennifer to search for and choose something that would be both self-fulfilling and of service to others. She wrote:

> I hope you come to find that which gives life a deep meaning for you. Something worth living for—and maybe even worth dying for—something that energizes you, enthuses you, enables you to move ahead. I can't tell you what it might be—that's for you to find, to choose, to love. Don't waste the gifts and opportunities you have to make yourself and other people happy.

Sr. Ita Ford's words could easily be used to describe the chartered members of the All Saints Club. For the saints are people who chose to respond to God's gifts and the opportunities he gave them. They found something or someone worth living for—and, in some cases, worth dying for. They were dreamers and doers.

Whatever that something was—a professional career, a civic cause, a humanitarian service, an artistic endeavor—it gave the saints some meaning and purpose to live for.

Whoever that someone was—their spouse, children, patients, students, co-workers, a friend, an outcast—they inspired and energized the saints to give themselves generously and selflessly.

In the gospel, Jesus tells us who become chartered members of the All Saints Club: "Blessed are those who hunger and thirst for what is right; they shall be satisfied. Blessed are the merciful; mercy shall be theirs. Blessed are the peacemakers; they shall be called children of God."

In other words, the saints are people whose set of values transcends their own petty concerns and whose agenda for action is dictated by the needs of God's people.

In his book *Motivation and Personality*, Abraham Maslow makes some statements about self-actualizing people that apply equally well to the saints:

> These individuals customarily have some mission in life, some task to fulfill, some problem outside themselves which enlists much of their energies . . . In general, these tasks are nonpersonal or unselfish, concerned with the good of mankind in general . . . Ordinarily concerned with basic issues and eternal questions, such people live customarily in the widest frame of reference.

Sr. Ita Ford was this kind of person. She became a saint because she had a dream of doing something grand for God, and then did something noble and selfless for his people in El Salvador. She was a dreamer and a doer.

Will her young niece Jennifer become a saint someday? Will she find something worth living and dying for, something that will inspire and energize her?

Will we become saints before we die? Will we experience some vision of greatness to which God is calling us? Will we find a dream to live by and do something beautiful for God? Are we dreamers and doers?

Immaculate Conception (A, B, C)　　　　　　Gn 3:9-15, 20　Lk 1:26-38

## FAVORED ONE

Back in the roaring twenties Gloria Swanson was a celebrated actress. To mark her eightieth birthday in 1980 she published *Swanson on Swanson: An Autobiography.*

She tells of her marriage in 1925 to a French marquis. Since she was already pregnant at the time, Gloria Swanson decided to have a secret abortion rather than jeopardize her career by creating a scandal. She was haunted in her conscience by that choice for the next 54 years.

But in 1979 Gloria Swanson went through a healing experience at a Buddhist temple. When she poured water and burned incense at the site of thousands of graves of babies, some of whom had died before they were born, she cried over the guilt she had carried for 54 years.

Today we recall another woman. She too is famous the world over—not for her films, but for her faith in an angel's message. She too married a man from a royal family—not some French marquis, but Joseph of the House of David. She too knew the sorrow of losing a child—not by abortion, but by crucifixion.

The woman we remember today is none other than Mary, the Mother of Jesus, and we remember her under her special title of *The Immaculate Conception.* Mary's title means that from the first moment of her existence at conception, she was preserved free of all sin, not only Original Sin, but also any personal sin.

Mary's unique privilege of being immaculately conceived is hinted at in today's readings. When God says in Genesis that he will put enmity between the serpent and the woman and between its offspring and hers, we get a preview of Mary and her role in the history of salvation.

We see the fulfillment of the Genesis prophecy in the gospel when the angel Gabriel declares that Mary is highly favored and blessed among women. This is the positive meaning of her Immaculate Conception—not only is she kept free from sin, but she is free to receive the fullness of God's gifts and favors.

In the Bible new names were often given to people by God to signify a new mission they would undertake for him. For example, when Simon was called to lead the apostles, Jesus changed his name to Peter, meaning "rock."

Since Mary is being called to play a new role in God's plan of salvation, she too is given a new name by God—"Favored One"—the "Immaculate One." Her impossible mission to be the mother of God now becomes possible.

Mary's mission today is somewhat modified, but it is still significant. The Preface of this Mass sums it up when we sing that just as she was a *sign* of favor to the Church at its *beginning*, so too she is a *promise* of its perfection at the *end* of time.

In other words, what she *is* by privilege, we are called to *become* by grace—namely, free of sin and filled with the Holy Spirit. What she is by virtue of her unique role as our *mother* in anticipation of Christ's redemptive acts, we are invited to become as her *children* in consequence of those acts.

In his book *The World's First Love*, Bishop Fulton Sheen says that by preserving Mary from sin, God gave hope to our weak humanity:

> One look at her, and we know that a human who is not good can become better; one prayer to her, and we know that because she is without sin we can become less sinful.

Maybe that was Gloria Swanson's experience when she made atonement for her sins. Perhaps this can be our own experience today. As we look over our own mistakes, foolishness and selfishness, we feel guilty, embarrassed and ashamed. But we don't have to stay that way. We can change our agenda and make a new beginning.

Mary's Immaculate Conception is an inspiration for us to have faith in our own special favors from God, to bring back into focus our vision of what we can become under God's grace and to make another effort in quest of this ideal.


Immaculate Conception (A, B, C)                 Gn 3:9-15, 20   Lk 1:26-38

# MISERY AND GLORY

Dorothy Day delighted to tell how she was inspired to become a convert. One day, as a young girl, she was looking for her friend Kathryn Barrett to play. In running through the long railroad-like apartment, she found Mrs. Barrett in the front room praying. Mrs. Barrett turned to tell Dorothy Day that Kathryn had gone to the store, and then she went on with her prayers.

Dorothy Day never forgot that incident. Later, when she became depressed by the problems of poverty and injustice, she would remember Mrs. Barrett. Dorothy Day writes:

> Though I groaned at the hideousness of man's lot, still there were moments when in the midst of misery and strife, life was shot through with glory. Mrs. Barrett in her sordid tenement flat finished her dishes at ten o'clock in the morning, and got down on her knees and prayed to God.

Dorothy Day's words, "in the midst of misery and strife, life was shot through with glory," are a splendid summary of the significance of today's feast of Mary's Immaculate Conception. As a result of Original Sin we are still "in the midst of misery." But Mary's Immaculate Conception, her preservation from all sin from the first moment of her life, is God's proof that no matter how bad things seem to be, life is still "shot through with glory."

Today's readings from Scripture reflect this note of optimism.

The first reading from Genesis attempts to describe how the Original Sin happened. Although the forces of evil win the initial struggle, God promises that we will win the ultimate battle—the woman's offspring will crush the head of the serpent.

The Original Sin introduced death. Nevertheless, life will continue and conquer: "The man called his wife Eve, because she became the mother of all the *living*."

These optimistic expectations are fulfilled in the gospel. The angel's words to Mary, "Do not be afraid," can be taken to mean that we no longer need to be afraid of misery and suffering. Through Mary, the Lord is now with us to overcome them. Through the Holy Spirit who has come upon us, "nothing is impossible with God."

Consequently, even though we still live "in the midst of misery and strife, life is shot through with glory." For one of our own—Mary—was kept free of sin and is full of grace, and her son—Jesus—has saved us from sin.

The misery brought on by Original Sin is still with us: casualties from war and revolutions, victims of floods and earthquakes, fatalities from accidents and killings. Yet, "in the midst of misery and strife, life is shot through with glory." Mary's Immaculate Conception is proof that God's power is stronger than the power of evil.

We still live in a world torn by strife: tensions between blacks and whites, Arabs and Jews, Irish Catholics and Protestants. Yet, "in the midst of misery and strife, life is shot through with glory." Mary's Immaculate Conception is evidence that harmony can exist within oneself as an individual—and, consequently, between individuals as members of society.

Cardinal Suenens once wrote:

> The sanctity of the Son is the cause of the anticipated sanctification of the Mother, just as the sun lights up the sky before appearing above the horizon.

Extending this further, we might say that the sanctity of Mary through her Immaculate Conception anticipates our own sanctity through the sacraments. What she is by privilege from the first moment of her life, we must approximate by grace before the last moment of our life.

As the Holy Spirit descends upon the bread and wine we offer so that they become the Body and Blood of Christ, may he come upon us again to make us more like Mary in bringing the presence of Christ to the world; and also more like Dorothy Day and Mrs. Barrett in announcing that "in the midst of misery and strife, life is shot through with glory."